MICK GRANT
TAKIN' THE MICK

MICK GRANT
TAKIN' THE MICK

Mick Grant with Mac McDiarmid

Haynes Publishing

First published in September 2010
Reprinted January 2011
This paperback edition published in May 2012

A catalogue record for this book is available from the
British Library

ISBN 978 0 85733 143 4

Library of Congress catalog card no 2011943929

Published by Haynes Publishing,
Sparkford, Yeovil, Somerset BA22 7JJ, UK
Tel: 01963 442030 Fax: 01963 440001
Int.tel: +44 1963 442030 Int.fax: +44 1963 440001
E-mail: sales@haynes.co.uk
Website: www.haynes.co.uk

Haynes North America Inc.,
861 Lawrence Drive, Newbury Park, California 91320, USA

Designed and typeset by Dominic Stickland

Printed in the USA by Odcombe Press LP,
1299 Bridgestone Parkway, La Vergne, TN 37086

*All photographs are courtesy of the Grant Family Collection
except where stated.*

CONTENTS

FOREWORD

by James Whitham

It was back in the mid 1970s that I first heard of Mick Grant. Back then bike racing was big – big crowds, big two-strokes, big facial hair and big personalities . . . especially to a 12-year-old kid. My dad took me to an international meeting at Mallory Park in our Austin 1800, the year was 1978. We queued to get in, we queued for a burger, we queued for the toilet and we queued to get out. All I saw was the back of some bloke's head, one in a crowd of 50,000.

The two biggest names that day, and in the sport at the time, were Barry Sheene and Mick Grant. The fierce rivalry between these two wasn't just confined to the track though – it was every bit as strong in the bleachers too. And you *had* to take sides! A good looking, articulate, and charming (if a little slippery it seemed to me) cockney with a Rolls-Royce, or the hard-riding, plain-speaking son of a Wakefield miner with a porn-star moustache. For most northerners it didn't take too long to figure out which side you were supposed to be on.

In an era when engine power far outstripped chassis design and tyre technology, with almost no thought given by race organisers to rider safety, the attrition rate was high. Riders *had* to be tough, and Mick was known to be as tough as they came. The press, as usual, turned it into a cliché – so much so that for some time I thought his middle name was Gritty.

I knew he lived close to us because it was mentioned with awe whenever we drove up the hill from Huddersfield to Wakefield. No local lad could pass Lepton Grange without observing 'that's where that racer, Mick Grant, lives'. A proper local celebrity was Mick. I'd no idea then that our paths were to cross in a fairly considerable manner before too long.

In 1981 I answered the phone in the family home and a voice said 'Hello, this is Mick Grant, is your dad there?' At the time this was akin to a 14-year-old lad who's into football answering the phone to Wayne Rooney. Apparently he – Mick, not Wayne – wanted to come and set up his race bike on the runway of the small airfield my dad was running at the time. He duly came and as a bonus asked if I'd like to go to a race meeting that weekend at Scarborough. Did I ever – and said nothing but please and thank you for two days. Although Mick had a nightmare meeting, with everything he threw his leg over blowing-up, I knew then that I wanted to race a bike one day.

A couple of years later when I started racing, Mick kitted me out with some of his old riding gear to get me going. It wasn't until some time afterwards, having realised how – er – careful he is, did I understand what a gesture this had been.

I ended up riding for the Suzuki team with Mick as team manager, for four years all told. We never had the funding we thought we deserved, but mechanic 'Butch' Cartwright and Mick worked miracles to make what resources we did have go a long way. The team was so small we all had to take on more than one job. I was surprised to discover during that time what a talented and savvy engineer, welder and fabricator Mick really is. Our success was in no small part due to his guile and the long hours he spent in his Lepton workshop making sometimes very un-competitive machinery into race-winning tackle. *His* determination and stubbornness somehow became the team's biggest assets. He always told me that the willingness to work hard was much more important than natural talent. Lots of times, both as a rider and as a team manager, he had fairly average bikes to work with but he always seemed able to tease the best from them.

He always spoke the truth as he saw it and, like any real Yorkshireman, was never afraid to tell you – or anyone else for that matter – what he thought. He expected commitment to the cause and hard work from us all. We ended up winning countless British Championship rounds and two titles in the four seasons we were together.

Mick is the type of self-reliant lateral thinker you just don't come across too often these days. He has unshakeable faith in the idea that if you put enough thought and effort into it, then no problem is insurmountable . . . and that applies just as well to him trying to coax more power from a motor as it does to him trying to talk his way out of a speeding ticket whilst sat in the back of a police car!

ACKNOWLEDGEMENTS

To the best of my memory, the pages that follow sum up my first 65 years, of which almost 40 were engaged in motorcycle racing in one way or another. That's a lot to remember for anyone and especially for someone as memory-impaired as me, so to begin with I should perhaps show gratitude to those who've helped jog what's left of my grey matter. Thanks, then, to Gerald Davison, Nigel Everett, Steve Plater, Russell Savory, Dudley Robinson and James Whitham for helping to plug a few holes. Thanks, too, to Mac McDiarmid, whose task it was to plug the rest and tickle it into something worth reading.

As a racer I have one man to thank above all others: Jim Lee, who took me out of self-sufficient obscurity and set me on my way to becoming a competitive racer and competent workshop fettler. I've been proud to wear his 'JL' logo on my crash helmet ever since he came to my aid. Jim died ten years ago, but I hope he thought my subsequent results were worth his faith.

Next to support whatever talent I possessed was the Padgett's Motorcycles dynasty, a name still familiar in British racing. They, too, taught me a lot (some of it unintentional) and put me on my way to my first British championship. They weren't half as chuffed as me when Norton's Frank Perris stepped on their toes to offer me my first works ride, but for all the Norton's shortcomings I'm still grateful to Frank. In passing I must also mention the willing support and advice of Phil Read, whom I first encountered as a Norton team-mate.

For most of my subsequent career I was a factory rider in one form or another, although George Beale and David Dixon stand out as private sponsors, often at difficult times. John Cooper, too – dear old Moon Eyes – loaned me the Yamahas on which I first really made a name for myself on a 'pay when you can' basis. Being considered worthy of such a deal by such a legend was compliment enough; being so generously given the hardware to prove him right was career-making. So thanks, John, you're a gent. So, too, is Brian Davidson, who supported me for the next two years as well as helping me in business. He remains a valued friend to this day.

From my years with Kawasaki the outstanding memory is of the technical brilliance of Mr Yashida, who I first met at Daytona in 1975 and who more than anyone put the triples on the pace. I also owe much to Kawasaki mechanic Rod Scivyer, formerly a talented racer in his own right.

As well as being a sound mechanic, Paul Dallas always provided good company, as well as extracting me from a few potentially bruising encounters in bars. I have Gerald Davison to thank for my next factory venture, the Honda NR500 project. The bike may have been a lemon, but working on the project under the brilliant Mr Fukui was something I wouldn't have missed for the world. Besides, the money was good.

Next, Suzuki, with whom I spent the last four years of my racing career. Steve Kenward, in particular, made that as enjoyable a time as any I had in racing, and was a steadfast supporter in later years when I moved into team management. Rex White was ever a friend and supporter, and a mine of useful information when I followed him into team management.

As a team manager – often a cap-in-hand manager – I have people almost too numerous to thank. Russell

Savory of Sanyo Honda stands out for his infectious and indomitable enthusiasm; his long-suffering sidekick, John How, was the ultimate Mr Fixit; riders James Whitham, and Steve Plater for their brilliant company and never-say-die approach; of riders no longer with us, Mez Mellor was a privilege to know whilst Smutty Robinson had talent to burn yet was one of the nicest guys in the paddock; Dire Straits's Mark Knopfler for his financial help and simply being a good bloke.

When racing's over all that's left are piles of pots and photographs, lots of good memories and – best of all – friends. Both Plater and Whitham also fall into that category, along with Roger Marshall, Russell Savory and John How, Billy McCosh, Tony Salt, Eric Boocock, Dudley Robinson, the obscure Derry Kissak and Johns Caffrey and Chapman. Riding trials has brought friends too numerous to mention. Clive Strugnall paved the way for my first visit to South Africa almost 40 years ago and remains the most welcoming host to this day. The most enduring – and long-suffering – must be Chris Bradley, with whom I took my first illicit steps on two wheels in a field near Wakefield and who's still a pal despite regularly beating me at trials. And when all goes wrong, Les and Steve Carroll from Emley Re-finishers continue to knock the dings out of my cars.

To my family – mum, dad, nan and sister Cheryl, of course – I'm especially indebted, not least for helping me keep my feet on the ground. Throughout almost all of my racing years there were two other constants that helped hold everything together. One was my mechanic, Nigel Everett, who invariably saw to it that my bikes, at least, were ready to race. I owe him a debt only exceeded by that other constant, my time-keeper, organiser and helpmate, on and off the tracks – otherwise known as Carol, my dear wife.

To all of you, heartfelt thanks.

CHAPTER 1

RHUBARB, RHUBARB, RHUBARB

'Gritty Yorkshireman.' That was me, or rather the cliché the media liked to pass off as me. At times in the Eighties, I was sometimes tempted to check my birth certificate just to make sure mum and dad hadn't slipped that old chestnut in somewhere. The image I read about myself truly suggested that I'd emerged from some West Riding coal face chewing a budgie, donned a crash helmet hewn from solid anthracite, stepped on to a racing Yamaha and emerged into the limelight.

The truth was rather different. I had no Davy lamp, and I didn't go to work in the bowels of the West Riding. Nor did I scrub away pit-muck in a tin bath by the front-room fire, although to previous generations of Grant breadwinners that was the daily routine. In fact, if I had props at all they were to do with another cliché entirely. The Aran sweater and scraggly beard I favoured were the uniform of art college. But that was a mistake too, and came much later.

On Monday 10 July 1944, as allied forces battled inland from the beaches of Normandy, in a small hospital in Wetherby, Dora Grant was engaged in some less publicised pushing of her own and, after a brief struggle, out popped me. I'm not sure why this momentous event took place at this relatively posh end of Yorkshire, since home was in Middlestown, just outside Wakefield. Although many people's image of the old West Riding is of grim grey woollen mills and ranks of belching chimneys, in the

Wakefield area 'King Coal' was – well, king. (Rhubarb, as you'll learn later, was queen.) Gordon – my dad, who everyone knew as 'Sammy' – had followed his father down the mines and, this being an essential part of the war effort, it qualified as a reserved occupation so he still worked in the pits. Not all kids were lucky enough to have their fathers at home.

Within ten months of my birth the war in Europe was over, although my contribution to Hitler's downfall was slight. For the first few years of my life we lived with my maternal grandmother at Number 3 Low Lane, a tiny rented cottage tacked on to the end of a stone terrace just down the hill from Middlestown which, if it had a horse, would be a one-horse town, about 100 yards from the main Wakefield to Huddersfield road and almost as far from its own outside privy. At the opposite end of the terrace was Mrs Spivey's shop, a tiny one-woman business selling everything from candles and cotton reels to beans and bacon.

Dad worked at several West Riding pits over the years, but mainly at Woolly, now just a distant memory off the M1's Junction 38. The site isn't far from the National Coal Mining Museum at the old Caphouse Colliery at Overton which, to the general disgruntlement of old colliery hands, once appeared as a South Wales noodle mine in an ad campaign for Pot Noodle. My first recollection of dad is also the most frightening. I can't have been more than a toddler at the time since he was throwing me up in the air and catching me. I can still see the great jolly grin on his face, although I doubt there was one on mine. Everyone was laughing, as I seemed to be flying as high as our gable end, and I was convinced he was about to drop me on my head. I was crapping myself, and maybe that's where my fear of heights came from.

From 60 years on, the dad I first knew is a bit of a shadowy figure, although mainly my memory's to blame since there was nothing vague about the man himself. He was a typical working man of the time, the archetypal family provider. He liked a flutter with the bookies and smoked heavily, which I didn't like. Mum kept at him to give up, and now and again he'd try for a few days, by which time he'd be so bad-tempered mum would buy him a pack of Woodbines just to calm him down and give us all a break. Maybe he thought that doing without the odd Woodie couldn't make much difference to a man who spent his entire working life breathing coal dust, but one day he startled all of us. At the time he was hunched by the living- room fire, halfway through a cigarette. Without warning or comment he threw the cig and the pack in the fire and never touched one again.

Ironically the only chest complaint I can recall in the family was mine. When I was aged about seven, mum noticed that I was losing weight. This, it turned out, was due to a collapsed lung. I spent the next few weeks covered in tanning cream under a sun lamp and doing exercises, which seemed to do the trick. Later I got a mongrel dog, Billy, which was fine except that I turned out to be allergic to dogs. Quick as you like, 30 years and four pet dogs later, I finally got round to seeking allergy treatment.

Dad loved working in the pit and seemed proud of what he did. I think coal miners in general thought of themselves as underpinning the country, providing the life-blood that for two centuries had been coal. In peace and war alike their work was vital to the country, and dangerous – so much so that I don't believe any of them thought in any way that being in this particular reserved occupation, rather than being shot at, was any sort of easy ride.

Like most working blokes he'd had only a minimal education, and probably neither he nor his parents ever set their sights on anything higher. So as soon as he left school he started life underground as a face worker. At the pit you got 'tickets' as you achieved different skill levels ... shot blaster's ticket ... deputy ... overman. He worked his way up – literally, since each qualification meant that he spent less time deep underground.

Gran, Ada Mallinson, didn't work in the pit, but she was as tough as anyone who did. She lived with us – or more accurately we lived with her – from the age of 59 until her death 30 years later. She was the boss, with dad second in command and mum more than pulling her weight but as 'other ranks'. She always used to say she lived with two bosses, gran and her husband, but never had the faintest inclination to boss anyone about herself.

Although you might think of a traditional mining area as all bleakness and grime, the valleys of the West Riding have a knack of hiding their industrial muck. The local pit was set in rolling countryside. Even today Low Lane is surrounded by green fields, farms and hedges and the lane running past it is still single-track, although it's now paved and every house has a car parked outside. Mrs Spivey's shop, inevitably, is now just another cottage.

Even more than most working-class women of her generation, Ada had led a tough life. Like her daughter, she'd also been married to a miner, Friend Mallinson, at a time when the pits were far more dangerous than they are now – partly because there are scarcely any left. Friend came from a large farming family, only going into the pits temporarily because there wasn't enough work on the farm to occupy all the brothers. 'Temporary' became tragically permanent when he was killed in an accident at Charlton near Pontefract early in the marriage, leaving Ada to bring up three daughters on her own. She was a tough old bird who got by taking in cleaning and any other odd jobs that would earn a few bob.

As you might expect she was a feisty and determined woman, but with a mischievous streak. As luck would have it, when I arrived I was the surrogate son that she'd never had, so within the ruling threesome at home – mum, dad and gran – Ada had a major part to play in my upbringing.

Today almost every house in the area has a car parked outside, but in those days there was only one, a Morris Eight belonging to Jackie Bird. Despite living yards from common folk like us, Jackie obviously had to be rich, at least in my fantasies. Dad made do with a push-bike, on which he'd cycle to and from the pit or the bookies. There were no showers at the pit until maybe 1960, so he'd pedal home after every shift covered in pit-muck, just the whites of his eyes visible in a face as black as spades. I remember being fascinated by the little rectangular tobacco tin he kept in his pocket, dented and battered but worn shiny over the years. Apart from the Al Jolson eyes peering out of the grime, it was the only thing about him that seemed to reflect any light.

Dad dug coal, but apart from the bits in the bottom of the tin bath after his post-shift wash, he didn't deliver the stuff. That was down to Walter Robinson, who made ends meet on his nearby farm by humping coal around the district on a horse-drawn cart, long after everyone else seemed to have gone mechanised. Generally, he had one shire horse pulling while two others ambled behind on tethers, all three being required only for uphill stretches when the cart was fully laden. Walter's farm, 'Newlands', was at the crest of a nearby hill and I'd sometimes go there to make a nuisance of myself – or 'help out' as I preferred to regard it. He tolerated my presence and the daft questions I asked, partly, I suspect, because he took a shine to my mum. By degrees, I took it upon myself to be in charge of the horses. Walter went along with it until the day he asked me to bring his biggest one down to his bottom field where he was chopping turnips. Yorkshire's answer to the Horse Whisperer strode manfully up the hill and climbed on its bare back only for the damn nag to bolt. The next Walter saw of me I was riding rodeo down the hill, too terrified to let go of the reins and a pitch-fork I happened to be holding. Not much later I had my first experience of grief and guilt when the same horse was missing, carted off to the knacker's yard.

As well as coal, post-war Wakefield's other big industries were council housing and rhubarb. Believe it or not, at one time the area produced 90 per cent of the world's forced rhubarb, becoming known as the 'Rhubarb Triangle'. Whilst we could take or leave rhubarb crumble, conditions at Number 3 were pretty cramped so one of the nice new council houses being thrown up all around us was an attractive proposition. Unfortunately for them (if not, as it turned out, for me) in order for my parents to qualify for a council tenancy, they needed to take grannie with them to score the necessary points. So in about 1950 gran gave up the Low Lane cottage to move with us into our council house, also in Middlestown. Years later mum and dad bought the same three-bedroomed semi under Maggie Thatcher's scheme. Although dad died a decade ago, mum, who's now 92 and still fit as a fiddle, lives there today. My sister Cheryl, who arrived in 1953, lives with her family just down the road.

Life – before the move and after – wasn't a lot to write home about but like most kids I felt secure and took what I had pretty much for granted. In the pre-television age you didn't yearn for luxuries you'd never heard of and, providing you were fed and mostly warm, everything seemed grand. Every Friday marked the usual ritual as dad brought home his wage packet of old white £5 notes – three of them. Even though this was a huge wage for a working man at the time, it was still the era of rationing and post-war hardship. Everyone made do as they'd had to during the war, and before that in the Great Depression. So you never wasted the little sliver of soap left when the cake had almost had it – you stuck it to the new one. Shampoo we'd never heard of – nor missed. Ordinary hand soap and vinegar did the job just as well. As kids, your biggest contribution, apart from not breaking things, was to eat every scrap on your plate. Even now, if a plate is put in front of me, I can't leave the table without eating every scrap.

Food certainly wasn't limitless, but our playground seemed to be. In the local fields and hedgerows we were commandos or cowboys, or we dammed brooks like Royal Engineers. Whilst I thought nothing of storming a machine-gun nest armed with nothing more than a stick, I left the tree-climbing to someone less fearful of heights. Despite our warlike antics, friendly-fire casualties were few. David Sissons once accidentally dropped a 1,000lb bomb – although to the uninitiated it may have looked more like a rock – crushing my finger. Mum and I took the bus to hospital, where apparently I was really brave. I'm not so brave any more but the finger still looks more like a courgette. Sissons was also responsible for cocking his father's shotgun, pointing it straight at my face and pulling the trigger – a memory that gives me the shivers more than any racing near-miss. Luckily, unlike my pants, the gun wasn't loaded.

Like most kids I was especially attracted to building sites, the true precursors of modern adventure playgrounds. Once, way past dark and hours after I should have been scrubbed and fed at home, I was lurking about instead in some half-built old folk's home when who should come plodding through the rubble but dad. Dark as it was, I could see he was absolutely fuming as I cowered behind a pile of window frames. Luckily in my imagination I was a commando on a daring mission behind enemy lines and dad was the Gestapo. Torture and certain death by firing squad awaited me if I gave myself away. In fact I wouldn't have been more scared if he'd had an entire Panzer regiment backing him up.

Another occasion found me climbing on the cloches in the back yard trying to retrieve a lost ball. Inevitably I fell through, smashing what seemed like acres of glass and ripping lumps out of myself. I tried to keep the carnage secret but mum didn't need to be a forensic scientist to work out what all the blood and broken glass amounted to.

Unless I'd been dim enough to make my pranks that

obvious, I usually got away with it – often with gran's connivance. Maybe because she'd never had lads of her own, she seemed to regard them – in other words, me – getting into scrapes as the normal order of things. She'd sometimes lie quite brazenly to protect me.

Not that there was ever much to protect me from. Taking your belt to your kids wasn't exactly unknown in the neighbourhood. Yet even though dad had quite a temper, and sometimes seemed stern and unyielding, he never actually hit me. In fact, apart from other kids, I can't recall anyone that did. Later, Cheryl occasionally felt the back of dad's hand, so maybe I was just better than most at not being found out. I wasn't particularly a bad 'un, although mum describes me now as being 'stubborn' and 'a bit of a monkey,' but perhaps I should have been clouted more often because I've made up for it since. Perhaps I'd already acquired a bit of the deviousness that came in handy when dealing with scrutineers in later life.

Of Ada's three daughters one, Marrion, was deaf and dumb, and lived with husband Harry in Agbrigg, near Wakefield. Until her demise, the other, Edy, lived with husband Bill Mannifield 200 yards along Ramsey Road on the same council estate as us.

Edy and Bill used to take me and my gran on holiday every year. They'd never had children, so I sort of became their part-time son, as well as my nan's. So – as much as a miner's lad on a skint council estate could be in those days – I was kind of spoiled. Year in, year out, our annual holiday was to go to the Yorkshire Riviera for a week, where we'd stay at Mr and Mrs Waller's boarding house in a back street in Scarborough.

The only other source of trips away was Horbury Working Men's Club. Every now and again I'd find myself dressed in my Sunday best and ushered to Horbury Bridge station, where all the local kids were issued with ten whole shillings (50p), a pack of egg sandwiches, and delivered to Bridlington for a day by the seaside.

Even though I never sang the hymn of 'school days being the best of your life', all this was in those early carefree days when you got fed, clothed and looked after, and all you had to do in return was to more or less behave. Only slowly did the realisation begin to dawn that there was going to be some sort of different deal later down the line.

It was a process I don't remember in detail, except for the time when our headmaster, Mr Yeomans, got the class together, and solemnly told us that if we had no qualifications when we left school we wouldn't be able to get a job. Most of us were sceptical, and what he said turned out not to be entirely true, at least for our generation. Of course I'd no idea what my future held, and as it turned out my eventual 'qualifications' were of a type no school could teach, but he was certainly right that education could give you options that most of our parents had never enjoyed.

He was also right in that the old working patterns were slowly changing, but it was still the case that many of the boys I knew would almost automatically follow their fathers into a working life underground. For generations that had been the normal run of events and, as far as anyone could see in the mid-Fifties, looked like continuing for generations to come. But like many working-class parents of the time, mine had aspirations that I should have choices they hadn't enjoyed. In other words, like Mr Yeomans they wanted me to reap the benefit of further education, of academic qualifications.

In one respect, at least, I was all for this. Before he retired dad took me down the pit where he worked. At the time it was considered pretty state of the art, with water sprays and other devices to improve safety and conditions, yet still you could barely see five yards. It was hot, cramped and unbelievably dirty. I can't imagine how anyone could enjoy that environment, yet dad and his mates lived in such conditions – and worse – for eight-hour shifts, year in, year out. I didn't have much of a clue what I wanted my future to hold, except that hewing coal out of 12-inch seams wasn't part of it.

Luckily for me – as it turned out – there was one fairly insurmountable obstacle to me getting on this educational gravy train: from Day One I utterly loathed school. When I entered Middlestown Elementary school we were still living at the Low Lane cottage and waiting for the big move to a council house. Because I'd been indulged as a child and the few friends I had were kids from the same small area, the prospect of joining a huge throng of utter strangers terrified me. I'd been literally dragged to my maiden day of education, clinging to lamp-posts and fences, screaming my lungs out, anything to delay the inevitable. Once there, I locked myself in the bogs and refused to come out.

The one saving grace – and it was a small one – was my first form teacher, a lovely woman named Miss Slack. I can still remember her writing 'A' for apple, 'B' for banana on the blackboard, and the trendy white shoes with brown inserts she liked to wear. (Maybe I noticed her footwear because my glance was usually downcast.) Most of all, her perfume, which would waft by me from time to time, was some relief from the pervasive pong of carbolic soap and boiled cabbage. As the school years passed Miss Slack was followed by the almost equally comfortable Miss Maude, and finally Miss Briggs, who was a bit of a tyrant in comparison.

Other than Miss Maude's habit of spraying everyone she addressed with spittle, neither had an interesting smell or choice in shoes. I guess that today you'd say that school was way outside my comfort zone. It was only years later that I realised what most people must – that to get on in life you have to be prepared to get out of that zone. But as a child with a comfortable existence I can't remember it being anything other than deeply traumatic. Looking back, I suppose it could easily have led to outright rebellion, but I was probably far too pliant and keen to please for that. If I rebelled at all, it was simply by opting out internally. In the meantime school became something to endure until I was old enough to do something else. In other words, even for someone brighter than me, it was probably not the ideal launching pad for a career based on intellect.

Nor was there always relief at home. The down side of Edy and Bill's otherwise agreeable attention was their religious commitment, which obliged me to join them at St Luke's church twice every Sunday which – far from making me godly – gave me a simmering resentment at having my weekends completely messed up. It seemed that I'd no sooner got out of my Sunday best in the morning than I was being unwillingly scrubbed up again for Evensong, with scarcely a break for play in between. (At least some of my prayers were answered, since where St Luke's church once stood as a monument to lost weekends now stands a block of flats.)

So, callow kid that I was, I spent the working week loathing school, Sundays hating church, and Saturdays, as often as not, resenting gran, because that was the day she'd often drag me along to see her deaf and dumb daughter in Wakefield, an expedition even more boring than the Book of Common Prayer. Happy, I wasn't.

As if school wasn't bad enough, within a year or so of starting there I'd suffered the additional indignity of moving almost into the playground with the shift to our new semi-detached council house on Ramsey Road on the Middlestown council estate. Was there no escape? True, it was a fine place to live after the four of us being shoe-horned into gran's cottage, except that it backed directly on to my loathsome primary school. Round the corner was the Savoy picture house, which later went the way of St Luke's – it's now Diva's hair stylists and the Grumpy Fryer chip shop. Approaching them you see a big sign bearing the legend 'Middlestown – Drive with Care', which also had no part in my formative years. Almost no one had anything to drive.

CHAPTER 2

THE ART
OF SKIVING

A car was out of the question but times were changing, even for dad. By the time I was eight or so he'd got fed up with peddling the push-bike and moved up-market to a 250cc JAP-engined antique with girder forks. This was a bit of a surprise because he wasn't into motorbikes in the slightest. In fact, unless it was a horse he'd got money on, he wasn't keen on anything fast-moving. If we went to the seaside, it was me and mum on the big dipper, never dad. Years later, on another bike, he took me along the narrow, winding lane from home to Horbury Bridge, with the throttle pinned to the stop and hedgerows rushing by at what seemed like warp speed, but was probably no more than 50mph. But that was an aberration. To him, a bike was just something to make life easier – at least in theory, since the damn JAP hardly ever seemed to run. Instead it languished unloved in the wash-house. If this was frustrating for dad, he didn't show it. But it was nothing less than a tragedy for me, since I was already passionate about anything mechanical, especially engines. Having a real one in the household seemed nothing less than magical. If only it had worked.

Dad's push-bike also lived in the wash-house. Sometimes I'd 'borrow' it, but since it towered over me like a penny-farthing, I spent more time falling off it than going anywhere. The only way I could physically mount it was by inserting one leg through the diamond to reach the opposite pedal, a posture ideal only for grotesque crashes and curvature of the spine. Thus contorted, I'd pedal off down the lane, as often as not ending up in a heap. Somehow none of this thwarted my enthusiasm for being in control, albeit briefly, of my own machine. Eventually, one Christmas, a bike of my own arrived.

At around the same time, something else unexpected – at least by me – arrived in the Grant household. Being wrapped up in myself, as usual, I hadn't noticed mum putting on weight. Suddenly, miraculously, the weight disappeared and in its place was a baby sister. I can't remember any complex emotions about what must have seemed a momentous event, just that I'd been perfectly happy being the centre of everyone's attention for the previous eight years and sharing any of it with Cheryl didn't seem a right good idea. It was probably the first major wobble in the self-centred life of Mick Grant. If nothing else, the introduction of a daughter into dad's universe seemed to soften him a bit, so it wasn't all bad news. In later years I managed to forgive Cheryl for the impertinence of existing, whilst she seems to have forgiven me for being a selfish sod. We get on great.

All sisters, of course, are soppy, especially to a nine-year-old as skilled in guerrilla warfare as me. My main comrade in arms at the time was Chris Bradley, who lived 400 yards along the road from gran's old cottage. He had a push-bike, too, and we must have pedalled across half of Yorkshire on expeditions during school holidays. Then, about three years after Cheryl's arrival, the two of us got a bike of our own. It was a 1936 Triumph Tiger 80 with girder forks and a big chrome tank which we polished till it gleamed.

Strictly speaking, Chris's father owned the bike, but this was a minor detail which we both took as an invitation to borrow it whenever no one was looking. As well as being a bit of a petrol-head – he was well into his trials and had an old railway carriage as a workshop – Mr Bradley was a civil engineer with the local authority. At the time the Suez crisis was in full swing, which meant nothing to us except that petrol was rationed and almost unobtainable. The Tiger had been bought mainly because a handful of fuel coupons came with it. Neither of us even knew of black market fuel coupons, much less could we have afforded them. And so my motorcycle career began as dodgily as it would continue, siphoning petrol out of Bradley Snr's Triumph Mayflower car. The car itself was dodgy enough, a large elastic band being the only thing stopping it from jumping out of second gear.

Even between us Chris and I hadn't the slightest clue how to ride the Triumph, or even start it. Eventually, and much to our surprise, after messing around with its magneto (as I later learned it was called) it fired up after a bit of energetic pushing. Even apart from allowing us the dangerous delusion that we had a special empathy with the internal combustion engine, this was bad news for the neighbourhood. Usually we'd hack it around the field facing the bottom of Low Lane, opposite the swankiest house in the neighbourhood, owned by Mr Fox. He was probably a very decent man, but to us he was plain scary. That being so, we were irresistibly drawn to trespass on his land and push his buttons a bit, even though being caught was a cast-iron certainty. After all, most people would probably notice a Tiger 80 with a dodgy silencer being crashed on their lawn.

To the best of my knowledge, Mr Fox never actually grassed on us to our parents, which surely deserves my belated thanks. Thus we continued with the delusion that our illicit grass-tracking was our little secret, although Mr Bradley would have had to be retarded not to notice that his bike was periodically covered in muck. Eventually he seemed to bow to the inevitable and let us use it openly – providing, of course, that we promised to be careful. So we'd carefully race each other for two laps each of the field, and just as carefully fall off, with the other timing on a battered Timex watch should we ever complete the distance. This at least had the merit of being legal and slightly safe. But since neither of these qualities were very high on our list of priorities, when no one seemed to be looking we'd also run the Tiger along the local lanes.

This first went pear-shaped when I rounded a bend at breakneck speed – possibly as much as 20mph – to find Mr Lumb coming the other way. This wouldn't necessarily have been a huge problem, except that he was in his ice cream van at the time. Skilfully I missed it, landing in a convenient ditch with no more damage than to my underwear. It was by no means the worst prang in the area. Some time later dear old Walter Robinson was killed in our speedway field when another of his horses bolted, pitching him out of his cart and breaking his neck.

Not long after, we had another bike in our stable, for the occasions when Mr Bradley was selfishly using his own bike. Dad eventually gave up on the lifeless JAP and bought a D1 BSA Bantam in its place. Since he usually worked nights, this was an altogether ideal arrangement. While he was sleeping I'd drag the Bantam out of the shed, pull the baffles out of the silencer (noisy bikes obviously drawing so much less attention than quiet ones), then thrash it around for a while in Coxley Wood. Then I'd clean the muck off it and announce, when dad woke up, that his dutiful son had cleaned his bike for him. Inevitably the local policeman, 'Bobby Davy' eventually twigged that he had an under-aged, unlicensed, uninsured lunatic on his patch, and the cat was out of the bag.

Chris and I remain pals, both of us still into trials riding and classic bikes. The oddest thing about our jinks around the field, considering what was to become of my life, was that Chris was by miles the more natural rider. He had – and still has in trials – better machine control, better balance. If we challenged each other to ride over something tricky, he always looked poised and in complete control. All I had was brute speed and the bigger collection of bruises. But I was invariably quicker on that old Timex watch.

Eventually the time came for me to move to the big school, Horbury Secondary Modern, having failed the 11-plus exam. Not surprisingly in view of their ambitions, this seemed to be a great disappointment to my parents, although I can't remember being the least bit bothered myself. If anything, the reverse was true, since most of my school pals were also 11-plus rejects so we'd be going to the same school.

Secondary school was just as onerous to me as elementary had been, except that you got to wear longer pants. I was bored and indifferent – not outwardly rebellious, but probably a sullen pain in the butt. Rather than dig my heels in, I was inclined to go with the flow, at least superficially, but at heart I generally suited myself. I was too chicken for major insurrection but seemed to be in a more-or-less permanent state of low-grade bother. In fact probably the only thing I had in common with my teachers was a mutual wish that I wasn't in their class. Like most kids, I had my moods and uncertainties, but never really doubted that my folks had my best interests at heart. They just weren't *my* interests. Their ambitions seemed to be about someone else.

There was a certain amount of bullying, too. For a while a lad called Kenneth Vale made my life a misery, until something truly miraculous happened. It was the day of the school boxing tournament. My first fight was against the class wimp, 'Froggy' Frogget, so I won. But this was a hollow victory for it pitted me in the second bout against – guess who – my nemesis, Vale. When the bell went I found something I never knew I possessed – desperation, probably. Convinced I'd get a right leathering, I went at him like a threshing machine and much to my surprise thumped the stuffing out of him. It felt wonderful. But not for long. The final bout was against

Ian Williamson, the hardest lad in Yorkshire. I'd no sooner walked into the middle of the ring than the world suddenly went black. I woke up – good practice for racing, this – looking up through a crowd of concerned people.

Then something else miraculous happened. Our art teacher, Barry Hinchcliffe, seemed to notice that I had a bit of a flair for art. He was actually quite excited about what I could do, which was even more surprising than knocking seven bells out of Vale. Whilst I wasn't altogether chuffed about the idea of being teacher's pet, I quite enjoyed the novelty of plaudits and attention, at least some of the time. At others I felt like an exhibit. They'd actually park me outside doing paintings of bits of the school like the boiler house, although I'd probably have been more comfortable slapping a coat of red lead on the boiler itself.

Then, by some mysterious process with which I wasn't entirely happy, Mr Hinchcliffe was instrumental in wangling me a transfer to the local grammar school on the grounds that I showed 'exceptional promise'. Suddenly, from being the object of a lot of head-scratching and frustrated dreams, all the grown-ups seemed to have my future mapped out: a successful time at grammar school, on to art college, and then move over David Hockney. I suppose I should have been grateful, but I wasn't, yet again. For all the enthusiasm with which my progress was greeted, the subject of it seemed to be someone else, not me. Worse still, the grammar school in question was at Morley, almost in Leeds. It was a balls-ache of a daily trip.

It certainly didn't feel like it at the time, but I suppose I was the first generation from my sort of background to have a choice in what I did as I grew up. Anyone older would have been destined for the pit or a trade, if they were lucky. I've no doubt now that my family saw what I was doing as a golden opportunity, and I suppose it was. But, like most youngsters, I had no more sense of the history or social context of my situation than I had of quantum mechanics. Ungrateful as I was, to me it all seemed onerous and irrelevant.

Yet on the face of it, I was doing well. I specialised in drawing and painting, with many of the results exhibited all over the country. But much as it was a pleasant change for teachers to pat me on the back from time to time, I had no real interest in what they seemed to be so excited about. So I did what I usually did – go with the flow and pretend it's not really happening. Intellectually I was never great shakes, and my memory has always been dire. At grammar school I'd do my best to learn, say, three pages of Shakespeare. But try as I might it just wouldn't stick.

One of my grammar school allies in this low-grade rebellion was a chubby, round lad named Stewart Pell, whose dad had a grocery shop in Kirkhamgate on the outskirts of Wakefield. His two main attractions were being a bit of a rogue and always seeming to have pots of money in his pockets which he was happy to lash out on ice cream or sweets. Later, as the hormones set in, his sweet tooth left him and he turned up one day in a bespoke teddy-boy drape jacket knocked up by a tailor in Morley. At around the same time the sweet shop made way for under-age trips to the pub. Preparations for one school speech day included a session at the Horse and Jockey to anaesthetise us against the boring bits. We'd probably had only three or four pints, but word got out and by the time two teachers arrived to drag us back to school I was completely wasted. Somehow Stewart still had enough wits about him to lock one of them in the Gents while we made our escape. Naturally this didn't go down too well with the headmaster. Both of us were threatened with expulsion, but luckily one of Stewart's uncles was on the board of governors, so strings were pulled and we avoided disgrace by the skins of our teeth.

At age 17, me and my two borderline O-level passes moved on to Batley College of Art. It may have been further education but I was still the reluctant student. It wasn't the art itself I disliked. In fact I quite enjoyed much of it. But it just seemed to exist in a bubble that had nothing to do with me – or my future. Years later, when I took up racing, I had a fairly clear idea of where I wanted to be at the end of each season. Even though I didn't necessarily achieve it, there was always a clear aim and a goal. At college that just didn't appear to be the case. Whatever the end product might be, it seemed to have nothing to do with me. In the meantime my parents were making real sacrifices just to keep me there. I felt as though I was living a total confidence trick.

Mind you, there were compensations – girls, for a start. And booze. If there was a party, the usual suspects – me, Headley Robinson, Chris O'Hare – would take a bottle to Booth's off-licence, where for about three shillings (15p) you could have it filled with cheap plonk from a barrel. It was ghastly gut-rot stuff, but it did the trick and you'd be pissed as a cricket before the party even began. Even the college's annual dinner-dance gave me another chance to throw my family's good intentions in their face. The do was always fancy dress and I decided to go as some sort of ghost. As luck would have it gran was a pretty organised lady, even to the point of already having her funeral shroud prepared. It seemed an ideal costume, so she let me borrow it, but one thing led to another and she never got it back. Years later, I felt a bit guilty that I'd no idea what she was wearing when we eventually put her in the ground.

If occasionally getting wrecked and making a prat of myself was a favourite pastime, my biggest passion was already motorbikes. When I'd been at school, and even after beginning college, I'd earned a few bob at weekends looking after the hens and driving the tractor on Desmond Lindley's farm on Ostingley Lane, near Dewsbury. It was just pin money, but I managed to save enough to pick up an old 600cc side-valve BSA M21 for a few quid. Me and

Chris and anyone else who was around used to mess about on it at Coxley Wood. Today, do-gooders have put the wood off-limits, but in those days mum used to walk the dog down there, and no-one batted an eyelid about us larking about on the bike. Everyone seemed to take it for granted that we had the run of the land.

Woods and fields were one thing, but there were roads out there, and that's where I really wanted to be. Trouble was, it would take more than a spot of hen ranching to pay for that. Then, out of the blue, on the eve of my 16th birthday dad announced that I could share the Bantam with him if I wanted – as if there could ever be any doubt. So on the stroke of midnight I'd already got all my gear on and was out on the bike until about three in the morning. And that was me, in my element. It was like coming alive. It was as though this was what I'd always wanted to do.

If I needed any collaborators in falling under the spell of motorcycles, I couldn't have found better than the Bradleys. The whole family were into competition, and from being eight until 15 or so, I'd join them in trips to scrambles meetings and even the odd road race. My first taste of road racing was a trip to Scarborough. Geoff Duke was riding, along with a very young Mike Hailwood on a Mondial. If that wasn't heady enough, the Oliver's Mount circuit put you so close to the action it seemed as though you could almost touch the riders as they roared past. It was magic, the biggest buzz I'd ever experienced. Later trips took us to other magical places like Oulton and Cadwell Park. Something about the noise and the speed terrified me, but deep down I knew that some day I wanted to give it a go myself.

Trouble was, for most youngsters like me racing was just something you read about, or watched from the sidelines, not something you actually did. You may as well have fantasised about being a Hollywood film star. Luckily, we had a couple of local role models. For the previous few years Chris and I had trekked half a mile or so to watch Eric and Nigel Boocock practising speedway in a muddy field. Later, we'd cadged their cast-off tyres for the M21. Now Eric also had a lovely Velocette. More impressively, despite being a few months younger than me, he was just about to start his professional speedway career with Middlesbrough. None of us knew it, but he'd go on to become British champion in 1974. So maybe it could be done.

In the meantime any ambitions I might have in that direction were more modest. On my 18th birthday Telstar, the first communications satellite was launched from Cape Canaveral, and my motorcycling ambitions also went into orbit when dad gave me £100 as a birthday present. These days that amount would barely buy a pair of tyres, but then 20 crisp fivers seemed an immense sum. So, first thing Saturday morning, I whizzed the Bantam over to Padgett's Motorcycles for the first of what would be many encounters with the Batley motorcycle dynasty.

Amongst the affordable items in the showroom was a 500cc MSS Velocette attached to a sidecar. At the time a 500 was considered a pretty potent device. I pretended to prod it knowledgeably whilst Peter Padgett hovered in the background telling me what a fine machine it was. I didn't actually need much convincing, so without much bargaining on my part we agreed a deal – without sidecar – and I went home pleased as punch. I fully expected dad to approve.

He didn't. 'It's too big for you,' he insisted. 'You can't have that.'

So back I went to Padgett's with my tail between my legs. Peter Padgett wasn't best pleased, either, especially since he now had to re-bolt the sidecar back on the Velo, but brightened up a little when I bought a unit-construction 250cc AJS Sapphire. It turned out to be a lovely little thing if you overlooked its habit of wrecking crankshafts every 6,000 miles.

Also on the same course as me at Batley was a mate called David Green, who I sometimes gave a lift to college. By this time I'd chopped the AJS in against a 350cc Velocette Viper from King's of Oxford (owned by Stan Hailwood, so I suppose that unwittingly I became a distant sponsor to his son, Mike). The breathalyser was still years away, so if you drank you generally drank and drove. One day Dave and I had both tied a few on, and as we rode up the hill to college he toppled off the back. I stopped and ran back, but he didn't move – just lay there with a blank expression on his face. My first reaction was that I'd killed him, but luckily he was pleasantly relaxed as he hit the ground, so once he'd got over the shock of waking up in the gutter and finished cursing me, he only had a few bruises to show for it. Naturally neither of us was wearing a crash helmet – they weren't compulsory for another decade – and we didn't have much by way of brains to protect. As to drinking and driving, it was generally assumed that if you could kick-start something as awkward as a Velo, you had to be sober enough to ride it. I've no idea where I got the money from, because I never seemed to have any, but there was always enough to put fuel in the Velo – and rot-gut in the odd pop-bottle at Booth's.

But something had to give. I could do the slobbing about in an Aran sweater, no bother, but the rest of the artistic stuff seemed more and more remote. By the time I was 19 I'd finally decided that the bohemian life wasn't for me. Further education was just prolonging the agony. I left. My parents were horrified.

CHAPTER 3

WORKING
TO RIDE

The downside of no longer being Yorkshire's answer to Canaletto was that I had to earn my keep. I wasn't by any means work-shy, but had no real idea what I wanted to do – except that it almost certainly didn't involve the creative arts. So somehow I ended up at Clayton Hospital, Wakefield, taking photographs and record-keeping. To me, and probably to the hospital itself, this was just a stop-gap, since the pay was rubbish and humping files about didn't seem to have such a glittering future. Still, it kept me in beer money for a while.

Whilst at the Clayton I answered an ad for a salesman's job, although even then no one in their right mind would buy anything from me. It wasn't even at the cutting end of the retail trade, but door to door, flogging anything from suits to carpets on hire-purchase. When customers defaulted on payment, the job included repossessing, which wasn't fun, especially when you had to scrape the carpet off the floor with a shovel. It actually seemed pretty mean: who buys manky second-hand carpets, anyway? The two attractions of the 'door-to-door' bit were that I wouldn't have a boss breathing down my neck, and the Austin A35 van that came with it. The downside was that I had to work Saturday mornings.

It was around this time, 1965, that I had my first taste of competition, a hill-climb at Baiting's Dam near Ripponden on the Viper. It was just a bit of fun since the last thing on my mind was a working life on two wheels.

If there had been any sort of career planning involved, it would have been a fairly stupid notion since – art excepted – I'd been no better than second-rate at anything I'd tackled in my life that far, sports included. If I'd thought about it for even a minute I'd have realised that the future earnings of a mediocre motorcyclist wouldn't even have paid for a trip to Booth's off-licence. Luckily, as it turned out, I was still largely running on autopilot and such logic eluded me. To begin with, me and the Velo hardly set the world on fire, but I loved every minute of the experience. Later, I sometimes won my class. And simply being surrounded by bikes and guys who knew what to do with them was an altogether thrilling new world.

Although I did the odd hill-climb over the next couple of years, riding off-road was what really attracted me. So later I tried motocross, or what was then known as scrambling. A mate who lived in Chickenly, near Dewsbury, had a 250cc Cotton Villiers scrambler, which I borrowed for a meeting at Post Hill. It was a bit of a knackered old nail which didn't run particularly well, but this beggar wasn't all that choosy.

Proper scrambles gear barely existed at the time. Instead you'd wear Belstaff waxed cotton pants, a raggedy old pullover and a pair of pull-on army surplus firemen's boots. Unfortunately for me the boots were surplus in more ways than one, since they fitted my feet the way a stall fits a horse. My feet barely touched the sides, and about three inches of leather flapped around ahead of my toes. With nothing to restrain them, with every lap they slid further and further off my legs.

The sensible thing would have been to stop and pull them up, but I was doing fairly well in the heat, and besides I wasn't very sensible. So I just plugged on with these things flapping around about a foot beyond my toes. Somehow, despite running over these appendages almost every time I dabbed, I qualified for the final. This time I really strapped them on good – but it made no difference, although I finished somewhere mid-field. It wasn't easy – and wouldn't have been even without those damn boots. You couldn't understand how some people were going so much quicker on much the same sort of kit as you. Yet somehow I felt that I really belonged in this world. Mum and dad would no doubt have thought otherwise, but since I didn't tell them what I was doing, that was OK, too.

The only person at home I confided in about my new life as a speed demon was gran. As ever, she supported me in every way she could – although sometimes it backfired. One weekend I entered a Saturday sprint at Esholt Park, where the entire Bradford sewerage system came together. As usual I was running late, rushed home from selling rubbish to reluctant customers, chucked the Velo in the back of the van and arrived just as they were calling me for practice. In a mad frenzy I threw the front wheel back in the bike – I had to take it off to fit the Viper in the van – scrambled into my leathers and stuffed my feet into my boots. But as hard as I pushed, they wouldn't fit. When they'd last arrived home in their usual soggy mess Gran, bless her, had stuffed newspapers into them to keep their shape. After a couple of weeks they'd turned into papier mâché. It had set like concrete and it took me half an hour to smash it out.

If bikes were involved I'd have a go at anything relatively local. My interest may have been more in trials and motocross, but that would have required a specialist machine. On what I was earning there was no chance of that. It was cheaper and easier to convert the Viper to road racing than to buy a 'crosser' and trailer. It didn't need to be very sophisticated.

My road racing debut was at Croft, just south of Darlington, for the last meeting of the 1966 season. I've no idea how I'd done it, but by this time the Velo was a 500. I'd bunged on a megaphone with a bit of copper sheet to give the exhaust a nice crack, made some clip-ons, a racing seat from some bits of plywood and stripped off all the lights. A pal named Malcolm Cooper, a garage mechanic, had a Mini-van, into which we shoe-horned the Velo. Also into the back went another mate, Dave Bottomley, so it was pretty crowded on the drive north.

By the time the early morning fog half-cleared there was time for only two laps of practice, during which I must have got the Velo up to as much as 30mph. This was probably just as well since my only front tyre, a ribbed Avon, had a huge blister in the right sidewall which would never have got through scrutineering. Luckily it wasn't so obvious after I dropped the pressure to around 10psi, then we blew it up again for practice. It was a stupid thing to do and I was a bit wary on right-handers, but it was a case of needs must. I was completely skint and a new tyre was about as likely as a new Manx Norton.

My leathers were borrowed from someone who must have been a foot taller than me, but the excess hide didn't seem to bother the scrutineers, either. Somehow I finished halfway down the field in my heat to qualify for the final.

The top man at the time was Robin Fitton, who had a pair of very quick Manx Nortons. Unlike the great unwashed at the cheap end of the paddock, Robin was an architect by trade and quite well-heeled. You've probably never heard of him but he was already a regular winner in International meetings as well as doing the odd grand prix. Two years later he finished an amazing second to Agostini's 500MV at the Ulster, ending the season fourth in the world championship.

Come the final, within a couple of laps all the quick guys have disappeared into the distance, leaving me in a world of my own, thinking I'm on it, the next Geoff Duke, redefining speed and grip. All of a sudden after about five laps … chuffing hell! … there's a roar and Fitton comes flying round the outside of me at Railway Corner at the end of the main straight, peppering me with sparks and dust. He seemed to be going 50mph quicker than me and yet I simply couldn't see how I could go any faster without falling off. I just couldn't believe a bike could be ridden that hard. It wasn't so much humiliating as plain unbelievable.

A couple of years later, on the same bike at the same circuit, I actually beat Robin, which he took in good part. But then he was a right gentleman. Tragically he was killed at the Nurburgring grand prix in 1970 after sliding off and clouting the newly-installed Armco at the Wipperman section. Denis Jenkinson later wrote an article in *Motor Sport* claiming that the steel barrier, installed at the behest of the Formula 1 car boys, was the direct cause of Robin's injuries.

For now, though, beating GP stars was a world away. Oddly, the Croft thrashing didn't deter me one bit so I decided to have a proper crack with the Velo the following year. For those first two years I didn't even win a club race, although there were plenty of top six finishes – when I managed to finish at all.

The guy to beat at the time was Ivan Hackman, who had an immaculate Seeley G50 Matchless. Ivan would invariably emerge on top, but as I got the hang of this new lark we used to have some right ding-dongs along the way. We'd probably have had more, but something always seemed to go wrong – mainly because I was riding what was basically a road bike, and I hadn't much of a clue how to set it up. Then there were the self-imposed handicaps created by hours of ignorant fettling.

Like all young racers, I was for ever on the search for more power – which might have been comical if George Formby had been the rider instead of me. And it has to be said that an appreciation of Renaissance painting is poor preparation for setting up a Velocette clutch. The bike became such a hodgepodge of half-cocked home-brewed ideas that I might as well have named it the Shuttleworth Snap. For instance, I bought a piston via a newspaper ad from a bunch of cowboys in Birmingham. This promised a huge increase in power, but showed more interest in locking-up and throwing me over the handlebars.

The next world-beating idea was Wal Phillips's so-called fuel injection. Since it had no means of regulating the fuel pressure, if you ever got it running right with a full tank – which I rarely did – it would run progressively weaker as the fuel level dropped. This usually made the engine seize – not that it needed much encouragement, thanks to its equally revolutionary pistons. Of course there were no dynamometers available to me then, just seat-of-the-pants trial and error, so learning from your mistakes was a slow and frustrating business. It took three disastrous meetings before I finally threw the injection system into a skip.

I'd also read somewhere – probably in my horoscope – that coil ignition could add as much as one horsepower, so off came the magneto. Maybe the myth was correct, but not with my home-made points system, which would progressively close up until I was left with no horsepower at all. At the time my workshop was a semi-derelict house I'd rented. To me, it was my tool room, but the biggest tool in it was me. In it I'd toil lovingly at my 'lathe'. This was nothing more than an old manual woodworking lathe, to which I'd attached a washing machine motor, bolted the lot to a couple of railway sleepers, and called it a metal lathe. On its best day, it could probably machine to a tolerance of plus or minus an inch. So when I tell you that this is what I used to make the contact-breaker system, you'll understand why it wasn't much good.

In the 1960s one of the biggest problems in racing was stopping – not retiring, that was easy – just slowing down for corners. Almost everyone had the same problem, and certainly the Velocette's biggest weakness was its feeble single-leading shoe front brake. So, having more ambition than know-how I'd knocked up a twin-leading shoe job – cams, back plate and all – without having the slightest clue about tolerances, concentricity or much else. It couldn't have been any less effective if it had been machined from a large cake of soap. Curiously, it worked best when going backwards – exactly what twin-leaders are supposed *not* to do. The truth probably was that it was more egg-shaped than circular, an esoteric detail that was a major mystery to me.

Dave Bottomley eventually threw away the entire sorry contraption. We ended up with a new backing plate, Hillman Imp slave cylinders and an Imp master cylinder on the handlebar – in other words, a hydraulic drum brake. It looked a bit Heath Robinson but worked pretty well for the first few laps. At about this time we'd met a guy from Sheffield named Eric Stanbra who, because he seemed very knowledgeable about bikes in general and Velos in particular, we christened 'Technical Tim'. He knocked up an enormous aluminium cooling disc around the hub, which made the brake fade after three laps instead of two. And eventually we threw away the drum and put a disc on. We must have had a thing about Hillmans, because this one also came from a Minx.

It was a typically roundabout way of learning what worked and what didn't. Mainly, it didn't. Eventually I ran out of brilliant ideas, threw away the fancy piston, bolted the magneto back on and set the bike up as Mr Velocette intended. It ran sweet as a nut – so much so that everyone else wanted to know what magic I'd worked on it. It was flying like it never had before. This was a major lesson. Factories, even British ones, generally know more about their wares than you ever will. The only thing that half-worked was a front disc brake I later fabricated, making my own rotor to go with a Lockheed caliper.

For the most part, though, it's not the bike that needs tuning, but the rider. As a novice you're never quite sure where the improvement comes from, but it does – slowly in my case. My best results in these early days were a couple of second places behind reigning 'club king' Steve Jolly at Cadwell. I also found myself leading a 'Stars of

Tomorrow' event at Mallory until I landed in a heap at The Hairpin and was carted unconscious to hospital. When I came round I did a quick runner without giving my details so mum wouldn't find out I'd been racing. So I wasn't winning, but if the bike didn't break I'd be there or thereabouts. And even if you managed to finish near the front, what did you get for your trouble? A cheap, nasty pot – when almost every one of us was skint and would have much preferred ten bob or so.

At least now I was earning better money, having joined the white heat of Harold Wilson's new technological revolution, or more exactly the heat and noise of the Woodhead-Monroe factory in Ossett, just a few miles from home. The plant was a rough, old-fashioned place, full of fire and smoke, with steel wire going in one end and suspension springs coming out of the other.

As the new boy I naturally got the worst job in the place: chief coiler, operating a clanking contraption into which wire was fed, emerging as a coil spring. The wire could be anything from 3/8in diameter wire, to bus springs size – mammoth things using iron bars almost two inches thick. The wire came white hot out of a long furnace, soft as butter, through a bar feeder, and on to me, in charge of what looked like two giant mangles. You picked up the bar, fed it into a dog, the mangles coiled it, then on it went to the quencher, belching out steam. Winter or summer, you never wore more than a T-shirt, yet sweat poured off you for the entire 12-hour shift. I'd work one week nights, the next days, each shift running from six until six. The hours were crap but the money was good, allowing me to afford two fairly full seasons of club racing but next to no time to work on the bikes. When no one was looking I also got the chance to practise a spot of welding.

If I was on nights, each Friday evening I'd take my Velo to work on a trailer on the back of a beat-up old Morris Minor I'd picked up cheap at Rothwell Car Auctions, and drive straight to meetings when the shift knocked off at 6am. It wasn't ideal but it sure beat repossessing carpets.

The Morris had a mere 86,000 miles on the clock, so seemed almost brand new. Much of the time it was shared with a couple of pals, Malcolm and Dave, who you've met before. By this time Malcolm was also racing, on a 500cc Triumph twin. He was a lanky lad who also hid behind a big red beard, so we became known as a sort of hairy Little and Large. Dave was mechanic and general gofer for the pair of us. On to the back of the Morris went a trailer knocked up from the remains of an old Messerschmitt bubble car. I used to drive it like a lunatic, especially over the Pennine mountain roads to Oulton Park, slithering round corners in a six-wheel drift while Malcolm and Dave clung on white-knuckled. If I'd rolled it down the fellside – which couldn't happen because I was the best driver in the world, obviously – I imagined the police hunting for the survivors of a grotesque four-vehicle accident – the Morris, the bubble car, and the unfortunate bikers on the Triumph and Velocette.

Eventually the Morris did a big-end, which Dave fixed. While we were at it I thought I'd enhance its value by clocking it, only for a bit of paper to flutter from the back of the speedo. Pencilled on it was a glum-looking bloke with a speech bubble saying, 'Oh, no, not again.'

The Morris was followed by an NSU Prinz, which at least slowed me down. It was the most impractical car you could possibly imagine. Instead of a boot it had a gutless 600cc air-cooled twin in the back. The gearchange relied on a nylon ball, which wore out every few hundred miles. And having no chassis, it wasn't the ideal thing to hitch a trailer to. The tow-bar was always a bit on the floppy side, a bit of a worry.

By this time my parents knew I was racing. Between that, and dropping out of art college, they were probably wringing their hands in despair. Whatever hopes they had left for my future, I couldn't see past the next weekend.

Yet I certainly didn't see racing as a career move, didn't even see it leading anywhere in particular, but for the first time in my life I felt fulfilled. I doubt that my folks had any sense of that. It was clear that they didn't want me to race, but neither did they try to hinder me.

Woodhead's wasn't the sort of place to attract the intelligentsia. If you pulled out a newspaper they looked at you a bit cock-eyed. So generally I kept pretty quiet about my art college background. Most of the blokes liked a drink or two, and that was fine by me. Now and again one or two would join me for race meetings. Usually we'd have more drama driving home blotto than I ever managed in a race.

My opposite number on the other shift was a right rough-arsed bloke whose hobbies seemed to be boozing and scrapping, which is probably why he always reeked of stale beer. Another guy, Laurie, was fond of telling stories about how he'd won the war on almost every front, with just a little help from Montgomery and Patton. It was all bullshit, but he did tell a good yarn. Yet another chap was notorious for never bringing sandwiches, so when we knocked off for a break he'd cadge other people's – until the day someone handed him two slices of bread and marg with a stick-on boot sole in between.

The foreman was a hard-nosed Scot. Unlike us, he was paid a productivity bonus, so it was his mantra always to keep the line running. The rest of us, of course, liked nothing more than to see it stopped. Occasionally I'd get my mangle-feeding wrong and the springs would tangle up in a great contorted mess, which raised a huge cheer from the shop floor, because everyone got a break until it was sorted out. Although there was a bit of a knack in setting up the machines, it was a real no-brainer of a job. So if I wasn't thinking about beer and women, in my head I was preparing my Velo in the wash-house at home.

As well as road racing I was still doing the odd hill-climb. My first win at National level came at a climb at

Barbon on the Velo, but repeating the feat on short circuits seemed to take for ever. Yet even if I had a good result, my attitude to it was similar to James Whitham's many years later. My first thought was never that I deserved it, more of a 'bloody hell, that was lucky'. It wasn't until much later in my career when wins started coming thick and fast that I truly began to believe I could win.

From about the time I'd started racing, the Velocette to have was the Thruxton. Over the next few years the Hall Green factory turned out about 1,000 of these special machines. A good Thruxton was capable of 120mph in race tune, well up with the fastest twins. Its reputation grew even stronger in 1967 when Neil Kelly and Keith Heckles scored a one-two in the 500cc production TT, Kelly averaging almost 90mph. This was obviously the bike I needed. Just as obviously, there was no way on earth I could afford one. But the main goodies – huge valves – were all in the cylinder head. I discovered that I could get one of those for around £32 – still a lot of money, but just about do-able. After two months' scraping I eventually assembled the readies to nip over to Ken Swallow's shop in Golcar, near Huddersfield, and in no time I was the owner of a poor man's Thruxton.

By the standards of the time the Thruxton was in a pretty hairy state of tune and needed setting up accurately. Its most notorious weakness was its inlet valve, the stem of which was for ever breaking from the head. Our old mate Technical Tim made a one-off replacement in nimonic steel. If you missed a gear and over-revved – which happened all the time since there were no rev-limiters then – it would bend but not break. You could just take it out, tap it straight, and put it back in again.

With a bit more oomph the racing was going rather better. The guys to beat in Northern nationals were Ken Redfern and Steve Machin, and whilst I rarely headed them, I enjoyed some great scraps with both. I was even getting the odd mention in the papers. 'Mick Grant on a well-turned-out Velocette was a comfortable second [to Redfern] in both races,' said *The Motor Cycle* of a Croft meeting in July 1968. Sometimes I'd drive home with £10 or £15 in winnings, which seemed like a small fortune.

So far all my racing had been at relatively local northern tracks – Croft, Cadwell, Oulton, Silloth, New Brighton, Aintree, Mallory, Llandow. By now I was still little more than a moderately handy clubman, but with an eye on new horizons. So towards the end of the 1968 season it seemed logical to have my first bash at the Irish roads for the Carrowdore 100. With me went a mate with another Velocette, Malcolm 'Cavvie' Calvert. I was allegedly his tuner which, considering my incompetence, probably wasn't a very matey thing to be.

After accepting our entries the organisers told us to get ourselves on the boat from Heysham to Belfast, where we'd be met and transported to the track. Cavvie had a race transporter of sorts, an MSS Velo bolted to a sidecar chassis with a length of RSJ in the middle to hold the race bike's wheels. I had my Minor 1000 with the Messerschmitt trailer. At Heysham we unloaded our bikes and pushed them on to the ferry. I was humping a bag of spanners, a can of petrol, two sleeping bags and girlfriend Dorothy Fisher. About a dozen other English racers on the crossing could barely suppress their mirth at our carry-on.

As promised, at Belfast docks our transport was waiting – a flat-bed lorry. We all manhandled our bikes on board and sat next to them for the journey to Ballywalter, where we spent the night on the floor of the village hall. It definitely wasn't de luxe but every one of us was excited at the thought of racing on the Irish roads.

The next morning I rode the three or four miles to Carrowdore, Dorothy on the back grimly hanging on to all the luggage. Naturally, as well as having no pillion footrests, I had no tax or insurance. Just as inevitably, a police car pulled us over. I was quaking but for them it was a normal day at the Carrowdore. 'Just be on your way and try not to do anything daft,' they told me after a brief and friendly chat.

I was beginning to realise that Irish attitudes to racing were a bit different from home, but I'd seen nothing yet. It was only when we trundled to the paddock – which was literally that, a field – that we learned they didn't see any necessity for practice. After all, what's the difference – you're still riding round the same bit of road? There wasn't even a warm-up lap. You just raced – over five miles of a narrow, bumpy road you'd never seen in your life before. That was just the way it was.

To you this may seem quaint and rather charming, but it threw me into a major panic attack. After a moment of not-so-quiet reflection I did what anyone would do in the circumstances, especially in Ireland, and found a pub and a pint. 'Can anyone give me a lift round the circuit?' I asked the rowdy throng inside. Most of them just looked into their Guinness. The only volunteer was a bloke with a scooter.

'Sure, I'll take you round,' he obliged, 'but let's just have one drink first.'

Another pint later – although it may have been more – off we went on his little Lambretta. My new mate was as good as his word and took me on a full lap – of the ten-mile circuit they didn't use any more.

By the time we got back there was an hour to go before my first race and my mind was totally scrambled. Luckily, Irish racing's a friendly sort of business and it wasn't long before a guy with a wild grey beard stopped by to help. His name was Chapman and he was a lecturer at Edinburgh University, a huge road race fan and an even bigger eccentric. He lent me his Triumph Terrier to make a final desperate recce of the real Carrowdore track. The big ends were dropping out, but I managed to do one lap. Trouble is, actually seeing this muck-splattered collection of lanes made me even more apprehensive than before, especially after someone crashed through a hedge and killed a spectator in the race before mine.

I had never been so scared in my life as I was on the Carrowdore grid. Halfway round the opening lap the magneto slip-ring jammed and the bike ground to a stop. I could have kissed it.

Naturally, having enjoyed my first taste of the Irish roads so much, we did Carrowdore again the following year. This time, as well as Cavvie, there was my new girlfriend, Carol. I must have really fancied her since we travelled de luxe, putting Cavvie's MSS outfit on the ferry, along with both our bikes. Carol was on the pillion with me clinging to one end of the RSJ. Having the MSS along meant that, after the previous year's shambles, I managed to get in two or three sighting laps, so had a vague idea of where the track went. It didn't do me much good, since I fell off on the first lap when I high-sided coming out of a corner and my home-made racing seat accompanied me into an Irish ditch.

I'd first met Carol earlier that year in the Midland, a Wakefield pub we'd regularly drop into. I liked the look of her but actually fancied her girlfriend, who had the sort of reputation that suggested she wasn't that choosy about who she enjoyed interesting times with. Luckily she was still selective enough to tell me where to go, so I ended up propositioning Carol instead. Someone less in a hurry might have asked if she fancied going out for a drink, but I think I invited her to come to Croft for the weekend. We quickly became quite friendly, which isn't hard to do if you're sharing a small tent, and from then on she was more-or-less ever-present when I went racing.

As well as racing, a bunch of us would regularly pile into a Mini-van for the drive up to Ingleton in the Yorkshire Dales for a weekend's potholing, and Carol became part of the same group. Living in primitive tents, covered in cave muck and smelling of stale beer probably wasn't very romantic but then no one ever accused me of being excessively starry-eyed.

Carol was a member of the wire-drawers union, a rather esoteric distinction which didn't mean she wore chainmail bloomers. At the time she lived with her gran, Mrs Rhodes, at Durkar on the outskirts of Wakefield. I was increasingly unsettled at home, so it wasn't long before I moved in with the pair of them. As well as cleaning my bikes after meetings, half of Carol's wages seemed to find their way into my racing pot, so I suppose that she and grannie Rhodes were really my first sponsors.

Since we shared the same room it must have been blindingly obvious that Carol and me were more than just pals. Grannie wasn't exactly a child of the Swinging Sixties, but maybe she thought if she ignored the fact, it would go away, until the day she found us sharing a bath. I was at the tap end facing the door when I heard her coming up the stairs, saw her spot us through the open door and let out a strangled yelp before shuffling back down stairs. I was convinced I'd be in for the riot act for corrupting her granddaughter, but not a word was ever said. That was fine by me.

By this time I'd given up wrestling with red-hot snakes at Woodhead's, moving to the Velmar carpet factory. It was just as no-hope a job, but now I got to drive a fork-lift truck, which was cleaner, cooler and a lot more fun. The fork-lift had a pole at the front to pick up the carpets. I got so I could charge full-tilt like a medieval jouster at the rolled carpets, slam into reverse just before the pole was fully home, and wheel-spin backwards, inch-perfect. Well, it impressed me.

Whatever money Velmar made always seemed to be dwarfed by the massive amount of pilfering that went on. The management responded to this by turning the site into a near-prison. It felt like Stalag Luft III before The Great Escape. Naturally the shop floor responded to this in time-honoured fashion, plotting ever more devious ways of knocking off the next bit of Axminster. For obvious reasons, the night shift was the one to work on since there'd be fewer management bodies about and darkness was the best ally. One chap, who lived across a field from the factory, wrapped himself in an entire roll of Wilton when his shift ended, then got someone to put his overcoat over the top. The plan might even have worked if he hadn't slipped on wet grass plodding home and rolled back down the hill to the factory. Completely unable to pick himself up, he just lay helplessly on the ground until eventually the dozy security man noticed and nicked him.

I didn't nick carpets ... well, not many. I just stole time. With absences for racing, not to mention injuries sustained whilst racing, I just didn't spend enough time pirouetting about on my fork-lift. The bosses were unaccountably unsupportive of my racing ambitions, so usually it was simpler all round just to lie. I once turned up for work with a broken thumb, which was bound to create more bother, until I pretended to drop a carpet pole on it and was sent home on full pay to nurse my 'industrial injury'. So for a while I managed to get away with it, until the day I asked for two weeks off to do the Manx Grand Prix. No bother I was told – just don't expect to come back to a job afterwards.

Having frightened myself witless the previous autumn at Carrowdore, for reasons which no doubt made sense at the time – I was younger and dafter then – I found myself entered in the Manx Grand Prix in 1969. With the optimism of youth I foresaw myself mounting a relentless challenge which would see me crown the fortnight with the coveted newcomers' award. I seriously believed I was in with a shout.

There were several flaws in this ambition. The first was my choice of machine, my trusty Velocette, which at that time was more sorted than it had been but still laboured with a few special tuning mods conceived and executed by one of the dodgier fettlers of the time, one M. Grant. The second was that I'd never even set foot on the Isle of Man before. This dovetailed neatly with the third problem: I was crap at learning new circuits.

Undaunted, four weeks before my Manx debut I set off for a reconnaissance trip on a borrowed Vincent 1000 with a knackered big end – my first classic Manx experience. Carol came along for the ride, although whether for a holiday or to keep an eye on me, I'm not sure. If it was the former, she was to be sadly disappointed, not least because she later became my wife.

Since no sponsors had yet recognised my obvious potential, I was skint: all we had between us was this rattly old Vinnie, two sleeping bags and about 3/6d in change. We spent the first night in a ditch on the climb out of Union Mills, the one section of the TT course I suppose I could claim to know intimately. The second night was spent on Ramsey Beach, which may sound romantic now although the only thing which prevented Carol from sleeping was fear of being washed out by the tide. In between times, the Vincent struggled around for just enough laps to show me I didn't know one end of the course from the other.

A month later I was back with the Velo for the real thing. This time I had proper accommodation, sharing a tent near the paddock with two friends from The Midland, Tom and Veronica Stead. I was Mr Gooseberry. Racing exhausts bellowing through the tent before scrutineering every morning made it less than a restful week, although I didn't know the half of it.

Come practice, I was hopeless. Although I'd always been rubbish at learning new circuits – something I never got much better at – with less than 40 horsepower the Mountain Circuit shouldn't have been all that tricky, with most bits flat-out. Unfortunately I didn't seem to have the knack of working out the odd bits that weren't. It was like navigating by braille.

Yet youth is a wonderful thing. Despite the glaringly obvious, by the middle of practice week I'd deluded myself into reckoning that averaging 87mph, which I thought I could just about manage, could win me the newcomers' award. On Friday practice, a week before my race, I'd lashed out on new tyres and new chains and planned to do just one lap to bed everything in, then put the bike away and spend a relaxing week getting my head together.

As a plan it wasn't altogether bad but the execution eluded me. Well, it was a bit damp. Hammering through the fast left-hander into Greeba Castle I clipped the white line and lost it, in a very big way. I slid for what seemed long enough to raise a family before clouting the big wall on the right, ricocheting across the road, and came to rest hanging like a rag doll over the wall on the opposite side. The bike was a mess, and I wasn't much better. Nothing important was broken but it was the most pain I'd ever experienced up to that time.

Mind you, I wasn't the only one. Another mate, Pete Laverack, had been on the same newcomers' bus lap as me. For May Hill, our guide had told us to peel in at the end of the black-and-white paving. I did as told on my first lap, and nearly hit the same wall Pete had clouted ten minutes earlier on the same wrong line. He ended up in Nobles Hospital with broken bones and a few lumps missing. He never raced on the Island again, so his entire career amounted to less than a lap. In the same session in which I dumped the Velo, another pal, Ivan Hackman, turned left instead of right at Glen Vine and ended halfway up a tree. In comparison I felt quite smug about getting as far as Greeba.

Naturally this left the week of ease I'd been looking forward to also dangling from the Greeba Bridge wall. Instead, I spent the entire time nursing bruises and rebuilding what was left of the Velo. Somehow, I manage to hobble to the start. The bike ran OK at first but spent three laps getting slower before finally expiring at Hillberry. I coasted down the hill to Governors, where the marshals insisted I had to push right through the dip and up the hill at the other side. By the time I reached the pits I was blue in the face and hyperventilating too much to explain to my crew what was wrong. Instead, I just collapsed in a heap. The culprit, of course, was Grant's Patent Points System, the only one in existence which made Joe Lucas look clever. After downloading the correct ignition mapping – prising the points apart with a screwdriver – we finally persuaded it to spark. And off I roared into history.

I finished 48th. Out of 48. I averaged a shade over 70mph with a best lap of 85mph. The winner, Gordon Daniels, was a mere 48 minutes ahead. After that things could only get better. And almost at once, they did: despite all the threats, my job was still there when I got back.

CHAPTER 4

JIM LEE AND ME

Despite the debacle of the Manx Grand Prix, 1969 was far and away my best season so far. Hard though it is to believe, I was better organised and even a bit better off. On short circuits, at least, the Velo was pretty reliable and I'd taken my first win on it in a Batley Club meeting at Cadwell Park.

Towards the end of the year I came under the wing of the man who would have the biggest effect on my future career. Jim Lee was well known in bike competition, mainly through his company, Jim Lee Racing Components, in Batley. Amongst other racing parts – aluminium tanks, clip-ons and so on – they turned out the well-known Dalesman trials frames. Jim was also one of the big noises in the Batley Motorcycle Club, which ran many of the meetings I'd been doing. Unknown to me he'd been keeping an eye on my racing progress and somewhere under my scruffy exterior had seen something worth nurturing other than my ginger beard. Out of the blue he approached me with an offer of sponsorship. The deal was that I'd go and work for him, which sounded more fun than stunt-driving fork-lift trucks in a carpet factory, and between us we'd build race bikes, which I'd ride. Frankly, I was staggered. Jim was my Santa Claus.

I'd first experienced Jim's products the previous year. He'd recently made a dozen frames for Stevens, the Velocette specialists. For £15 I managed to get hold of a spare one which had been kicking around the workshop for a while. A proper modern cradle in Reynolds 531 tubing and thus much lighter than the original Velo chassis, it also allowed the engine to sit much lower than before. It was never going to turn the Venom into a world-beater, but it had certainly given the old girl a new lease of life.

Getting someone like Jim on my side was a major event, every bit as crucial at the time as getting a full factory ride would be later down the line. I'm still a bit baffled about what Jim thought he saw in me. Never at any time in my career did I regard myself as a natural rider. I always felt that to get a similar result to the next guy I had to apply myself harder. This was maybe part of the reason I spent too long making only slow progress in club racing. It also didn't help that I was invariably more or less skint and running my bike on the proverbial shoestring. On the other hand, I'm sure the same factors gave me a resilience and determination that would pay dividends in later years.

So maybe Jim recognised something about my attitude rather than my skills on a bike – for I definitely wasn't a quitter and always gave 100 per cent, even if the result was occasionally farcical. From the beginning I had an insatiable desire to pass people, even on the road. In normal life I was never outwardly aggressive, but at the track a complete stranger seemed to climb into my leathers. Nor did I try to ride unfairly – but if the bloke in front left even half a gap I'd be in it, and if that caused the other guy to fall off, that was his problem, not mine.

I was driven. I just had to be in front. It wasn't something I was particularly aware of at the time, but other riders have mentioned since how focused I would be before a race. I wasn't a rider who smiled and nodded 'have a good race' to the next guy on the grid. The only guy I wanted to have a good race was me. All I'd offer anyone else was a glare. At the time I was just doing what came naturally, but years later, on a light-hearted event called The Tour of Man, it was clear that Carl Fogarty was exactly the same. As a racer I've rarely been troubled by deep insight, but on that day the penny dropped. Whatever our respective skills and achievements, we at least had in common that deep yearning to be in front. Foggy, though, probably had a better glare.

I suppose luck also played a part. It's easy to be fearless if you never suffer pain, and many's the promising young racer who has a big one and never shows the same promise again. I was fortunate – it can't have been skill – in going a long time without breaking any bones. In fact I never did break one in all my time on the Velocette. For the first year or so I barely fell off at all and later all the tip-offs I had were little ones. It doesn't take much of this to convince you that you can walk on water, which is when it begins to become really dangerous.

At Jim's I wasn't called as much, but was effectively a machine shop apprentice, learning my trade. After a succession of soul-destroying dead-end jobs, this was a priceless opportunity almost as valuable as the help with my racing. I was doing work I actually enjoyed, with an end-product I actually cared about, and learning real skills along the way. After all my years of bodging and making do, it was eye-opening to watch people who genuinely knew what they were about, using kit actually designed for the job. There were no botched-up spindle lathes at Jim's.

Jim had three other guys working for him, but being part of such a small set-up meant I had to be hands-on and contributing, so I spent much of my time making jigs, bending tubes, and so on. The main output was Dalesman frames and light alloy tanks, which were delivered for assembly up the road in Otley, initially by Pete Edmondson until Wassell took over the Dalesman concern. Although this meant a regular flow of work, it also put nearly all Jim's eggs in one basket. He was effectively working for Wassell, who constantly squeezed him on price. There were lots of other jobs – clip-ons and rear sets, Commando frames for the likes of Tom

Rutherford and Harry Thompson, racing tanks for anyone who wanted one.

Unless he was going to make several, in which case he'd make a proper jig, Jim's approach to making frames was simplicity itself. He'd just put a piece of wood on the floor, draw the lines he wanted in chalk and bend his tubes to the shape he needed. He had a brilliant eye for line, and the technique almost always seemed to work. He was a very clever fellow, not that it did him a lot of financial good.

Jim's right hand was a machinist, Jeff Thorn, and between them they seemed to be able to make almost anything. Mind you, Jeff wasn't infallible. He once made me a wheel hub from scratch. It was a beautiful piece of machining, but proved bafflingly difficult to lace to the rim. When we finally counted the spoke holes, we found that the hub had one less than the rim. Jeff spent the rest of the morning wondering where the other one went, before Jim welded up all 19 and started afresh. For a bodger like me working with him was both an eye-opener and an education, and it's impossible to describe how much I learned and how much I owe Jim. Some of it, at least, I was able to pay back, at least to Jeff: a decade or so later, Colin Appleyard and I sponsored his son, Chris.

My first Jim Lee race bike was based around an old 500cc BSA Gold Star engine he happened to have lying around. By the time we finished with it the Beezer revved to about 8500, far more than it was designed for, so it needed new pistons every few meetings. The engine and gearbox were located on four rubber bushes, so it wobbled about a bit in the frame, but at least didn't make your fillings fall out.

Compared to my old Velo the Goldie was lighter, a bit faster and handled better. It was also easier to start. This was something else I'd spent hours practising, something else which paid off in future years. Just three paces and a bump would see the Velo on its way. With the BSA, I got that down to two. Whenever the flag dropped, I was almost always one of the first away.

With Jim's backing my racing stepped up a gear and I set about doing regular National meetings, against the likes of Steve Machin, Tony Jefferies, John Barton and Ken Redfern. With a properly prepared bike under me at last, the 1970 season got off to a flier. The Beezer proved quite successful – for a Gold Star which, after all, had last been produced in 1963. First time out I placed fourth in a Croft National meeting behind local ace Steve Jolly who the year before had placed fifth in the 750cc Production TT (the same race in which Malcolm Uphill, on another Triumph, had become the first man to lap at over 100mph). Peter Williams finished just ahead of me.

After my Fred Karno workshop, it was astonishing what Jim's could produce. In no time a 350 appeared, an air-cooled Yamaha TR2 engine bought from Padgett's, mated to a spine frame Jim knocked up for the job. There were other novelties. At the time, apart from a few trendies such as Lance Weil, leathers came in any colour you wanted so long as it was black – until the day Jim presented me with a set of lurid lime green ones (almost the same shade I'd wear years later for Kawasaki). Much to my embarrassment his race bikes were no less vivid – always candy apple green, set off with bright orange Sperex-painted exhaust pipes, which went nicely with my green leathers and ginger beard. This was also the time the 'JL' logo, also in bright green, first appeared on my helmet. I've kept it since – along with the number 10 plate, although that arrived much later – partly through loyalty to Jim, but equally to make myself identifiable.

After four years of racing nothing but barely-modified road bikes, the Yamaha was a revelation – light, fast and nimble. At one stage in the season I knocked off a run of 16 consecutive wins and began to get noticed. In the 1000cc final at Aintree in July I lapped everyone including the guy in second place, yet I'm not sure who was more surprised – the rest of the field, or me. After all the years of scratching around with cobbled-together kit, suddenly it was all coming together.

Also in July we debuted Jim's 750cc contender, a Norton Commando engine I'd acquired slotted into another of Jim's lightweight frames. At Croft first time out I started the day by winning both 350cc races on the Yam – just ahead of a hard-charging Scot named Alex George in the second – but the Norton was a disaster. In its first race it lost a cylinder, and in the second the front disc brake was binding and I couldn't even push-start it.

That year's TT, my first, was a similarly bitter-sweet experience, although not such a farce as the previous year's Manx Grand Prix. For some reason I took the Velo for the Senior, although we'd pretty well finished with the old girl by then. Maybe she knew it, for she broke down early in practice week. Since I still needed a qualifying lap I borrowed Carl Ward's Manx Norton. Like almost everyone else I'd always assumed the Manx to be the dog's bollocks, but couldn't believe how heavy and slow it was and actually lapped slower than on my tired old Velocette. As it turned out it was all for nothing because the Velo was too sick even to start the race.

Not long after I made my peace with the Norton single after breaking Jim's Gold Star in practice at Croft. Mark Butterworth kindly lent me his 350 Manx for the unlimited final, explaining that it was on its last legs before a rebuild, so I wasn't to rev it beyond 7000rpm. For once I did as I was told, despite which – it must have been one of those magic days when you feel totally in tune – after a couple of laps I was wondering where everybody else was. I went on to win at what seemed like a canter.

But at the TT the Yamaha looked more promising. Apart from Ago's lonely MV Agusta, most of the likely runners were either on TR2s like mine or single cylinder Aermacchis. Practice was pretty frustrating since although the Yam always ran sweet as a nut on short circuits, the extreme changes in altitude on the Mountain Course meant that, try as we might, we couldn't get the jetting right on the Isle of Man.

The race, not to put too fine a point on it, was a piece of piss. Along with a feeble memory and fear of heights I've always had a weak bladder, and nowhere in racing quite tests that like those moments of panic on the Glencrutchery Road before the start of a TT race. Eventually, after about a dozen trips to the loo, none of which produced more than a mortified dribble, the flag dropped. After a couple of steps the Yam rattled into life and off I screamed down Bray Hill. So far, so good.

By Quarter Bridge, barely a mile into the first lap, I needed another pee – desperately. But this was a five-lap race on a typically wet and miserable Manx day, and the nearest loo was over two hours away. No way could I last that long. I decided to just grit my teeth for a reconnaissance lap and check out somewhere quiet where I could stop and take a leak second time around. A lap later I was none the wiser, but in even more pain. Now it may sound like a sick joke but coming round – you guessed it – Waterworks, there's a bloke holding out a bit of card saying 'Ago Out'. Bloody hell, I thought, if he's out, everyone else is going to be riding that bit harder, so the attrition rate will be higher and I might get a bit of a result. So, whatever happens, Granty, just don't stop …

I've never been in so much discomfort but decided to grin and bear it. If I was still going on the final lap, I reckoned, I could just pee in Jim's new green leathers. My reasoning for not doing it earlier was that with bikes being so unreliable then, the last thing I wanted was to be broken down halfway up the Mountain like Billy-No-Mates, stinking of piss. Come the start of the final lap, I just couldn't do it, couldn't piss. So I just went for it, if only to get back to the bogs that much quicker – for a glorious 18th place. This isn't something you'll have read in any TT 'Who's Who' blogs, but ever since then one of my biggest worries on the Island has been my bladder. The other was flies – on my visor.

Eighteenth may sound pretty average, although even Joey Dunlop, in his first Junior six years later, would manage only 16th place. But at the time, particularly after going so well on short circuits, I was disappointed. But I was in good company in a quality field. Tom Dickie, Vin Duckett and Geoff Barry were all behind me. Agostini, incidentally, wasn't a DNF at all, but won, five minutes ahead of Alan Barnett's Syd Lawton 'Macchi'. Barnett lapped at just a shade under 100mph, a remarkable feat.

If working for Jim took some of the uncertainty out of the quality of my race bikes, it also helped with race transport, since I could usually borrow the firm's J2 Morris van. Inevitably it was also painted candy apple green – as you've noticed, Jim seemed to have a thing about green. I was able to borrow it most weekends and it proved reliable enough except for a habit of overheating. This was one of the few signs that anything significant was going on in the engine bay, since it never did more than about 55mph, even downhill. Getting to far-flung circuits like Lydden or Thruxton seemed to take the best part of a week. Jim's response to the overheating was to take out the thermostat, which I thought was there for a reason so stuck it back in, whereupon Jim would have taken it out again by the next weekend.

Some bits, though, had a knack of simply unbolting themselves. Once, coming back from Thruxton, there was a big bang as a front wheel fell off and the corner of the J2 hit the ground in a torrent of sparks, followed by an even bigger bang as the errant wheel tried to smash its way through the floor of the van, before disappearing off into the night. It took us an hour to find the bloody thing. It turned out that Jim had had the wheels off to do the brakes, and had forgotten to tighten them up.

Like any cash-strapped young racer, my own transport was the usual sorry collection of hacks it would have been kinder to sling on the scrap heap. Typical was an Austin Princess I bought in Bradford via an ad in the local paper. It looked sound enough but guzzled petrol at an alarming rate – four gallons in the fifteen-mile drive home – until Dave Bottomley, my mechanic, discovered that both breathers on the twin SU carbs' float chambers were blocked because the gasket was on upside-down. After that it ran a treat, and since it had only cost about £50 I wasn't all that bothered that large parts of it were on the verge of falling off. On her first trip on the M1 in it I treated Carol to her maiden ton-up run, both front wings flapping like Dumbo's ears. Later we took the same old heap to an ACU dinner in Harrogate, where a bloke done up to the nines had the job of opening each guest's car doors as though we were celebrities. I was keen that he didn't try ours, since both hinges had rusted to oblivion years before, and the entire door would simply have fallen on his feet.

By this time Carol and I were a serious item. At race meetings she always mucked in and became part of the team, but always with the good sense not to poke her nose in where it didn't belong. She may have known her place on race day, but was otherwise pretty feisty and direct. Partly through shyness she could come across as hard as nails on the outside, but was soft inside, which not everyone got to see. She was in charge of catering and all the domestic stuff needed at meetings – stuff I was completely useless at. If it had been down to me the entire team would have starved if they hadn't succumbed to exposure from lack of bedding first. Her special talent was timing. Initially, she just used a stopwatch, which I could just about understand. Years later she'd have a computer and was able to log the practice times of each of the top ten riders. Since to this day I'm still as familiar with computers as I am with Chaucer's tales, this seemed nothing less than magical.

So far the Norton had been neither particularly fast nor reliable. So for the start of the '71 season I spent £80 having it tuned by Mick Redfern, brother of Ken, whose own Commando always seemed to go well. At its first outing, at Oulton Park in mid-March, we struggled to set it up and came away with nothing, especially as I also binned the Yamaha. After all the promise of the previous year, it wasn't a great start to the season.

From Cheshire we drove cross-country to Cadwell for another National meeting, threw up the tent and worked on the bikes until well into the small hours. Charlie Sanby was the acknowledged boss in the big class, riding one of the Gus Kuhn Commandos which at the time seemed to be winning everything. Despite my Norton jumping out of third gear I managed to beat him fair and square to take my first ever National road race win. Jim, bless him, was in tears, but I was more interested in the £60 prize money – almost enough to pay for Mick's tuning job. For once *MCN*'s reporting was right on the button: 'Mick Grant smiled and stroked his ginger beard at the thought of the £60 first prize.' Nor was it a home-track fluke. Although Charlie turned the tables shortly later at Lydden – hardly my local circuit – the Lee Commando clocked up over 30 wins in the season.

The 350 was flying, too. In that class the man to beat was reigning British 250cc champ Steve Machin. I had my first real go at him in a championship round at Croft in early April, finishing third. I might have given him a better fight if the cheap stick-on sole covering the hole in my old boot hadn't come lose and kept fouling the footrest. I could hardly change gear. I'd lashed out on new tyres for the meeting, but should maybe have treated myself to a pair of boots as well. But I at least had the consolation of beating Phil Haslam in to second place in the 1,000cc race.

The other up-and-coming Yorkshireman was, of course, Tony Jefferies, father of David. Tony also rode a 750 and a 350 – a Triumph triple or Commando Metisse and a Yamsel – so we had plenty of tussles during the season. For the most part it was friendly stuff. In the warm-up area at Thruxton, Tony's mechanic – who went by the unflattering name of 'Twit' – was larking about with a steel tape pretending to measure the Lee frame. Then he 'measured' the exhaust – by pushing tape up it. At the precise moment the marshals waved us through to the grid, the tape hooked the exhaust valve – and stuck. That was about the point I realised how he'd got his moniker – although to be fair I've never seen anyone get a Commando exhaust system off so quickly.

At that age Tony could be a bit wild. Probably, we both were. He once passed John Cooper on the inside over the start line at Scarborough, where Coop was the reigning boss. It was a very ballsy, not to say hairy move. Coop was highly unamused.

On the shorts I usually felt I had the edge on Tony, but that year's TT was altogether different. In the Formula 750cc race I did OK, ending one session fifth on the leaderboard. But getting a result was always going to be an uphill task. Jim's Commando did 132mph through the speed trap compared to 147mph for Ray Pickrell's factory BSA. As it turned out this didn't much matter.

Race day was one of those occasions when I felt I could fly, felt invincible, which I was still too daft to know would probably end in pain. Coming out of Cronk-ny-Mona I could see Keith Heckles's Norton a long way ahead. All that went through my mind was that if I didn't get him at Signpost I'd be stuck behind him all the way to Governors and could say goodbye to my first 100mph lap. So – to hell with the physics – I took a big lunge and collected Keith halfway round the corner, mangling his bike and breaking his collarbone. He was a lovely fellow and I felt quite bad about that, but not as bad as Jim felt about me scraping his new green leathers. Tony had no such bother and won by 26 seconds from Pickrell, with Peter Williams riding the top Norton into third place.

It was a great year for Tony. In a sodden Junior he took full advantage of Agostini's retirement to win, whilst I splashed into seventh place. However well I was doing on the mainland, I clearly still had some way to go on the roads.

Still, there was consolation to come. Against a really high-class field at the Mallory post-TT meeting I chased home John Cooper to place second on the 350, backing that up with a solid sixth on the Norton in the Superbike race. Also causing a stir at the same meeting was a southern smoothie named Sheene, who finished second to Ago in the 500cc race.

A month later at Scarborough, it got better still when 'Mick Grant, the man with the red beard and bright green leathers' (I suppose it was a public image of sorts) won his first international race, leading Steve Machin over the line in the 350cc race. It was Machin, though, who set a new lap record. I was all set to follow that up in the 750 race until the gear linkage fell apart, handing Dave Croxford the win.

The most memorable race of the year – to bike race fans if not to me at the time – was Mallory Park's 'Race of the Year' in mid-September. This was the legendary day on which old 'Moon Eyes' Cooper on the BSA triple stalked Agostini's MV Agusta, overtaking the Italian world champion at the hairpin on the last lap, to the hysterical delight of fans and bike press alike. As I went through the Hairpin on that same lap, I could hear the crowd yelling wildly, but couldn't fathom why my mid-field exploits were so exciting. They were actually cheering at Coop overtaking Ago just behind me ... but almost a lap ahead. My part in the final festivities was a modest 12th place on the Norton – but then with Pickrell, Paul Smart, Percy Tait, Phil Read and a young Jarno Saarinen in the field, being on the same stretch of tarmac was almost achievement enough.

I already knew Coop a little from work, since Jim Lee would often entrust his two-stroke crankshaft building to him. Six years older than me, he was already a bit of a legend, but what impressed me most was what a gentleman he was, yet always down-to-earth and forever smiling. What I didn't know was how big a part he'd play in my subsequent career.

CHAPTER 5

BATLEY VARIETY CLUB

By any standards 1971 had been a massive season for me. I'd had short circuit wins galore and people were beginning to take notice. True, getting there may have been a long, slow slog and at 27 I wasn't exactly a youngster anymore, but I'd arrived. But there was one problem and it was a ticklish one. For all the huge debt I owed to Jim Lee, I began to wonder if riding his bikes was in my best interests in the longer term. Jim's race ethos was more about machine development than race-winning, although he was as delighted as anyone with a good result. Yet looking around the paddocks, it was obvious that the guys with relatively standard machines – stock Yamahas or Yamsels – had fewer issues but were at least as competitive as me. All they seemed to do was throw away the original Yokohama tyres, put on a pair of Dunlops, and fast laps were there for the taking.

Although I don't think I'd worked it out in a very coherent way, by this time it was also dawning on me that racing might become some sort of career – if I only had something resembling a strategy, rather than bouncing about from opportunity to cock-up like a demented pinball. On good weekends I was earning more in prize money than I got in my pay packet. Not all prizes were so convenient. After taking triple wins at Croft I came away with 28 bottles of Strongbow cider, but I'm sure I found a good use for them, too. Not all weekends were good, by any means, but even I could work out what the sums meant.

I'd even advertised for a proper mechanic – nothing fancy, just a slot in the Batley Club's magazine. It offered 'inexpensive weekends and even cheaper mid-week entertainment'. There was no mention of cider. Or wages, come to that.

Yet I still didn't see racing as a living, much less a career. In my background, like most people's, you worked your 40-hour week, paid your tax and stamp, and the rest they gave you each Friday in a brown envelope to give to the missus or sluice down the loo. Left to my own devices I don't think I had the self-belief to take what seemed like a giant step into the unknown and become an independent privateer. But I'd seen other local guys like Dudley Robinson, Mick and Derek Chatterton, who I didn't think were any better than me, just pouring petrol in their standard Yamahas, jetting them, riding and doing pretty well – whilst we were mucking about trying to make prototypes work. If they could do it, I thought, then why couldn't I? Inevitably, Jim Lee's main interest was in developing his business, not my racing career – although he never did anything but help that, in his way. So I realised I had to move on, try to make a move to the next level, and keep my fingers crossed that it would work out.

The biggest name in bike racing in my area, then as now, was the same Padgett's from which I'd almost bought the 500cc Velocette before dad put his foot down. Late in 1971 we hatched a deal for me to ride their bikes for the 1972 season, which was duly made public in *Motor Cycle News* on 8 December. It was probably the most painful decision I've made in racing. Yet I was convinced that if I wanted my racing to develop, I did need to move on.

Although I had huge respect for Jim Lee and we got on well, not surprisingly he took it badly – not least because he always saw Padgett's as one of his main competitors as a supplier of racing parts. In fact I suspect that was the heart of it. He wasn't so much bitter that I'd left him to better myself, which I think he understood, but that I'd deserted to join his arch rivals. In fact I'm sure this was also one of the reasons Padgett's were keen to poach me from Jim – his loss was their gain. They were one of the two big Yamaha race dealers in the north of England, the other being Dugdale's in Cheshire for whom Charlie Williams rode. Even without the local connection – their Batley showroom was only 15 minutes away from home – it was the obvious place to go.

Along with the ride came a job. As well as racing for them at weekends, I'd spend the working week in one of their workshops, which I moved into late in the winter of 1971–72. As well as selling road bikes, Peter Padgett had a thriving business building Yamaha race bikes from spares, and much of my work was doing the assembly, as well as straightening frames and forks and any fabricating jobs that needed doing. By now I wasn't quite the botcher I'd been before joining Jim Lee. The racing arrangement was that Padgett's would provide me with a 250cc TD3, a 350cc TR3 and occasionally a 354cc Yamaha for the 500cc class. I'd pay for getting the bikes to the circuit, entries, tyres, chains, fuel and I'd look after the bikes, other than the engines, which was Peter's territory. Any prize money I won we'd split down the middle.

After each weekend's racing, the deal was that if I had an engine that needed fixing or refreshing, I'd drop it off with Peter on Monday morning, get it back and stick it in the bike. Often it didn't work out quite as smoothly as that. Usually Peter's priority seemed to be the engines he was building for customers for money. Like most racers I gave little thought to where the cash was ultimately coming from and thought my needs were more important.

Then there was the famous Batley Variety Club, then in full swing. Peter seemed to be an addict, especially for Shirley Bassey, with whom he was obviously in love. At any rate, he practically lived there, which wasn't entirely conducive to building engines. So it might be Friday night before I got the engine back, giving me barely time to slot it into the rolling chassis, load the van, and get to Cadwell Park or wherever first thing on Saturday. It wasn't the happiest set-up.

The weekly grind also had its drawbacks. Padgett's main shop was then in Wellington Street, Batley, but I was mostly banished to another workshop half a mile away. I'd get in at eight o'clock on the dot, but often it wasn't until Peter or his brother Don wandered in, anything up to two hours later, that I'd have anything to do. Don soon realised that this meant that in the meantime they were paying me to do nothing, which filled him with horror. The most obvious solution would have been for them to get in earlier, or at least give me my instructions the previous day.

Now all Yorkshiremen have a reputation for being tight, and the Padgett brothers were nothing if not true Yorkshiremen. So Don came up with a better answer. He installed a clocking-in machine at the main shop and handed me a time-card. This was ideal, at least for him, since it meant that I couldn't clock in until they'd opened the shop. Not that I seemed to have much control over the time-card, anyway. Every lunchtime, Don would considerately clock me out and disappear for his lunch, a process repeated every evening.

If that wasn't very funny at the time, sometimes the tragi-comic double act between the brothers was. The pair of them shared an office upstairs from my workshop and were forever falling out over the most trivial things. From my standpoint downstairs the clunk of phones hurled across the room was regular background music. Don, who had a gammy arm, always referred to himself as 'me', as in 'I've got nothing, me'. Given his enormous Ford Galaxy parked outside, not to mention a fleet of personal bikes, this took some believing. 'Him there,' he'd say, pointing a finger in the direction of Peter, 'he's got everything. I've got no money, I've got nowt. If it weren't for my arm, I'd go in the army, me.'

'Aye', Peter would counter. 'Dad's Army.'

Undeterred, Don would carry on his lament to poverty.

It may have been a well-worn script, but eventually it became too much for Peter. 'You fucking what? You want some fucking money? Here,' and he put his arm in his jacket, pulled out a bundle of notes as big as your fist and flung them across the workshop. Suddenly the air was full of lovely fivers floating slowly to earth.

At this both brothers dashed outside in a huff – one to each external door, like a Brian Rix bedroom farce. For a merciful instant there was silence. And then, as the greater danger dawned, each cried in unison: 'Bloody 'ell, Granty's in there with our money', and both shot back in before I could snaffle a single note. Money may sometimes have divided the Padgett brothers, but when it looked at risk it united them powerfully, too.

Despite the drawbacks, it seemed that nothing could stop us on the track. The bikes were as good as anyone else's, and from March until the TT we were winning pretty well as we pleased, although Ken Redfern and Derek Chatterton sometimes had other ideas. The 350, especially, was a gorgeous little machine. By late May I'd clocked up about 30 wins and put Padgett's 350 at the top of the British championships, with the '500' only one point adrift in second place. I'd also finally got rid of the beard and – these facts may have been related – become engaged to Carol.

On one level I was happy – who wouldn't be with results like those? I'd suddenly got a purpose in life and was saving as much money as I could to better myself. But between Don's bloody clock-cards, late engines, handing over half my winnings and paying for tyres – even though a pair of Dunlops cost only £14 at the time – I seemed to be barely better off than I'd been the previous year. I felt that the brothers were getting the better half of the arrangement. I pleaded with Peter to ease our deal just a little bit, but he wouldn't budge.

I consoled myself with two weeks without time-cards and

flying telephones as Padgett's main man at the Isle of Man TT. It was a watershed event in many ways. On a personal note I claimed my first podium finish, and my second, but that year's races are remembered for a far more momentous event. On 9 June in atrocious conditions, Morbidelli's Gilberto Parlotti was killed at the Verandah on the last lap of the Ultra-Lightweight event, a race which should never have been run. The Italian was only competing at all because his main world championship rival, Angel Nieto, refused to ride on the Island, giving him a chance to gain an edge in the point standings. Parlotti himself wasn't a big TT name, but his close friend Agostini certainly was. Ago came close to boycotting that afternoon's Senior, but changed his mind and won the race. But he never rode a TT again.

A lesser light in Ago's last TT was me, one of the usual Brits hoping the MV would break down – although it rarely did since it was never pushed hard enough. After half a season on Yamahas I'd been pressed against my better judgement to ride an air-cooled Kawasaki triple in the Senior rather than the 354cc Yamaha. Apparently Padgett's had some tie-up with John Durrance of the then UK importer, Agrati sales. At the time the Yamaha was definitely a better TT bike than the Kawasaki, which was a huge wide thing, scarcely any quicker despite its extra 140cc, and didn't handle half so well. Worse still, while the Yam used normal triangular tyres of the sort I was used to, for some reason these wouldn't fit the triple, so I had to use some strange rounded Dunlops in which I had no confidence. Even so, it may have paid dividends because this was my first contact with Kawasaki, with whom I'd enjoy some of my best years from 1975 onwards. I finished a wobbly but otherwise fairly uneventful race in third place behind the MVs of Ago and Alberto Pagani. Pagani was only 1½ minutes ahead but his team-mate beat me by almost half a lap.

The Junior was altogether more interesting, especially when I clouted the bank at Laurel Bank, a corner I've always hated – but at least it stopped me sliding. To be on the safe side the Yamaha needed two fuel stops for the five-lap race. At the first stop, after two laps, there still seemed to be a fair bit sloshing around in the bottom of the tank, so I decided to risk the last three without stopping. Only fumes and prayer got me down the Mountain for the final time until finally the bike spluttered to a halt leaving Governor's Bridge dip. Luckily most of the slope was behind me and I managed to push in to beat Jack Findlay into fourth place by just 12 seconds. What I didn't know was that one of the piston ring pins was about to fall out, having been bodged after coming loose in practice. Tony Rutter was 40 seconds ahead of me with Agostini, as usual, some way in the distance. The only downside of my first TT podium was missing the 100mph lap by four seconds. In the Senior I'd come even closer, just 0.4 seconds off that magic milestone. I failed to finish both the 250 and Formula 750 races, but two out of four wasn't bad.

Back in Batley I asked for my wages for my two weeks' labour, which I thought was pretty reasonable. Although Don and young Clive Padgett were present, Peter handled negotiations on behalf of Padgett's plc.

'Oh, can't have that,' he replied smugly. 'You've been on holiday.'

'Holiday?! I've been working for you,' I squeaked, a bit nonplussed.

'No, you've been on holiday.'

'OK, then,' I said, recovering slightly, 'how's about some holiday pay?'

'Now, lad, we can't be doing that.'

'Well can you at least put a stamp on my card?'

'Oh, nay lad, not when you were on holiday.'

By now I'd got the picture. 'OK, then, but you're not going to like it. I won £600 on the Isle of Man, and half of it's yours, right?' (At the time TT prize money was still scandalously low. For winning the Senior, Agostini got the same as Stanley Woods had exactly 40 years before.)

'Right.'

'Well tough shit, I'm keeping the lot.'

And I did.

Worse was to come. Shortly after the TT, a telegram arrived from John Player Norton inviting me down to Andover to discuss riding for them for the second half of the season. At the time there was huge public interest in the newly formed Norton team, using a bike based on the 750cc Commando engine. So far that season Tony Rutter had been the third rider in the factory Norton team with Peter Williams and Phil Read, but for some reason didn't ride for them at the TT. By this time I'd got to know Tony pretty well since he was one of my main opponents in the 250 and 350cc classes. He was a quiet and pretty reserved bloke who kept very much to himself, and I suspect all the razzmatazz in the Norton squad didn't exactly agree with him.

Whatever the reason, around TT time he left the team. This was the vacancy on offer. Sheene had been in the running for short-circuit meetings, but had just ruled himself out by breaking a collar bone at Imola. Apparently Perris and Williams had both been impressed by my showing on Jim Lee's Commando the previous year, so I was next in line.

So far, at least, Norton weren't setting the racing world alight. They'd begun brilliantly when Read briefly led at Daytona, before finally finishing fourth (ahead of him, ominously, were three Yamahas of less than half the Norton's capacity, with Don Emde's in first place. No two-stroke had won the event before). From there the project seemed to run out of steam, with chronic gearbox problems sidelining both bikes in the Formula 750 TT, although Williams's Commando placed second to Pickrell's Triumph in the 750cc Production race. Despite all this, it was a proper factory effort with a big-bucks sponsor, so from my point of view there was nothing to think about. For an art-school dropout who'd been scratching to afford to go racing at all just a year or so before, it was a major opportunity. Naively, I rushed into Peter's office to break the tidings, expecting him to be as chuffed as me.

He just knocked me over cold. 'There's more arses than saddles,' he growled. 'If you put yours on their bike, you won't put it back on ours.'

Sod 'em. I wasn't about to turn down an offer like this. So the next day Carol and I went down to Hampshire to see Frank Perris. He took us to a swanky restaurant for lunch, a whole new world for both of us. The menu may as well have been in Urdu for all it meant to me, and each place setting had more tools than my workshop. Still, if Frank thought I was retarded, it didn't stop us striking a deal. In no time at all we'd agreed terms and a fee of £1,200 for the second half of the season, subject to a couple of shake-down tests. It was heady money for me.

A day later, back in Batley, I broke the news to Peter. I phrased it something along the lines of 'You'd better get some of those arses you talked about in gear, because I've signed for Norton.' At this, he began to change his tune, no doubt seeing Padgett's lead in the two British championships evaporating before his eyes. After a bit of finger-pointing and bluster, I agreed to ride their bikes in championship events for the rest of the year, but in no other races. And there was to be no more shilly-shallying about waiting for Peter to prep his engines: they'd prepare the bikes and take them to meetings ready to race. It was quite hard-nosed and acrimonious, which is not what I wanted at all, if only they'd been squarer all the way through. Ironically after that I was as right as rain with Peter.

On 28 June, after I'd tested their bike at Mallory and Thruxton, the bike papers broke the news of me signing for Norton. My first factory outing would be the Formula 750 round at Anderstorp in July. In the meantime I had to come up with bikes to ride in non-championship events. Another fairy godfather came to my aid.

It had started, appropriately enough, with a call from Jim Lee early in the season. He'd heard from John Cooper, who'd just had two huge wins in America. He'd bought from his winnings a brand-new Yamaha 250 and 350, which were far cheaper over there than in Europe. Both came with a full spares kit, ready to race and raring for a competitive rider. Over a year earlier at the Mallory post-TT meeting I'd pushed Coop all the way to take second place. Evidently he'd been impressed and had been keeping a quiet eye on me ever since. Coop asked Jim if he thought I'd be interested in taking the bikes.

At the time I was still tied into my deal with Padgett's, anyway, so – as flattering as Coop's offer was – I turned it down. I think Coop understood. His parting words were something along the lines of 'OK, but get back to me in a couple of months when you and Padgett's fall out.' Now was obviously that time.

Trouble was, there was no way I could afford one new Yamaha, let alone two, and anyway I'd never been brought up to do anything on tick. Like many working men of his generation, my dad's motto was 'If you can't afford it, you can't have it', and it stuck.

Coop didn't see it in those sort of terms at all. 'Just take the bikes,' he insisted, 'and pay me when you can.' I was a froth of indecision. I only had to fall off and break a leg, I reasoned, and I'd be in debt forever. But eventually, after asking lots of other opinions from mates and other riders, I agreed at least to take the 350 for a test in a Lincoln Club meeting at Cadwell. It was a missile and I led by a mile before pulling over to leave the club lads to it on the final lap. Just to be sure I lent Jack Machin the bike for another race. He won. Job done.

So the next day, 10 July, I rang Coop to accept his generous offer – a pretty fine birthday present for me. I suppose it could still have gone pear-shaped, but it turned out to be the best gamble I ever took. For the rest of the season we had a fantastic run, never finishing out of the top three in major internationals, even against the likes of Saarinen, and never failing to finish. I can't over-stress how much Coop's generosity and faith in me launched my career. I've a lot to thank old Moon Eyes for.

CHAPTER 6

BRITISH IS BEST –
ESPECIALLY WHEN
IT'S A YAMAHA

The factory John Player Norton I'd be riding was basically a cut-down version of the road-going Commando using a lighter, lower version of the standard Doc Bauer/Bob Trigg tubular frame. Petrol was carried in 'pannier' tanks alongside the cylinder heads. Much of this was clever, if not quite revolutionary. The same couldn't be said about the engine, which had started life as a 500 in 1948, so wasn't exactly cutting-edge. The race bike's engine was based on the production racing Norvil.

Mind you, it did look good. The Thruxton test was the first time I'd ridden anything 'factory'. I now realise that all factory bikes feel a bit special. Partly, I'm sure, this is just something in your head, but they all feel bespoke, precious. They even smell different from other bikes. At the time, of course, the only bikes I'd ever ridden were ones I'd prepared, so I didn't really have any sort of yardstick to apply. Either way, it seemed to me to handle like nothing I'd ridden before.

There were, though, a few fundamental problems. One was the crankshaft, which had cast iron flywheels which weren't, I'm sure, designed for the sort of revs they were asking from it. Secondly, the pannier tanks fed to a tiny header tank via a mechanical pump actuated by the swing-arm's movement – and so on the start line you'd always see the mechanics bouncing the bike up and down to move the fuel. On every car in the world the same type of pump worked perfectly, but could Norton get it to work? Not on your Nelly. The petrol ran from the panniers to the top tank in plastic pipes alongside the engine, and I can only surmise that it used to vaporise and gas-lock with the heat. For whatever reason, we were always plagued by misfires.

The misfires usually stopped when the gearbox broke – the bike's big weakness. This wasn't so much because it was basically at least 25 years old and full of neutrals, although that didn't help. The issue was that the clutch was way outboard of the gearbox main bearing, and the overhang on the shaft caused flex which used to play hell. Either the mainshaft or the gears themselves would break under load. All sorts of mods were tried to correct this, until they finally did the job properly and put an outrigger bearing on the end of the shaft.

And it was slow. I think my Jim Lee Commando was actually quicker, if only because it was a good deal lighter – as well as being a lot less complicated and not having the misfire problem. Otherwise, it was a lovely thing to ride.

My first Norton race outing was at Anderstorp on 22 July. Frank drove from the Harwich ferry, he and Peter puffing away like chimneys. I'm a poor traveller at the best of times, so went through several shades of green all the way through Sweden. Come practice, the bike made even more smoke. Hammering along the back straight at about 140mph, its antique cast-iron flywheels exploded, ripped through the back of the crankcases and sliced through the back tyre like a chainsaw. All I knew was that there was a bloody great bang, a choking plume of smoke, and I was sliding along on my arse at an exciting rate of knots. The bang occurred just before the braking point, so as I slid along I was actually catching Dave Potter's Kuhn Norton, although luckily I didn't quite.

The remains of the flywheel had actually emerged in three main chunks. One took out the camshaft and another the ignition. The third tore through the tyre. Luckily I suffered little more than a cut and blistered hand, but that was me out of the race: as the third man in the team, there wasn't a spare bike for me. So my first factory race was as a spectator.

I was also a bystander of sorts at our next meeting, at Rungis just outside Paris. This was a strange venue – just a one-off race along a cobbled-together circuit centred around the town's market place. The track started with a first-gear hairpin, then another, followed by a switchback straight with four blind humps. Yes, four humps. Definitely four.

Practice wasn't much help. For the first session it poured down. The second was dry but the Norton succumbed to its usual misfire, so by race day I've barely got in a flying lap. Phil Read, bless him, really took me under his wing. 'Look,' he told me, 'Kent Andersson will be first away on the Yamaha, with Ago not far behind. We can't let them get away.' What he was saying was that the big Norton would be harder to push-start, but if we didn't get away somewhere near the front, we'd be too far behind to catch up. So the logical thing would be to go a bit manic through the opening two hairpins, otherwise we could kiss a result goodbye.

Ready was spot-on. When the flag dropped, Andersson and Agostini took off as billed, but I was on a mission and by the second hairpin had barged my way into third place. Then we hit the humpback straight. Approaching the third hump I could see the back end of Ago's MV wagging as he hit the brakes over the crest. 'I've got him … he's braked too early,' I practically screamed to myself as I tore flat out in his wake. Wrong. I'd miscounted. There only ever were three humps. I came down the hill like a dive-bomber and hit the umpteen-times world champion square amidships as he tipped in to the turn.

Usually, when you're sliding along the road you want nothing more than for it to stop. Not this time. I'd have slid 'til Tuesday rather than get up and face the wrath. Both of us ended up tangled in the bales, but unhurt. I dusted Ago down, helped him pick up the MV and bump-started him away before firing up the Norton. I'd have ironed his shirts, too, if he'd asked me. Further embarrassment was spared when my bike ground to a halt a few laps later.

Afterwards I apologised profusely to Ago. I was so mortified I probably curtseyed, before enquiring how the rest of his race had gone. Since the track was located in a market area – one section, Garbage Corner, actually stank of rotten cabbage – there were lots of broken crates and other bits of debris littered about. One of these had ended the Italian maestro's race, but he had a different slant on it.

'Not good,' he said, 'I have a puncture', brandishing a nail removed from his tyre. 'It came from the Norton.' To this day I don't know if he thought we actually nailed them together or was taking the piss. It didn't end there. Frank happened to be married to Alberto Pagani's sister so, quite apart from mangling Nortons, whacking Italians was very bad news. I left France in the doghouse.

The next two Norton outings were better: I finished. Fifth in the Hutchinson 100, the 'wrong way' around Brands Hatch, felt pretty good. I followed that up with another fifth – and first John Player Norton – in the Silverstone International. On a Yamaha. It might have been even better if I hadn't run out of fuel and coasted round the last corner.

One of the stranger and more agreeable parts of my Norton deal was that, as third rider, if anything calamitous went wrong in practice I'd be the one without a ride. The team simply didn't have enough spare bikes for all of us and Williams and Read had priority. As something of an afterthought my contract stated that under these circumstances I could ride my own bikes. So sometimes I'd be in the happy position of being paid by Norton to beat them on one of Coop's Yamahas. But if you remember that Silverstone meeting at all, it'll be more for Jarno Saarinen's two wins and an absolute lap record on his 250 and 350cc Yamahas.

Dad was still uncomfortable with the idea of me hurtling around race tracks every weekend, but he was my dad and offered what support he could. At heart he was just a working bloke so didn't have the means to help, and probably didn't really understand what was going on. But he had the good sense to let me get on with it and never tried to hinder me, which is all I could have asked. I suspect that a lot of youngsters in the sport today are only there because of their dad's enthusiasm. Yet in the long run the will to do it has to come from within, otherwise you're not likely to last the distance. The higher up the ladder you go, the harder it gets, and if you haven't had to fight to get there you're less likely to survive when it does get tough.

Dad was there that day at Silverstone, along with a friend, Michael Preston. Jarno and me cleared off in the 350 race. I knew full well that he could leave me any time he felt like it, but he was making it look good for the crowd, dad included. Dad was still smoking at the time, and according to Michael had two on the go at once. Sure enough, with two laps to go Jarno pulled the pin and disappeared into the distance, but at least this time I didn't fall off.

Mother wasn't a fan of the racing at all. 'Michael,' she'd begin – I was always Michael when I was in bother – 'I wish you'd stop this racing. You'll get nowhere and you'll only get hurt.' Now and again in the Velocette days it even crossed my mind that she was right. Then I'd think, 'Hang on, you've brought me into this world and it's my life now, you've got to let me live it.' She wasn't best pleased but there wasn't much she could do to stop me. Gran, for once, wholeheartedly agreed with mum. She didn't like the racing at all, although she became quite proud later on when I began to come good.

Being paid to ride Yamahas for Norton might seem an odd state of affairs, but the truth was that if I'd depended solely on the Commando I'd have been short of racing miles – and I've always been the sort of racer who needs track time to keep on form. Riding Coop's bikes put me at the top of my game and actually helped my Norton efforts, at least when they had a bike to ride.

Two weeks later it was Snetterton for the Race of Aces. In the main event Peter brought his Norton home in third place behind Coop and Agostini, with me in sixth. But the day was more memorable for my best dice so far with Sheene. Two weeks earlier I'd pipped him in the 350cc race at the Hutchinson meeting, but today we had a right ding-dong on our 250s. In this class Barry definitely had the edge, since his was a special factory six-speed job compared to my five-speeder, but lap after lap I just wouldn't let go. In those days Russell's, the final corner, was a fast left–right rather than the miserable slow chicane it is now. I've never seen it before or since but the pair of us must have had complete faith in one another, for on the last lap we went through there literally side by side. At the line we were credited with exactly the same time, but Barry just got the result. He beat me in the 350cc race, too, but I got the last laugh: BP Man of the Meeting.

A day later at Oulton I managed second place behind Rod Gould on the 250. Rod had been world champion just two years before, so this was also pretty heady company. On the 350 I went one better, winning with a new outright lap record to claim man of the meeting and was later crowned 'BP Superman of the Year'. It may have been a naff sort of title, but at least I didn't have to ride in a cape. Most of all, it confirmed the improbable: from almost nowhere I was one of the top men in UK racing. Next, home turf: Scarborough.

Unforgiving though it was, I'd grown to love the Oliver's Mount Circuit. Two months earlier I'd racked up two wins and a third place there and reckoned to have the beating of anyone – if I was allowed to. There's still a bit of a dispute about team orders for the meeting. My memory is that I was told to finish behind Peter, although Frank Perris later denied this. Either way it didn't much matter.

For once all three Nortons got to the line and all were on the pace in a classy field including Tait, Jefferies, Coop and Pickrell on the factory triples. I got a pretty good start before overhauling Pickrell for the lead at Mere Hairpin on lap two. As the race settled down it was me, Peter in second and Ready in third. So far John Player Norton hadn't won a single major race, so Frank must have been chain-smoking and wetting himself back in the pits – especially when Phil slid off at Mere. I was just wondering whether to let Peter pass when his over-pressed gearbox saved me the bother. He pulled out with a broken mainshaft, leaving me and my big grin to take a comfortable win in front of 30,000 delighted fans. It was almost 14 years to the day since I'd watched my first bike race at the same circuit, so I was about as emotional as I'd ever been after a win.

The bike papers went potty: 'Grant Gives Norton First Superbike Win'. John Player must have been pretty chuffed, too: on the same day Emerson Fittipaldi took the JP Lotus to his first world Formula 1 crown with victory in the Italian grand prix. A chap named Mike Hailwood was second in the Surtees-Ford.

Great as the result was for me and Norton, it was a bigger day for someone else. Although he had no superbike, it was that man Saarinen who really took the meeting by storm, winning three races. On his 350 he trashed Cooper's lap record, which had stood for no less than seven years, with the first lap under two minutes. I was second to him on both my 250 and 350, so had the best view in the place of how well he rode. However good I was feeling about my riding, this Finnish bloke was in a different class.

A week or so later, at Thruxton for the 500-miler (run for some reason over only 400 miles that year), Norton

81

got another big win, this time on a production Norvil Commando. I was teamed up with Dave 'Crasher' Croxford, who'd been second at Scarborough on his Seeley BSA and won the 500-miler the previous year on a Triumph when Peter Williams's Norton had crashed out whilst leading.

This time the drama was all Croxford's, which was actually nothing new. We led from lap one, only for the engine to cut out coming into the final chicane for the last time. Dave was never the fittest rider – he preferred a pint to a workout, every time – but paddled furiously on to the straight before hopping off to push and almost landing on his face. He was practically on his knees as he took the flag, just ahead of Rex Butcher and Jim Harvey on the other official Norton.

Crocket was one of racing's real characters. Like James Whitham years later, he was a non-stop stream of funny stories which were no longer funny after the third time you heard them. On the eve of the race we'd met up for a meal in a hotel near Andover.

'What shall we have to drink,' asked Crocket.

'Anything you like, but don't forget we've got a long race tomorrow.'

'How about a nice bottle of Mouton Cadet? That should hit the spot.'

By the sixth bottle we were utterly legless. How we rode, let alone won, I've no idea. But riding through hangovers seemed to be a Crocket speciality. I remember that whatever his normal race preparation usually involved, his wet weather set-up called for twice as many bottles.

Crocket actually started his motorcycle career as an original Ace Café rocker before becoming a racer of legendary exploits, some on a bike but mostly on his arse or in the pub. He used to ride at Scarborough fairly regularly, so I knew him from there. We'd had a bit of a disagreement once when the fog rolled in from the North Sea. It was obviously too dangerous to practise – you could barely see one side of the track from the other. But being young and stupid I wanted to practise, anyway – partly because the whole meeting would be canned, and with it my start money and winnings, if practice didn't get under way by lunchtime. Crocket, on the other hand, thought it was too dodgy – an unusual position for someone as mad as him. Inevitably, half an hour after Peter Hillaby abandoned the meeting, it was a glorious sunny day.

Although you'd usually call him 'Crocket' to his face, Dave wasn't called 'Crasher' for nothing. In a career spanning something like 100 get-offs his worst injury was a small cut requiring two stitches. He was obviously made of rubber. Years later, around 1995, the two of us were invited to race Triumph triples in the 'Past Masters' match races at Mallory. I wasn't keen, but Crocket was. 'Come on,' he urged, over the phone. 'You've got to do it. We'll make it look good for the fans and have a laugh.' He was always on for a laff. I was unmoved, but went just to watch. When I arrived, the first thing I saw was Crocket with his arm in a sling. He was spitting. After walking away from all those crashes, the front brake caliper had fallen off his Triumph going into the Hairpin. Down he'd gone for crash number 101 and broken a collarbone.

Meanwhile, all that was left of the season was to wrap up the British championships at Snetterton in mid-November. Going into the meeting I led Steve Machin by 54 points to 43 on the 350, but was just two points ahead of Jim Harvey in the 500cc rankings. A mere three points would give me the 350cc title, but I won fairly comfortably. The 500 race was a different proposition. The bike ran roughly from lap one before finally grinding to a halt with a seized crank at Coram's on the final lap. Harvey took the title.

Certainly 1972 had been a great season in every way – a factory ride, that first Norton win, umpteen wins on Yamahas and a national title. How much better can life get? After Snetterton I handed over £2,200 to Coop for his Yamahas and wondered why I'd ever been so frightened of the deal he'd offered. Mind you, he charged me 'interest', nipping in to pinch my Norton ride after BSA pulled the plug on him.

Being neurotic about where the next fiver was coming from, I was also still working. After my arrangement with Padgett's collapsed I found a job working alongside a guy called Alan Capstick for a big Irishman named Bob Brolly, who installed sprinkler systems in industrial premises. I was the welder on the team, working on pipes which were often 30 or 40 feet in the air, even though I'd no head for heights (and not much of a head for welding, come to that, since at the time I was completely self-taught).

If I wasn't hanging from the roof with a welding set, I'd be clinging to a Hilti gun, banging bolts into roof beams. The posher guns had a trigger and weren't so bad to use. Ours wasn't posh, but a great heavy thing with a percussion pin at one end. So you'd load the gun, climb 40 feet up a ladder to the cross-beam with the gun in one arm, put your other arm through the rungs so you couldn't fall off, then belt the pin with a hammer in your third arm – simple. There'd be a huge bang, the gun would recoil out of your arms to the ground. With any luck you hadn't riveted a part of you to the beam, so could clamber down again to repeat the process.

But at least this job was racing-friendly. Bob, partly because he was Irish and therefore had bike racing in his genes, was a star. Whenever I needed time off for racing or practice, he'd think nothing of fibbing to his partner, who had a less benign view of dangerous days off, that I was grafting away at another site.

CHAPTER 7

DIFFERENT CLASS

After the musical chairs of the previous year, I began the 1973 season with a proper sponsor, Brian Davidson, who ran a company producing industrial piping. Racing began unusually early, too, with an invitation to the first of many race visits to South Africa, which definitely beat hunkering down in Wakefield. The deal was a two-race series – the South African TT at the Roy Hesketh circuit in Pietermaritzburg, followed by the South African GP at Kyalami. The races had no real world standing, but the fields were pretty classy – right up to Ago on the works MV. All I had to do was crate up my bikes, get them to the airport, and the organisers would foot the bill. Unknown to me, the trip would eventually take me to Italy.

The only drawback was the flight, which lasted 14 hours. Apart from being 13 hours longer than any I'd endured before, I was no happier up in the air than I was climbing ladders with Hilti guns. So I was obviously delighted to be met at Jan Smuts airport in Jo'burg with the news that my onward flight to Pietermaritzburg was all arranged. I simply couldn't face it and instead used all the cash I possessed renting a VW Beetle from Hertz. South Africa's just a little bump on the bottom of Africa, I thought. Surely Pietermaritzburg couldn't be very far.

Hours later it's getting dark and I'm becoming paranoid about rogue lions and rhinos, so I pull into a hotel in the middle of the veldt. It was a gloriously de luxe place and I had only about a fiver in my pocket, but needs must. The bill, including breakfast, came to about half that. There was enough left to fill the tank for the rest of the drive.

The race organisers obviously had a sense of humour so I'd been billeted with a South African ex-racer called Mike Grant, which was a bit confusing. Two other guys, Tony Day who worked for Olympic Motors in Durban, and a Yamaha dealer named Errol Cowan in Jo'burg, were also helping out. I was leading my first race at Roy Hesketh until I dumped the 350 and just about wrote it off. Mike and me worked like crazy to make one good 350 out of the 250 and 350, which were almost the same. Since they'd paid me to come all this way, I suspected the organisers wouldn't be starting without me, so I left Mike to finish the job and took a shower, arriving on the grid like Joe Cool while the rest had been sat sweating in the sun. It worked: I won.

Because of the altitude at Kyalami, Phil Read had told me to go down six jet sizes, say from 280 down to 220. Wakefield not having much by way of High Veldt, this was hard to believe. As usual, Phil was right – in the first practice session, the 250 was horribly rich and wouldn't pull. Come the race it was running better. Ago won the 500cc race but in the 350cc his MV packed up early on, leaving me and Coop to battle it out. I was just thinking that I had him when a factory 750cc Ducati came thundering past. That twin was *fast*. On every straight it would hammer past. Luckily the Yamaha had the edge through the twiddly bits and I managed to hang on to win the race.

That Ducati, though, had been impressive, so I wasted no time sending a telegram to Bologna saying how impressed I'd been by their V-twin. And, by the way, is there any chance of borrowing one for the 200-miler at Imola? This was the year after Paul Smart had given them their first big international win there, so the fact that the bike was good wouldn't have been much of a surprise to them. It was cheeky, something I wouldn't have had the nerve to try even six months earlier. I fully expected to be told to naff off, if I got any reply at all. But much to my surprise a telegram came back inviting me to try the bike. So off I toddled to Bologna.

Ducati took us to Modena to test the bikes. All the top guys were there, including Fabio Taglioni, the father of Ducati's desmodromic engines. Also there was a pair of Brunos – Spaggiari, who placed second to Smartie the previous year, and Kneubühler, who at the time was winning the odd grand prix for Harley-Davidson. And, out of the blue, my old mate Tony Jefferies, who seemed to have turned up on spec.

The 750 had come on a lot since '72. It was smaller, lighter and altogether much more of a racer than the modified road bike Smart had ridden. We spent the day getting quicker, with me always about half a second behind Spaggiari. Eventually he thinks he's got the job done and slips into his slick Italian suit. I go out for one last-ditch effort – and go quicker still. So off comes Bruno's suit. Eventually I went tits-up, but Ducati must have thought they'd seen enough so I got the ride.

Ducati's was a smashing set-up, run by people who so obviously loved their bikes. Even though it was then a relatively new motorcycle company, there was an aura about the factory that you just didn't get in Britain. Even the little things seemed important, like the visor screw I'd lost from my helmet. Almost before I knew it, one of the mechanics, Giorgio, had jumped on to a lathe and knocked one up from scratch. This was also the first time I'd encountered espresso coffee, for which I got a serious taste and spent much of the trip walking around like a wide-eyed zombie.

Most of all there was Taglioni, who was revered almost like a god by everyone around him. He was very gentle and refined, and took great pride in showing me around his projects – triple cam 125s, wooden patterns for a racing four, all kinds of exotic kit – a far cry from the superannuated road bikes the factories were racing at home. With my Jim Lee background, this was all fascinating stuff. More exciting in the short term was a 500cc racing twin, a six-speeder which revved to 12,000. It looked fast, stable yet flickable, a perfect formula for the Isle of Man. It was also economical enough to do full race distance without refuelling. I was pretty confident that if it could last a TT race distance it was a sure-fire winner, but under the circumstances it was probably never going to happen.

At the time racing politics were way above my head. My horizons didn't extend much beyond riding, revving and the odd bit of healing in between. If I'd thought about it, I'd have realised that at the time the Italians had a big down on the TT following Parlotti's death and Ago's subsequent boycott. Yet for a while the factory seemed keen for me to ride the Senior TT on the 500 before Bruno de Prato rang to say the deal was off.

It probably didn't help my case that my Imola performance didn't altogether impress. In practice I slung the bike away at Aqua Minerale, where there's no such thing as a small crash. In fairness it wasn't altogether my fault, since I'd been sent out on old tyres, but a crash is a crash.

Then, on the eve of the race, Kneubühler and Romy, his missus, took me out for a meal with another couple, the curvier half of which was drop-dead gorgeous. Later I'm in my room and who knocks on the door but the gorgeous half, dressed very slinkily and in a very friendly state of mind. You may not believe this, but somewhere a little voice told me this maybe wasn't altogether on the level and I packed her off to her room. And it must be said that if it was an attempt at sabotage it was the most agreeable I've ever had. Ironically, she needn't have bothered, for in the race the clutch went before the bike even got off the grid. Bruno finished in the top three or so. And that was the end of my factory Ducati career.

But as one door closes ... Also staying at the same Imola hotel that weekend was Frank Perris. One evening he wandered over at dinner to ask a favour. 'Jesus, matey,' he started – that was his catch phrase – 'can you ride for us on the Isle of Man?' The deal was, as usual, that I was supposed to finish second to Peter, which wasn't a problem because at the time he was certainly quicker than me around the Mountain Circuit. We agreed a fee of £2,000 and shook hands on the deal there and then.

That year's Imola 200-miler was won by my old mucker Jarno Saarinen on the new liquid-cooled 350 Yamaha, hot off another huge win at Daytona. He just had this amazing ability to go quick right from the off, which couldn't have been more different from me because I was always a dunce at learning new circuits. Within three laps of first seeing Daytona, he'd been on lap record pace.

That Daytona meeting was my first around the Florida speed bowl, so I was well placed to see just how good he was. I'd gone there with Rob North, the man responsible for those lovely frames on the factory BSA and Triumph triples. He flew out as my mechanic, but can't have liked the job since he never came back. Since prices were so much lower in the States, I bought a new 350 Yamaha over there for the meeting. It was a good machine with an absolutely lousy front brake. After two laps it had faded so much all it could do was stop the bearings from falling out of the hub. Even so, I managed to finish sixth, the first privateer behind the factory bikes, which wasn't a bad performance. Jarno, though, was racing on another planet.

He was so confident and so cool, and such a thinker. On his air-cooled Yams, which then had a habit of overheating and losing power during a race, he'd sometimes sit on the grid whilst everyone else cleared off on their warm-up lap. When the flag finally dropped he was confident enough – and good enough – to know that he could stay with the pack on cold tyres until the extra lap of full power from his cooler engine gave him the means to get away.

Before he got the full works ride he'd go from meeting to meeting in a VW camper van with a box trailer for the bikes, and a tent they used as a garage. Inside, there'd be just Jarno and his mechanic, Vince French, a generator humming, shadows moving and light spilling out of the tent until well into the night. Although his factory Yamahas were always a year ahead of our customer bikes, basically they weren't all that special. But as a qualified mechanical engineer, he knew what he was about. I always imagined he and Vince were filing and fettling, but in fact they were simply fitting new bits – rings, pistons, barrels, cranks. This is what gave his bikes the edge. Nothing was allowed to wear out. That was the secret for keeping the bikes sweet. Derek Chatterton was another rider who always had quick Yamahas, and his 'secret' was similar. He'd do a few meetings, then sell the bike and buy a new one, so his kit was always crisp.

Partly through a limited budget, partly through ignorance, my approach – and that of most other British riders – was totally different. Rather than fit, say, a new crank, I'd rebuild the old one. After all, Yamaha sold big-end kits and in the back of my van was a press for rebuilding them with new rods and big-end bearings. I was blithely unaware that, although I might be giving them a new lease of life, I wasn't making them any quicker. Strictly speaking, the Yamaha cranks weren't engineered to be rebuilt at all, although the likes of Hoechle after-market cranks were. Every time a new rod assembly went in, the tolerances would go off and the performance would suffer. It was years before I worked this out, and when I finally ran a TZ Yamaha on a decent budget – George Beale's 350 eight years later in 1981 – that's exactly what we did. With the 'secret' out of the bag the bike was a missile all year.

At Scarborough the previous year I'd seriously thought I could have a proper go at Jarno. After all, I was riding well on a good bike and knew the circuit as well as anyone. No chance. On a tricky, hairy circuit he'd never seen before, he whupped the lot of us. As usual he'd pulled me along away from everyone else, then with two laps to go summoned an extra something from somewhere and left me for dead. I had a chance of winning, all right – but only if he broke down. He was just too good to beat on level terms. The only guy I can recall who ever gave him a real battle was Ray McCullough at Dundrod, and that had been a couple of years before when Jarno was learning his craft.

As well as immense ability he also had the nerve and hunger needed to be a winner. Later in the '73 season he had a fierce dice with Ready at Hockenheim. Phil was on the MV, Jarno was on the new four-cylinder 500cc Yamaha, which at that stage wasn't anything like as good a package. On the infield the Yamaha went into a huge slide on the power out of a corner, yet Jarno didn't roll it one bit, just kept it pinned in pursuit of Read. It was striking because you just couldn't do that with the power and tyre characteristics we had in those days – yet Jarno did. Maybe his speedway background helped. He was definitely the most impressive rider I ever came up against. I had huge respect for Read and Agostini, but this guy was head and shoulders above the lot of them – and I believe even Ready feels the same.

Although I'd raced against him on and off in previous seasons, I didn't really get to know Ago until 1973 when he regularly came to the UK for International meetings at Scarborough and elsewhere. At Cadwell, with him on the 500 to my 350, I pushed him all the way when we both recorded the first 80mph lap. What I didn't put into the equation was that he was maybe riding at eight-tenths, whilst I was on a mission. In grands prix he was a totally different proposition. Being a typical Italian heart-throb, he was also my sister Cheryl's hero.

Having such a turncoat in the family didn't go down too well, but I always found him a gent. And considering the enormous success he's had, he's stayed pretty level-headed. It was a surprise if he ever said anything controversial – the complete opposite to Phil Read.

Ready's had a lot of bad press over the years but he was always good to me, right from that ill-fated encounter at Rungis. Not that this stopped him taking the piss – from the first time he took me out for a meal and ordered moules marinière, which to me looked like a bowl of beach.

Being a southerner with a few airs and graces – even though he was really just a working-class lad from Luton – he'd take the piss out of my accent. I was never all that broad-spoken and knew enough not to fill post-race interviews with 'na' thens' and 'ee by gums'. It was obvious you had to speak a bit more 'proper' if you wanted to be understood – unless your name was Joey and you didn't give a monkey's about the press. This went well enough until a hotel receptionist in Daytona, remarked that 'Gee you've got a wonderful accent.' I was just preening myself on sounding such a gent when she added, 'Are you Australian?' After that I spoke with a broad accent whenever Ready was around.

As a rider, Ready has to be up there with the all-time greats. In 1971 when he won the 250cc world title on Helmut Fath's bike, I'd watched him win the Lightweight TT from the bank at the 13th Milestone, where he looked 10mph faster than anyone else yet so smooth and neat. Mind you, it can't have been all that captivating. A bunch of Irish fellows with an empty crate of beer slept through the entire four laps. I don't think Read had much by way of technical nous, but on sheer ability he was top drawer, right up there with Hailwood in my book.

But there was always something about him that made you want to prick his bubble. On the eve of his controversial TT return a few years later the journalist Chris Carter rang me for some preview copy.

'Does Phil Read pose a threat?'

It was one of those rare moments when you actually think of the clever line in time: 'Pose, yes. Threat, no.' It was just a joke and I made Chris promise not to use it. Inevitably it was the headline on the next day's back page.

Whenever I bumped into Phil throughout that TT, not a word was said. We'd nod and exchange greetings, cordial as you like. Eventually he told me I was a bastard, but didn't seem particularly upset. That's the lovely thing about him: he's so hard to offend. Things just seem to bounce off him. I've a lot of time for the man, and as a rider he was very special.

Yet, in the UK at least, by 1973 I definitely didn't fear Ready on the track. It was the same whenever other grand prix stars came over to England. At Mallory Park and Brands Hatch the likes of John Dodds and Walter Villa rarely gave me a problem. So, setting out for Hockenheim and my first grand prix in May, I reckoned the same must be true on the Continent.

Did I get my eyes opened?

It was chalk and cheese. In England people played at tuning, but nothing like the way they did for GPs. At home power wasn't that critical. The game was all about stuffing it up the inside. In Europe, at fast circuits like Hockenheim in particular, racing was almost a different sport. Their bikes were quicker, which really showed on the old, super-fast German circuit. Until Saarinen came along, Dodds and Villa were the two classiest guys, the ones who impressed me the most. They'd use bits of tarmac I'd never even thought of. Their track was wider than mine.

One of the bends which gave me the biggest problem was the big long Ost-Kurve at the far end of Hockenheim. There I'd be with the bike completely on its side, everything scraping, and guys riding round the outside of me like I was parked. I simply couldn't see what more I could do.

I was baffled and asked Ready for help. He told me to tag along behind him in the next practice session. So an hour later I'm right up the MV's chuff as my problem corner hurtles towards me, just thinking about braking – and he changes *up* a gear. I'd been aiming for the typical British short- circuit line, tight around the inside. Ready was yards away, keeping it wide and high and maintaining his speed. Amazing. A big lesson. Yet even with that I managed only tenth in the race, which Saarinen, inevitably, won. I was so disgusted I didn't even bother picking up my prize money.

Although Chas Mortimer and a few others were having a proper go, many Brits had a major problem in grands prix. Although there were two-stroke 'tuners' about at home, most were really just skilled assembly men, able to put an engine together correctly and blueprint the tolerances. In Britain, at least, there was simply very little engine development going on that the factory hadn't already done for you. The only fettling we ever did was to be ultra careful to get the compression ratio and squish band correct and, obviously, to get the jetting right. The plus side of this – and to riders like me it was a very big plus – was that if you knew what you were doing with the jetting and basic set-up of a 250 or 350 Yamaha, you had the makings of a British championship bike right out of the crate. But at the same time Continental tuners such as Helmut Fath and Harold Bartol were able to eke out significant extra horsepower from their Yamahas. Since they seemed to have no genuine counterparts in Britain, this placed home riders at a major disadvantage in grands prix. At any fast circuit we simply couldn't get near them.

At Hockenheim Team Grant also suffered a power struggle of a different sort. With me were Paul Dallas, now my mechanic, and Carol and – big-time – they didn't get on. Eventually Carol gave me an ultimatum: 'Make your mind up – it's me or him.' Since the next stop was the grand prix at Monza, for which I needed a mechanic more than a girlfriend, we put her on the plane back home. Not that she ever reminds me of that.

The first mechanic I actually paid – although not very much – was Alastair Taylor, who later moved on to better things, eventually working for Harold Bartol. He'd been followed by Paul Dallas, another Huddersfield lad. Paul was a bit of a wind-up merchant but since he was always smiling and not even as physically imposing as me, people often thought of him as a pushover. What they didn't know was that as well as being handy with the spanners he had a black belt and umpteen dans in judo. In a pub in Finland a huge Viking oaf started shoving him about and was on his arse before we even noticed anything had happened. For a wimp like me, Paul was priceless company.

Some time later at Monza the two of us were winding down in a bar on the night before a race. For some reason the barman, a powerful-looking fellow, seemed to take an instant dislike to us. Naturally, we responded by taking the piss. He couldn't have understood a word we said but obviously got the general message, because suddenly there was an ear-splitting crash as he slammed a cosh into the bar inches from my head.

Having missed with his first salvo, Sr Friendly Barman leaps round the bar for a better shot and a big hairy fist whistles past my chin. Now this is not my territory. This is scary. I can't fight my way out of a paper bag. Meanwhile, this gorilla notices that Paul's just standing there chuckling and takes a swing at him. Big mistake. In an instant he's completely horizontal, five feet off the floor, with a startled look on his face. After he thudded to the floor, Paul just sat on his chest and grinned.

Carol at least got to go home from Hockenheim in a bit of style. Paul and I headed south in the battered blue Transit I'd bought from Smartie the previous year. It went well enough, since a previous owner had shoe-horned in a V6 engine and higher-ratio differential. The speedo didn't take account of this so indicated about 70 while the thing battered along at the best part of 100mph, which gave us no end of introductions to traffic cops. To pass the time on long trips, Paul and I had competitions for who could drive the thing flat out the longest, while the caravan flapped around like a mad thing behind.

Monza turned out to witness my most impressive burst of speed all year. At this time Phil Read had been widely reported for his attacks on the TT, which many of the top riders were boycotting. I thought this was a pile of hypocritical bullshit and had said so in a column in *Motor Cycle News*. The real issue, I reckoned, was money, not safety as he claimed. So who should I see as I emerged from the back of my Transit with a plate of fried breakfast but Phil and wife Madeleine gliding by in their Rolls-Royce. Phil probably wasn't all that bothered, but Mrs Read could be fierce. With a shriek of 'You fucking …' she leaped out of the Roller and set off in pursuit of me while I took to my heels in the opposite direction, leaving a trail of spilt egg, bacon and beans. Dignified it wasn't, but I escaped.

That was the only light-hearted part of a meeting which infamously claimed the lives of Saarinen and Renso Pasolini in the 250cc grand prix. In the previous race, the 350, Walter Villa's Benelli had been allowed to continue despite dumping a load of oil on the track. So far as I know, no serious attempt was made to clean the track between races. I didn't know it at the time, but at least one rider, John Dodds, tried to persuade officials to delay the race and clean up the mess. They responded by threatening to have him thrown out of the circuit and the race got under way as planned.

Although this was only my second grand prix meeting (other than the TT), the one thing I was good at was push-starts (and running away from irate wives). It was rare that I wouldn't get away in the first two or three, but luckily for me this was one of those times when I didn't.

As usual the bike started instantly, but I stalled it, which quite possibly saved my life. I was still paddling along in disbelief as the pack roared away. The two seconds or so it took to restart it seemed like a lifetime. As I trailed the pack into the Curva Grande – then blisteringly fast, unlike the modern chicane – the scene ahead was like nothing I'd ever seen.

Normally, in this sort of situation I'd have hit the brakes and laid the bike down, but for some reason a voice in my head was screaming to stay on board, so that's what I did. As I was weaving through the mayhem, bikes were ricocheting in all directions, bikes burning, riders tumbling about or just lying prone on the track. A flying petrol tank almost took my head off. Yet, somehow, I made my way through the carnage unscathed and toured back to the grid.

After I parked the bike Chas Mortimer came over, looking grim, and broke the news that Jarno and Paso were both dead. It was truly horrible. I was in shock. It was one of the very few times in my career that I wasn't sure if I could actually race, but the meeting was promptly cancelled so, mercifully, I didn't get to find out.

Apparently Paso had led in to that first corner but slid off, bringing down Jarno. Another 12 riders went down in the mêlée. Still photographs later showed bodies sickeningly cartwheeling like rag dolls into the trackside barrier. No convincing inquiry was ever conducted. The organisers first claimed that Pasolini's engine had seized, then that Saarinen's had, neither of which was true. Two months later, at another Monza meeting, a circuit doctor asked for an ambulance to be stationed at the Curva Grande. He was ignored. There was another multiple pile-up, to which it took the ambulance 20 minutes to respond. Three riders died.

Although most of us were only half-aware of it, if at all, this was an era in which riders' lives came pretty cheap. A few men, such as Ago, were making noises about safety, and the Grand Prix Riders Association had been formed not long before to campaign for better safety and prize money. But many of us, especially the younger ones, didn't seriously question the circumstances in which we raced. We were too busy making ends meet and dreaming of stepping up the ladder. The culture had changed 21 years later and there was a very different reaction to Ayrton Senna's death at Imola, although at times even that was more like a witch-hunt than a serious look at safety.

The practice of laying a bike down, or not, was horribly reinforced three months later. At the time Kim Newcombe was going great guns in grands prix on the four-cylinder 500cc König. At the World Formula 750 round at Silverstone he was riding a 680cc version of the same machine when he half-high-sided right in front of me at Stowe. Somehow he stayed on the bike as it hurtled towards a bank of railway sleepers. If he'd got off the bike he'd probably have been out in the next practice session, quite possibly on the same machine. Instead, he stayed on board and hit the bank head-on. He died three days later in hospital. Whatever I'd thought before, from that moment onwards, whenever I was in a dodgy situation my first reaction was always to get off the bike.

Saarinen's death robbed racing of its brightest talent. He was a nice guy, cheerful and engaging, although like many Finns he tended to keep himself to himself. Despite being a factory rider, at most meetings there'd be just him, his lovely wife Soly, a van and a mechanic. Things were different then.

CHAPTER 8

TRUST ME, I'M A PROFESSIONAL

Even with the one-off Norton factory ride, the 1973 TT wasn't quite the breakthrough I'd hoped for. This was my sister's first visit to watch me race on the Island. I reckoned I was pretty neat round Cronk-ny-Mona, so suggested she watch the Junior from there. In those days you'd take it as fast as you could get there out of Hillberry on a TZ350, in a two-wheeled drift all the way round.

By the Bungalow I was leading by a comfortable margin when a broken split pin left me with no clutch. To even contemplate another five laps without a clutch would be madness, so I just cruised down the Mountain, which was duly reported over the radio. Then, as I reached Creg-ny-Baa, I remembered Cheryl had come all this way to watch, so put in a bit of effort down to Hillberry, and came through Cronk-ny-Mona with the Yamaha sliding as usual. That done, I pulled in at the pits and was just stepping off the bike as Geoff Cannell came trotting up with his microphone.

'What's happened, you were leading by ...'

'Problem with the clutch, Geoff. Had to pull in.'

About an hour later Cheryl arrived, mascara running down her cheeks, almost hysterical.

'You frightened the life out of me,' she blubbed.

I was nonplussed. 'How come?'

'They said you were only cruising but it looked terrifying to me.'

I don't think she ever watched me at the TT again.

The Senior gave Cheryl an easier time – she'd gone home – but was even more disappointing for me. On the third lap I was ahead of Jack Findlay's Suzuki by around a minute when I slid off on oil at Parliament Square, leaving the Aussie veteran to take the first Senior win by a two-stroke since Scott in 1914. I had a little rant about my misfortune to *Motor Cycle News*: 'It's not good enough … previous riders were shown the warning flag, and riders after, but the marshal wasn't there when I arrived.' I did have the consolation of setting the fastest lap, 104.41mph. Not that that, or the rant, made me feel much better.

I'd been having a bit of a running battle with Cannell for the previous two weeks. Throughout practice he'd been complaining about my front wheel landings off Ballaugh Bridge, where he'd been commentating. Apparently they were dangerous. After a few days of this nonsense I got the chance to tell him the landings were completely deliberate and intended to protect the chain and transmission. Whether or not he knew what he was talking about he was always an opinionated character and, typically, wouldn't be budged.

Sure enough, on the first lap of the Senior, when I was in even more of a rush than usual, he was at it again. 'Grant still hasn't learned,' he lectured as I plopped down the TZ's front wheel.

By the second lap I had a healthy lead and took Ballaugh much easier, landing on the rear wheel

'At long last, Grant's got the bridge right.'

By the third lap, the lead was even greater. I pottered over the bridge so slowly the Yamaha didn't even leave the floor. But it did give me time to stick two fingers up at Cannell's commentary box.

'He's so confident he's even waving at me.'

However, he had the last laugh, when I slid off on Rutter's oil at Ramsey.

Before the same race, Tom Arter had been voicing concerns about 350s in the 500cc Senior race. A TZ '350' of course measured only 348cc, so wasn't eligible for the Senior class. Not all riders bothered to increase the capacity enough to make them legal. Putting his money where his mouth was, Tom stuck in a blanket protest before the race to have the first seven finishers measured. I was one of the ones who'd gone to the trouble of putting in eccentric crank pins which made my engine 351cc. When I fell off at Ramsey it became academic, but I was still keen to show that the bike that had been leading was in every way legitimate. The instant we got it back to the paddock I took it to the scrutineering bay and insisted the scrutineers measure it. The result didn't exactly fill you with faith, since they reckoned it was 360cc. Which was wrong, but OK by me.

Despite the disappointments this was the year I truly got on the pace on the Island, although at least one guy was faster. Peter Williams ran away with the Formula 750 race on the other Norton. That left me battling with Tony Jefferies for second place, neither of us really enjoying the experience. As well as having me to contend with, Tony was sitting in a puddle of petrol from a leaking tank, so his crown jewels were giving him a pretty painful time.

I'd had a bit of a misfire since the start, which on the last lap turned into a typical Norton death rattle, but I managed to nurse it into second place. Peter's best lap was over 107mph, the fastest since Hailwood's day, leaving me, Tony, Charlie Williams and Stan Woods all over three minutes behind. When the crew stripped my Commando they discovered that the main bearings had indeed been rattling, but not for the usual reason. The crankcases were actually cracked all the way round, right through the bearing housings. Only the frame was stopping the engine falling in half. More worryingly, I noticed that it still used the same cast-iron flywheels which had spit me down the road in Sweden the year before. To my mind that was inexcusably dangerous. Norton surely had the means to make something better.

It was around this time that I packed in the day job and became a full-time racer. It wasn't really as though going professional was a conscious career decision, but some time in mid-season it dawned on me that I didn't seem to be going to work very often any more. The process – if it was a process – was fairly typical. Throughout my entire career I may have had a vague sense of where I might be a year or two down the line, but never consciously looked that far ahead. I certainly never planned for it in any strategic way. By and large the Grant master plan was still to muddle along from one season to the next.

The truth was that I just wasn't a grand ideas sort of bloke. And some of the ones I met were enough to put you off. One of these was Rudi Kurth, who I'd met with girlfriend Dane Rowe during an Assen grand prix. Rudi was at heart a sidecar man, so a bit potty at the best of times. Being Swiss, he'd have been right at home in a cuckoo clock. He was also a bit of a boffin, full of radical new ideas.

Over the months we became good friends and eventually he invited me to ride his new project, a one-off racer called the Monark. As well as being good value around the paddock, Rudi was an absolute genius at technical innovation yet a total disaster at race-bike preparation. The Monark used a full 500cc engine based on a three-cylinder Crescent, at a time when almost everybody was running 'big' 350s in the 500cc class. I first rode it in practice at Mallory Park with a view to using it in the 500cc race instead of my usual Yamaha.

The engine had begun life as a marine outboard and had what I presume was the original bank of Tillotson carburettors, which seemed incapable of mixing air and petrol in a ratio that would actually burn. Heaven knows how many boaters these engines had been responsible for casting adrift.

The chassis was no less wondrous. It had cast magnesium wheels, twin discs at the front, Norton forks, and a pneumatic rear suspension strut borrowed off a Citroën car.

This was something Rudi evidently felt at home with because his race transporter was also a Citroën estate into which his usual sidecar outfits fitted – just. The screen of the bike can't have been much more than two feet off the ground, and you sort of contorted yourself behind it as though getting ready for a rectal examination. If he'd made it as a kneeler it might have been better, but as it was you needed to be double-jointed from the arse down. I ended up putting about eight inches of padding on the seat and still had to crane my neck to look up at Kreidler 50s.

The obvious attraction of the outboard engine was that, being a full 500, it produced about 70bhp – I think Rudi later claimed 75bhp – maybe ten more than a good TZ350. A similar concept developed by Dieter König was already going well. It would finish the season second in the championship, as well as giving Rolf Steinhausen back-to-back sidecar titles a couple of years later.

The Monark was definitely fast when it got into its stride but the carburetion was miles out and the forks were sticking, so it was slow into turns and even slower out. All it needed was a good mechanic to spend a week sorting the damn thing out, rather than a nutty professor with ever-more radical ideas, so I raced my Yamaha instead. But Rudi wasn't easy to put off, and a couple of months later he somehow wangled me an entry to ride it at the Swedish GP at Anderstorp, complete with the embarrassment of wearing the Number One plate.

By then the Monark wasn't exactly competitive but it was working a lot better than it had at Mallory. In practice I heard Ready's MV growling behind me on the long straight. Rather than get in his way I pulled over to give room into the long, long right-hander at the end. Phil thundered past, really on it, the big Agusta chopping and sliding through the turn. Yet I was amazed to find I had no great bother keeping up with him. The bike clearly had potential.

Putting an entire lap together was another matter, so on the start line I found myself about two-thirds of the way down the grid. Because of the dodgy carbs it was a bugger to start, so you really had to clean it out with lots of revs before killing the engine. 'Ring ... ding ... *dung*', it went, as the Krober ignition exploded. Half the grid ducked for cover as bits of rotor flew everywhere.

Also at the meeting was Crescent's PR guy, Per Grönvall, a stylish-looking chap with a crisp summer suit and a dolly bird on each arm. Despite working for an engine company, this was obviously not a man familiar with the inside of any device more oily than a nose-hair clipper. He chose this moment to shuffle over to the bike.

'What's happened?'

'It's buggered.'

'Oh, surely you can just lead for a couple of laps and then stop.'

Sometimes, no words are appropriate.

I believe that Yamaha later bought the Crescent from Rudi and it was never seen on a circuit again. It's a pity they didn't buy the PR guy, instead. The bike showed more promise.

Otherwise, good results seemed to come thick and fast: a double at the Cock o' the North at Scarborough in July (it might have been a triple if the clutch hadn't given up in the main race); four wins at the Hutch a couple of weeks later; two wins at the Snetterton Race of Aces meeting; followed by a new lap record at Oulton in early September. No one in British racing was putting together better results.

At Scarborough in September I had another of my occasional John Player Norton outings. I'd already had a first and a second on my Yamahas but as usual the deal was that I had to let Peter beat me in the Superbike race. This actually helped. After a few laps I was lying about fifth, with the best view in the house of Peter and Percy Tait having a right old ding-dong in front of me. With my orders in mind I let them get on with it, until they had a coming together at Mountside hairpin and landed in a heap. I nearly fell off from grinning, but kept it together to catch Sheene's Suzuki. After a few laps dicing he retired with a cracked fork yoke, leaving me to grab Norton's second Scarborough win in as many years.

At around the same time, Norton's £2,000 TT money still hadn't arrived so I rang Frank Perris to ask where it was. 'Jesus, matey,' he said, 'we didn't agree any money.' Eventually he reluctantly said that if I thought we had an agreement, then Norton would pay me, and a cheque arrived. But it was grudging. Not surprisingly Scarborough was my last ride for Norton, despite a bit of a press campaign to keep me in the squad. Mick Woollett wrote of the John Player team's 'long bleak summer' and urged Norton to sign me for 1974. 'The irony of the situation,' he noted, 'was that Grant raced for the team in 1972 but when they were cut from three to two riders he was passed over in favour of John Cooper.'

With no contract from Norton or anyone else in the pipeline, 1974 looked like being another year of the same, still with sponsorship from Brian Davidson. The season began in March at Daytona, and getting there was unconventional, to say the least. After Daytona 1973, Rob North had ended up working for Bill Toosher, the main Yamaha dealer in San Diego. So I flew to California to buy my 1974 race bikes, two TZ700s and a pair of TZ350s. Bill had one of those cool Airstream buses, converted to carry race bikes, with a workshop at the back and – by the standards I was used to – luxurious living quarters up front. The plan was to drive the 3000 miles from San Diego to Florida.

Americans don't do things by halves, so Bill had grafted an enormous 700-gallon fuel tank into the Airstream. After preparing the bikes and nipping down to Mexico to fill up with cheap petrol, four of us drove coast-to-coast non-stop – almost literally. We'd even change drivers on the move, one sliding out of the driver's seat as another shuffled in. There was me, Rob, Bill and a carrot-coloured guy called Big John, who was about three inches smaller than me. John's diet consisted entirely of carrots, which probably explained his hue.

Our one stop came, in a roundabout way, courtesy of the Yom Kippur war. Because of the resulting oil crisis the US had just brought the speed limit down to 55mph, so naturally I got pulled for exceeding it whilst crossing Texas. It cost us a couple of hours and me a few dollars, but I did get to see the inside of a Texas courthouse which was exactly like something from the *Dukes of Hazzard*.

Apart from that and Big John's strange complexion, all went well until we actually got to Daytona. The big TZ was a disaster. It was fast all right, but handled like a tea-trolley, partly thanks to the KR97, a new rear tyre Dunlop had developed specially for the 200-miler. The tyre's crown was completely flat, with a zigzag pattern, and actually slid *up* the banking. It was so scary that when the exhaust pipes simply fell to pieces 13 laps in to the race, I almost prayed in gratitude.

After the Daytona disaster, we arranged that Rob would send the four new Yamahas over to the UK, along with one of his own 350s, which I'd arranged to sell to a bloke called Rutter – no relation to Tony – from Manchester. Later, before actually sending off the shipment, Rob rang me full of gratitude for arranging the sale.

'Look,' he said, 'I want to buy you a present.'

There was no need, but when I failed to change his mind I said, 'OK, I'll have a …' and mentioned something British customs probably would not want me to bring in.

'Righto,' responded Rob, 'I'll put it in the back tyre of the 700 you rode at Daytona. The bikes should be in Manchester by Friday morning.'

Now, being an incurable Yorkshire tight-wad, I'd put a ludicrously low import valuation on the bikes for customs purposes. A few days later I had a phone call.

'Mr Grant? Manchester Customs and Excise here. I believe you have a shipment of motorcycles for collection.'

'Yes, that's right.'

'Could you just come over. There are a couple of things we need to clarify.'

With a sinking feeling, I agreed to drive over to Manchester airport.

They received me cordially enough, then sat me in the sort of windowless room where you give your name, rank and serial number.

'Now,' said the meaner of the two, 'stop fucking us about. Just what are you playing at?'

Oo-er. 'Pardon?'

'Look, you can do it the easy way and admit it, or we'll give you more grief than you can believe. You know and we know those valuations are bollocks.'

I nearly kissed him. It wasn't about the contraband in the wheel. It was about the valuation. But it didn't end there.

Next they took me to the warehouse to identify the bikes while they considered whether to give me a public flogging or just a fine. Inevitably the one bike they'd removed from its crate was the dodgy one. There it sat on a rear-wheel stand with the back wheel free to spin, although needless to say it was a bit heavy on one side. But no one seemed to notice and I was allowed to drive back home.

For the next month I practically crapped myself every time the phone rang. All it needed was for someone to idly spin the TZ's back wheel and notice it wasn't exactly balanced, and the game was up. Matters worsened when I got a call from Rutter, much brassed-off that *he*'d had a visit from Customs who'd turned his place over but found nothing – mainly because there was nothing to find. 'Christ,' I thought, 'I'm next.'

Finally, the phone call arrived. 'Mr Grant, Customs and Excise here ...' He went on to say they were going to fine me so many pounds for being a lying Yorkshire git – easy for them, they'd be Lancastrians – plus the duty due on the bikes' real value.

All I could think driving the van over the Pennines was that they were tricking me. They were just trying to lure me to the scene of the evidence so they could lock me up. But no, nothing happened, nothing was said. All for a damned present I didn't even want. That night I lobbed it in the local reservoir.

By far the worst upshot of the whole affair was that by this time I had a company, Mick Grant Racing Ltd, which handled the money side of all my racing. For convenience, the books were overseen by Brian Davidson's accountant, John Little. I can only presume that Customs passed on word of my little faux pas to the Inland Revenue, who put two and two together to make five, because the next I heard they were tearing apart Brian's business accounts. If the whole episode taught me anything, it's that you don't muck about with the Excise. Or the Revenue. If only I'd been better at heeding lessons like those.

As it turned out, there was something else hidden in the tail of the TZ700 – a sting. At Brands for my first year of Transatlantic Match Races it spat me off at Clearways and broke the scaphoid bone in my right wrist, the first break I'd suffered while racing. Somehow I saw out the rest of the weekend's racing before visiting Clayton Hospital in Wakefield. When a junior doctor finally condescended to see me two hours later, there was the usual tut-tutting about 'dangerous motorbikes' and he put me in an enormous plaster cast. It went from the tip of my fingers almost to my shoulder, looked like something Henry Moore might have come up with, and handled about as well as the Yamaha.

The next day I went back to see the orthopaedic consultant, who was no more impressed than me.

'Who the hell put that on?' he asked. 'It's ridiculous.'

I was in complete agreement. 'Whoever was working in your casualty department yesterday.'

So off came the cast and on went one which reached only from my knuckles to just above the elbow.

It was better but I was still worried. The scaphoid's the slowest-healing bone in your body and I had a living to make. Riding with even the slimmed-down plaster just wasn't on.

Luckily my mate Eric Boocock knew of a speedway enthusiast named Carlo Biaggi who also happened to be a private bone specialist. He was happy to tend to crocked racers on the National Health. So off I toddled to Galashiels for a free consultation. It was like Groundhog Day.

'Who on earth put that on?'

Carlo understood. When I'd booked the appointment and explained who I was he'd asked me to bring with me a clip-on handlebar. The plaster he came up with was moulded neatly around the handlebar, weighed next to nothing, and wasn't much longer than a gauntlet. With it came a letter from him: 'To whom it may concern. I consider this person completely insane but fit to ride a motorcycle.' Part of that – I'm not saying which – I just made up.

Galashiels wasn't so far from Brian Davidson's place. He's always been a guy for picking up waifs and strays and giving them a leg-up, which is probably why he sponsored me. At the time his latest project was a herbalist who made up exotic potions when he wasn't having too much to drink. Brian suggested I drop by to see this tame healer on my way home from Carlo's.

I don't have much faith in snake oils, but dropped by anyway. After chatting for a while the healer knocked up some tablets which I took for the next few weeks. Five weeks and one TT week later Carlo removed the plaster and was astounded at how quickly the bone had healed.

Trouble was, I still had little more wrist movement than I'd had before the plaster came off. Two hours later I'm sat on Brian's settee, next to his herbalist who spent 20 strange minutes rubbing in some powder he'd concocted. There was no manipulation, just the most gentle massage. I'm still not sure I believe it, but by the time he finished I had full movement again, and almost no pain.

John Williams had been in the wars, too, jumping off during early morning TT practice. In the same session I was going round with Tom Herron, both of us on 250s. On the longer straights we could see John's Triumph triple in the distance ahead of us. As we came over the jump at Kerrowmoar, a Triumph tank lay in the middle of the road with other debris scattered everywhere. Tom stopped, then me, but I was not looking forward to what I might find.

It looked like a plane crash but could only have been John, of whom there was no sign. Aliens? Manx fairies? It was very mysterious.

We heard John – assuming it was John – before we saw him, a low groan emanating from somewhere beyond a stand of trees. As we edged towards it, the groan said that its toe was hurting which, under the circumstances, was pretty good news. Apparently as he'd landed off the jump John's twistgrip had literally fallen off the handlebars, and his hand with it. He'd been thrown over a stone wall, miraculously found a way between some very stout trees, and landed on someone's lawn.

It's an ill wind … With John crocked, Gerald Brown, John's sponsor, kindly offered me his Yamahas. The broken wrist still wasn't 100 per cent, but on the smaller bikes not too big a handicap, and I was well pleased with second place in the Junior, albeit miles behind Tony Rutter who lapped at a brilliant 106mph. Wednesday's 250cc TT was an utter shambles which brought a similar result on the Fowler Yamaha. Rain and bad visibility caused the start to be delayed by hours. When we finally did get away, Charlie Williams disappeared into a lead he never lost. Mind you, he had an edge – only his left wrist was in plaster. This left me to dice for second place with Chas Mortimer.

This was all going to plan when I went into the Creg a bit too hot with the back wheel hopping and skittering and buried the front end in the bales. As I landed I turned round to see Chas riding past with a big grin on his face. Chas was a lovely bloke but a bit of a toff and a bounder who always reminded me of Terry Thomas. I cursed a bit, dragged the TZ from under the bales and set off again. On the drop down to Brandish I could smell burning rubber, so something was obviously bent but by the time I got to

Hillberry it seemed to have gone, so I just thought 'bugger it' and carried on.

After a once-over at the pits I got my head down, and found myself promoted to third place when Bill Rae slid off at Brandywell. I was pushing hard – my last lap was the fastest of the race – but had more or less settled for third when who should I see pushing out of Governor's Dip but dear old Chas. Apparently his filler cap was leaking and he'd run out of fuel. 'Take that you bounder,' I thought. 'Now it's my turn to grin.'

By that time I was already basking in the joy of becoming a TT winner, thanks to Slippery Sam. Sam already had a great TT history with consecutive wins – two for Pickrell, one for Jefferies – in the previous three years. So when its owner, Triumph dealer Arthur Bennett, invited me to ride it, I was only too happy to oblige. Lovingly built and cared for by Les Williams, the bike was called 'Slippery' because it was notoriously oily. I suspect it was also as legal as a bent copper – a real factory special full of bits that appeared in official Triumph parts lists but were unavailable to Joe Public at any price. It certainly felt a lot lighter and a lot faster than a standard Triumph triple.

In fairness Sam was only slippery – oily slippery – if you caned him. So if ever you wanted to win at the slowest possible pace, the time was now. The omens, though, weren't good. Throughout practice we'd had all sorts of engine and gearbox problems, including running a big-end before Braddan, and never seemed to manage a trouble-free lap. Les tried all sorts of quick-action throttles but yanking open three Amal carburettors with a dodgy wrist also didn't help.

The race had a Le Mans mass start. Although this was a stupid idea round the Mountain Course, at least your position on the road was also your position in the race, which actually helped. The Triumph definitely had more power than the Norton twin, but at that time Peter Williams was still faster than me around the TT course, so it was obvious that the biggest threat would come from him and his Kuhn Norton. My particular weakness was on the climb up the Mountain, so if I could get to the Verandah first, I reckoned, I'd be in with a shout. As luck would have it I got away in front of Peter, who retired before the Mountain on the opening lap.

After one lap I pitted for fuel but was back in front by Ramsey. My signals gave me all the good news I needed … +15 … +30 … +45 … then+1! What? Where did that come from? I took a peek back over my shoulder – nothing. It took me half a lap to realise that '+1' meant plus one minute, which should have been '+60'. Even with that worry gone, it was still one of my toughest TT races. Because of the plastered wrist I couldn't tuck in as much as I wanted, and by lap four had so many flies on my visor I could just about make out the edges of the road but not much more. It was literally a case of keeping it on the slightly grey bits between the two fuzzy green bits – frightening. Luckily no one was pushing hard and I hung on to win by almost two minutes from Hans-Otto Butenuth's BMW. Sadly, David Nixon was killed when he slid off just behind me at the corner before Glen Helen.

That first TT win was special, particularly on such a British institution as Sam. In truth it wasn't the most competitive TT ever run: there were only 24 starters, half of whom didn't finish. And of course it didn't have the status of the Senior or Junior. But it was a win, fair and square. Sam went on to win for Alex George and Dave Croxford the following year, but that was it. Since the production rules barred any bike more than five years old, that was Sam's last TT, and there wasn't much prospect of a new triple taking his place since by then the BSA Group was down the toilet.

On the surface, having a TT winner in the family didn't seem to impress anyone very much – Yorkshire folk are like that. But underneath, I think they were all proud of me, if a little mystified at the strange way I earned a living. Mum only ever came to one race meeting, at Cadwell, where I landed on my knees right in front of her at the Mountain. I can't blame her for not wanting to witness any more of that. A year or so later I did the same for my sister at Mallory, against Sheene and company in the Superbike race. I was leading coming out of Gerrards, lost it, caught it, lost it again and ended up head-butting the banking. As I tottered to my feet cross-eyed I came face to face with our Cheryl, stood about ten feet away with a mortified look on both her faces. She didn't come to watch much after that, either.

I may have been professional by now, but that didn't mean the money was rolling in. Apart from pay-days like the TT, life on two wheels was a hand-to-mouth existence. As time wore on I got better at negotiating start money. Race promoters were tough old sods, so you had to be as hard-nosed with them as you'd be stuffing the bike under someone on the last corner of a race.

There simply wasn't much money around in UK racing. I'd touched on the subject in an interview with Peter Kelly for one of the motorcycle papers (which dubbed me the 'Yorkshire Flyer' – true grittiness was obviously some way ahead). 'You can eat out your heart in England,' I'd said, 'but it won't get you a works ride. Forget the British shorts … the money is so pathetic you can hardly afford to race anyway.'

As a relatively late bloomer in racing – by this time I'd be almost 30 – this was something I felt particularly. It was also true that I'd probably stayed racing at home for too long, although my late start also had something to do with that. On the other hand, after five years or so in which privateers had grands prix almost to themselves (only MV was making a consistent factory effort), more factories were now getting in on the act. Privateers would never again have it so good.

One short-term result was that any extra fiver you could scratch was a bonus. Every so often on the way to European meetings I'd drop off at Fort Dunlop to stock up with race tyres. They cost something like £7, but you could usually sell them on at circuits for double that. At least, that was the plan, because within half an hour of arriving at the next meeting the stock had usually been pillaged by mates who I hadn't the heart to charge over the odds.

I just wasn't the entrepreneur type – unlike others in the Continental paddock who could make a profit on any old tat. At the time Dunlop had recently changed their standard T1 compound for the much stickier 534. One afternoon at Tilburg Chas Mortimer skidded to a halt outside my van on the look-out for tyres. All that was left was a solitary, obsolete T1. Over my protests he insisted on buying it for the usual £7. Half an hour later he was back. I expected a bollocking for him going tits-up on the antique Dunlop.

Chas always had a good line in flannel and it had paid off. 'Good deal that T1', he grinned. 'Just sold it to some mug for 12 quid.'

A few years later I managed to get my revenge. Me, Carol, Chas and his wife Jackie were out for a meal at the Coach House at Ballasalla on the Isle of Man. Carol isn't usually a high-roller, but decided she'd have the lobster. Since no one else wanted to lose out with something cheaper, that settled it: lobster for four.

Usually in such situations I'm the mug the waiter homes in on when the time comes to pay the tab. But since this promised to be an especially painful one I went into stealth mode, pretending to be deep in serious conversation with Carol. The waiter duly dropped the bill on Chas, instead. You could tell from his expression that it was hurting, but being a good public schoolboy he wasn't going to protest in front of the women. The following morning I bumped into him in the paddock. He was still in pain.

''Kin' hell, Mick. I thought you'd help me out with that bill.'

'I did, mate, in Tilburg. Remember that T1?' I bet even today he can't eat lobster without it tasting of rubber.

CHAPTER 9

GOING GREEN

During 1974 I'd ridden a couple of times for Stan Shenton on his Seeley-framed Triumph triple, although it didn't amount to much on my CV because I'd decked it out at Gerrards and launched it into the Leicestershire scenery in a very big and expensive way. The bike they dragged back to the paddock was six inches shorter than the one which left. So Stan and I knew one another.

The previous December I also happened to track-test for *Motor Cycle News* Percy Tait's race bike based on the two-stroke air-cooled 750cc H2 Kawasaki roadster. The bike had handling problems but the engine was impressive – a big soft, powerful lump. 'With the right jockey,' I'd concluded, 'there's no reason it can't be a winner.' At around the same time I'd partnered Percy on a production Kawasaki Z1 four-stroke at Amaroo Park in Australia, placing fourth.

So, along with a podium position two years before in the Senior TT, almost by accident I'd accumulated something of a Kawasaki pedigree. As it happened Stan Shenton ran Boyers of Bromley, one of the major Kawasaki dealerships. For the '74 TT he provided me with one of the same H2-based triples. It worked out better than the Seeley, but not much. It was a bit of a handful at the best of times, let alone with a broken wrist. A docile old lump like Slippery Sam was one thing, but the Kawasaki was something else. I struggled home in 17th place, the only bronze replica I ever earned. I went so slowly that I actually oiled a plug, which was a bit embarrassing.

By mid-'74 word was going round the paddocks of a major factory push from Kawasaki for the following year, so I was keen to keep well in with Boyers and rode the bike for the rest of the year. Mostly, it was a frustrating experience. At the Cock o' the North at Scarborough the chain broke when I was lying second. This was the same meeting in which Phil Haslam, brother to Ron, was killed. He was leading when his Pharaoh Yamaha suddenly slowed and he was rammed by the following pack. Bizarrely, when the race was red-flagged he was granted a posthumous win on count-back.

The H2-based bike was still raw and unsorted but had potential. At Silverstone, I was howling around with Smart and Yvon Duhamel when 'ignition troubles' – the end of the crank fell off – sidelined the bike. A few weeks later I set a new lap record at Snetterton, nipping past Peter Williams's Norton on the last lap to take my first win on the bike. At the same meeting Barry Ditchburn won the feature event, the Race of Aces, on Ted Broad's TZ750.

In early October we took the H2 to Ontario in the States. The place didn't have great memories for me, since I'd ridden one of Bob Hansen's 750cc Kwackers there the previous year and seized after four laps. Although the Boyer triple spent most of practice detonating and seizing, in the race it hung on to finish seventh in a quality field. Then, back home for the last meeting of the year at Brands, I battled through from a lousy start to grab the lead from Sheene with two laps to go. But it was Barry's day. He took three wins on the 750 Suzuki and nipped past to take the win when I was slowed by a backmarker at Clearways on the final lap.

All in all, though, I felt I'd done pretty well on the bike and for once my longer-term planning paid off. In November I signed a Kawasaki contract for the '75 season, as team-mate to Ditchburn who'd signed the previous week.

Domestic life was forging ahead, too. Just after getting back from Ontario, Carol and I were married at Wakefield Register Office on 14 October (she reminds me). The local paper ran a headline something like 'Local Ace Jets Back to Wed', which makes it sound like something from *Hello* magazine, although it was more like something from the *Beano*. The paparazzi were conspicuous by their absence. Instead there were just Carol's mum and dad, Ronald and Dorothy Rhodes, my parents, sister Cheryl and Steve, her husband-to-be. Overton church hall hosted a fine reception with a buffet prepared by my mum. And not one of them had a camera. We rounded that off with a no-expenses-spared honeymoon in Criggleston. Carol paid for the wedding licence.

During the previous winter Carol and I had finally moved out of her gran's, buying a house at Station Cottages at Crigglestone – yes, it does sound like something out of *The Flintstones* – just south of Wakefield. It had cost £4,500, which seemed a fantastic sum and terrified me almost as much as Carol could. True, by now I was making a decent living racing, but had scarcely any savings. And, after all, racing wasn't like being a doctor or even a plumber, where you had a pretty good idea what was coming in each week and would continue to do so. Besides, living on 'tick' wasn't what I'd been brought up to do.

Although it was in a pretty, rural location, it wasn't even that much of a house – just two rooms downstairs, two above, and a cellar below the lot. Half of the kitchen was taken up by an enormous chimney breast. We'd hardly moved in when, without so much as a by-your-leave, dad arrived with a big hammer and a wheelbarrow, and within an hour we were all standing on a pile of rubble. The kitchen now seemed huge, but so did the hole in the roof.

Station Cottages was a row of three terraced houses at the end of a narrow dirt road. Ours was the end cottage, which meant that if anyone parked outside the others, we couldn't get in or out. Eventually we had Carol's brother, Paul, bring down his digger to widen the track. It did the trick, but only briefly, since the extra space only encouraged the neighbours to buy more cars. It seemed that he could have excavated halfway to Bradford and we'd still have been stuck.

A year or so later the bike journalist, Chris Carter, arrived in his old Mercedes to interview me about something or other. He stayed for dinner – Chris had a figure to maintain and liked his food – and left at about 11pm full of clam chowder. I was just about to go to bed when who should ring but Carter. After a bit of quizzing we established that he was on the forecourt of Ringways, a big Ford dealer near Leeds. His Merc had a puncture.

'Well, why are you telling me? Just put on the spare.'

'That's flat, too.'

So off Carol and I set in an old Standard 8 I'd bought for £150, with a spare wheel off the Transit which had the same size tyres and with a bit of luck might fit the Merc. Halfway there, the flywheel clutch fell off the Standard. After tramping for miles I found a phone box, called Nigel Everett, my mechanic who was staying with us, and told him to jump in my Mazda and come and rescue us. This would have been a better plan if Nigel knew how to drive. By the time he reached us he'd already driven into my Transit and ricocheted into the caravan. Everything I owned seemed to be dented.

Eventually the three of us reached Carter and put a new tube in his tyre. We were just about to inflate it when the sound of sirens filled the night and the forecourt lit up with blue lights. Some concerned citizen had reported a car being nicked. All in all, it wasn't a hugely successful night.

Nigel had joined me earlier that season, although we don't agree on exactly how it came about. I seem to remember him answering an ad I placed in the bike press, but he has a different version. Since my memory's been shot since I was in short pants, he's probably right. What we can agree on is that he was with me every year to the end of my career, which says as much about his staying power as his skills at building bikes. And mine – because he could be a cussed little git.

Whatever the background, I remember being impressed by his attitude more than his CV, since he was barely out of school and didn't have much by way of experience. As a kid he'd skived off classes to hang around Mick Wheeler's bike workshop in Witney, later working at the same place. Later still, Rod Skivyer joined the firm and Nigel started to help him at meetings, eventually becoming his full-time mechanic. I first encountered him when he helped Paul sort out some problems with my bikes at Imatra. Two weeks later at Silverstone he asked me directly for a job. He was keen, definitely – he didn't stop asking for three days. I'm not sure whether I'd have relented, but after I threw away the 350 in a big way I was too crocked to drive home. Nigel drove me back, set about preparing the bikes for the next meeting, the Ulster Grand Prix, and never left.

He was raw but bright and keen, which often matters more than pure technical ability. And dedicated: to get from Witney, near Oxford, to Crigglestone, he'd take off his L-plates and whine up the motorway – on a moped. Eventually he more or less moved in with us during the race season, staying until the end of my riding career in 1985.

Race mechanics don't stand on ceremony. They're hands-on guys who live a pretty strange sort of life and can be a merciless bunch – not the ideal place for a downy-faced youth. So until he found his feet Nigel was usually pretty reserved. It was only as the years passed that he became the paddock's chief bolshie and wind-up merchant.

I mean this kindly, but Nigel is the only person I've met in racing who's dodgier than me. But what mattered more was that he was never less than 100 per cent behind me. His strength wasn't tuning. It was being unbelievably quick and thorough with the spanners. Once, I was lined up on the Donington grid when it started raining heavily. In the time the other teams had just about managed to change wheels, Nigel had whipped in a set of different yolks, as well. It barely seemed possible, but I not only had the best set-up of any rider in the race, but was absolutely confident the job had been done right.

The beauty of having such a long relationship is that over the years he came to understand me and the way I rode a bike. Once, when we were running Dunlops on the Suzukis, they came out with a huge fat front wet tyre. It gripped brilliantly but, largely because I never had a hang-off style, I just couldn't get it into corners. I was over a second off the pace. Nigel switched fork yokes to add about 5mm more trail, and the bike was transformed. From being miles off the pace I was suddenly vying for pole.

Sharing the same pit at the time was my team-mate, Rob McElnea. Rob did hang off – he had a lot to hang off with – and hauled the bike round after him. But like all racers he was always on the lookout for the latest magic ingredient. He had his mechanic try the same fork mod. Off he went, and came back a few laps later shaking his head. He couldn't tell the slightest difference and lapped at exactly the same speed.

Like even the best mechanics Nigel wasn't immune to dropping the odd clanger – like a sprocket falling off whilst I was leading at Macau. But they were few and far between and I was always confident of the bike he put under me. Sure, there were occasional fallings out and the odd cross word – there couldn't not be in such a high-pressure existence. But nothing stood out. Hiring Nigel was one of the brightest decisions I ever made in racing.

Meanwhile, back in Green Land, Kawasaki seemed reassuringly serious. In February, at simultaneous press conferences in Tokyo, Los Angeles and London, they announced their plans for '75. Their target was a triple assault on the 250cc and 500cc world championships, as well as the major international Formula 750 events. At home, our priority was the *Motor Cycle News* Superbike championship.

On the face of it their kit was equal to their ambitions. After years of Kawasaki making do with bikes derived from roadsters, all three bikes would be purpose-built racers, all water-cooled. The one that really took my eye was the KR250 twin – which would go on to do great things, if only they'd realised it sooner. Then there were two KR triples, of 500 and 750cc.

As usual the season began at Daytona. As well as Ditch and me with our four bikes, there was the Kawasaki USA squad of Duhamel, Art Bauman and young Jim Evans. Between us we reckoned we had a pretty formidable team and were optimistic. Trouble was, the KR750's gearbox was made of chocolate – or something like it – and would only do a couple of laps before falling to bits.

As it turned out, only doing two laps at a stretch was a major health benefit because the tyres just couldn't cope with the power of the 750s and the loadings on the Daytona banking. This was brought home in spectacular fashion when Sheene had his huge crash – right in front of the cameras, since the BBC was filming a documentary about him at the time. I happened to be standing on the banking with a stopwatch, saw his back tyre explode, the bike spit sideways and launch him up the road at enormous speed. It was the most horrendous crash I've ever witnessed and seemed to go on forever. As he bounced and flew, you wanted it all to stop and see him get to his feet with a thumbs-up, but he seemed to just cartwheel for miles. When he did finally stop, nothing seemed to be moving at all. I think even my heart had stopped.

Later, when I went to see him in hospital he was seriously knocked about and obviously in a lot of pain, but – typical of the man – he had a fag in his mouth and was laughing and joking.

It was no secret that at Daytona tyres were a problem. We knew it, and so did the tyre companies. Goodyear, the

American outfit, was the one which had come closest to finding a solution, largely because these speed bowls were in their back yard. But we were contracted to Dunlop, so I'd been especially keen to touch base with their man, David Buck, before practice even began.

'What tyre have you got for us this year, Bucky?' I used the singular because no one gave a stuff about the front tyre. The rear was the one that kept you alive.

'KR97.'

Terrific. This was the same tyre I'd hated so much on a TZ700 the previous year.

'You can shove that up your arse, for starters.'

'No, no,' he insisted. 'We've redesigned it. It's different.'

'Not bloody different enough.'

I was no more impressed when I saw it. Like the 1974 tyre, its trouble was that it was so fat and flat that it just wasn't going to be stable – either on the infield or the banking. I told Bucky that rather than use the same rubbish again I'd pay for Goodyears out of my own pocket – which, for any Yorkshireman, is a pretty serious indication of discontent. But Bucky pleaded and pleaded, and in the end I agreed to try the Dunlop for just one session.

He was right. The weird flat shape, which I was convinced was the root of the problem, was still the same. But somehow they'd altered the tyre structurally so that it gripped on the infield and didn't weave on the banking. It felt a totally different tyre. God knows why they continued to call it by the same name as the useless KR97 of the year before, but they did. Whether it would last race distance – or rather half race distance, since in deference to the tyre issues the organisers had turned the 200-miler into two 100-milers – we never found out, because after three laps of the race the 750's gearbox did its usual impression of a hand grenade without the pin. Gene Romero went on to win the race for Yamaha and none of the other Kawasakis fared much better than mine. In fact the KR750's brittleness never allowed it to win Daytona. The factory didn't post a single win until Scott Russell in 1992. We never even got to ride the KR250.

If there was one highlight from the meeting it was finding Mr Yashida, Kawasaki's resident pit genius. There was nothing he could do about the metallurgy of the KR's gearbox, but after puzzling for half an hour decided that he could at least get more oil to the gears by scrolling the shafts. This normally required a lathe and a fully-equipped workshop, but he laboriously made do with a tiny hand grinder. Before that, he'd made an accurate protractor from a piece of scrap metal. It was beautiful work but was never going to make the box last race distance.

Only a few weeks later at the opening round of the British championship at Cadwell Park, two astonishing things happened. After the debacle of Daytona, Kawasaki turned up with a redesigned, remade, gearbox which to the best of my recollection never had another problem. And Sheene, barely out of a hospital bed, turned up with his three-cylinder Suzuki.

Maybe I was still gob-smacked on the grid, because I completely fluffed the start, howling away flat last in pursuit of the pack. I managed to get past most of the field but the hardest of all to pass was Barry, who was leading the race. Eventually I did get past him – he retired in pain a little while later – to post the team's first domestic win. My team-mate Ditchburn slid off at Barn and couldn't start for the second race. But Sheene was always the big threat on his Suzuki triple. A few weeks later he was still hobbling but obviously back on his game and we shared a win apiece at Brands.

At Continental meetings Kawasaki often used the same hotel as Dunlop, and Bucky – their top tyre man – had by this time become a good friend. A couple of years earlier I'd been with him at a circuit near Marseilles to test the latest Dunlops, including their first slicks. At the time Michelin runners like Sheene were using PZ2 and PZ4 tyres, against which Dunlop hoped to pitch their new

KR124. So there's Bucky with a folding table, chair, clipboards, and stopwatches; Dunlop France's Dave Lamb to change the tyres; and Nigel, as ever, keeping my Yamahas sweet. I'd be riding the Dunlops and Michelins back-to-back to see which were best.

Except that some piece of mischief got hold of me, so when I was running on Dunlops I used 1,000rpm less than when running the Michelins. By mid-afternoon Bucky's got his head in his hands, having spent months designing a new tyre that obviously – or so he thought – wasn't working. His world had collapsed under him, but he put on a brave face.

'That's it, then. Back to the drawing board. We may as well test the slicks now.'

He didn't see the point but I pressed him to give the KR124 one more go, this time using all the revs. I actually went a bit quicker than I had on the Michelins. As I passed Bucky's table on the second flying lap his face contorted into a grimace. 'You bastard, Grant' was written all over it. You couldn't get away with that sort of larking about today. Testing is too costly and too precious.

Next, we tried the new slicks, which had never been run on any bike before. They were simply amazing – probably the biggest single leap in grip in the history of motorcycling. Grip, though, isn't everything. Precisely because they gripped better than the suspension system had needed to cope with before, they gave the most horrendous chatter. At first the only way to ease it was to use narrower tyres, which of course no one wanted to do. Despite this I didn't have much problem getting under the circuit's 350cc lap record, so Bucky was happy with our day's work.

But not for long. Based on this test Dunlop soon produced scores of the same tyres, but they never worked in British conditions. The same thing would arise time after time over the years, even 30 years later with the Sanyo Hondas. We'd smash lap records at, say, Almeria, then get to Donington Park and find we had no grip. Just because a tyre was brilliant at one circuit didn't mean diddly-squat at another.

My last big run-in with Dunlop black magic came a decade later at Macau in 1983. Bucky was gabbing on about these brilliant new tyres he'd supply me, half the weight of anything else and more grip than velcro. Since they were in short supply, for practice at Macau I used the tyre that had finished my last meeting, at Brands the month before. By the end of testing it was scrap.

It was a seriously stupid thing to do, but I began the first race on one of Bucky's completely untried magic tyres. The bike handled like a camel and within half a lap Ron Haslam, my only serious rival, had already disappeared into the distance. For the second leg, we put back the shagged old Brands tyre, and I won. It was the sort of cock-up only a novice should make. I sometimes wonder how I managed to win even a club race.

The next big outing after Daytona – and the next lesson about tyres – was the 1975 Transatlantic series, my first on the Kawasaki. On the whole it went well. I think I finished around third in the home team's points standings, but not without some hairy moments along the way. At Mallory Park I was lying second to Roberts, both of us on slicks. Then, halfway round Gerrards, a place where you don't lose the front – ever – the front went away in a fearsome slide. Somehow I hung on to it, but it unnerved me so much – I was convinced something was badly wrong with the front end – that I pulled in. We found the problem, all right. A match was sticking out of the surface of the rubber. It had been moulded in at the factory – by a bloke who shortly wouldn't be working there.

I later visited Fort Dunlop to see the process by which the race tyres were made. It was very archaic, not especially clean, and not all that surprising that bits of debris could end up in the carcase. I suppose I should be grateful it had been just a match and not somebody's packed lunch.

One of the things that's always amazed me about tyre companies is that their products have their own unique signature. Michelins, for instance, always took a little longer to warm up but, if one of their tyres had a designation number on the sidewall, that told you exactly how it was going to work, whichever batch it came from. With Dunlop it couldn't have been more different. You'd feel differences even within the same batch. So if you got a good tyre, you tended to hang on to it. In the days before tyre warmers, the big advantage with Dunlops, which worked in my favour in my battles with Sheene, was that after one lap you knew they'd be up to temperature, whereas with Michelins it might take two.

The biggest surprise the Americans gave anyone in any Transatlantic I was involved in was in the wet at Mallory Park in '77, and also tyre-related. In the States, if it rains, racing's abandoned. So hardly any of the Yanks had turned a wheel in the wet. We, on the other hand, were supposedly the world's wet-weather specialists. There were two flaws in this argument. One is that most of the Americans were raised on dirt-track ovals, so they never felt more at home than when the back wheel was hanging loose. Guys like Kenny seemed to have no fear of the wet at all. The other flaw was tyres which, by modern standards were pretty primitive. At the time there was no such thing as full wets. When it rained we'd put on what were virtually road tyres with racing compounds and carcases.

The Yanks didn't have any of these so turned up with what they presumably thought was the next best thing – a pile of Goodyear flat-track tyres. They were probably the only tyres in America which weren't slicks. When we saw these chunky things, which looked more like trials tyres than something you'd sling on a TZ750, we simply laughed. But we soon stopped when the flag dropped and they all disappeared into the distance. By accident, the Yanks seemed to have discovered wets.

The Transatlantic itself is something I look back on with mixed feelings, quite apart from the bones it helped me to break. To my mind the series never got better than when Smarty, Pickrell and the rest rode the BSA and Triumph triples. What a noise! In later years I have to admit that the politics of the series often pissed me off. At the time, like many others who made the British team, I was a regular at Daytona. To race there you paid your own way, everything from fares and shipping to entry fees and insurance. In contrast, when they came over each Easter, the Americans would have everything paid and get a fair whack of start money as well. I don't blame their riders in the slightest, but the imbalance left a bit of a sour taste.

At the time, if a circuit thought you'd bring punters through the gate, they'd pay good start money – typically about £2000–3000 a meeting for the top men. In comparison, the actual prize fund was pocket money. It also begs the question of why, if they could pay that sort of start money then, they can't pay it now. Someone's trousering a lot of money today, and it isn't the riders.

The other odd thing about the Transatlantic was that it was supposedly a team race in a sport which is all about individual performance. Bike racing's not like rugby. There's no jolly sitting around in baths together and fighting for the common good. It's all about number one. Oddly the Yanks did seem to have something of a team spirit, maybe because they were miles from home and were being paid to have one. But despite all the hype in the bike press, and a lot of dodgy quotes from riders saying what the media wanted to hear, with the Brits it wasn't like that. No one had the notion that finishing last wasn't so bad as long as the team won. For any bike racer, there's absolutely nothing good about being last.

That's not to say you are not pals off the track. But on it, it was almost like riding in a normal two-man team, except in this team there were eight: whatever else you did, you had to beat your team-mates. And the idea of adopting tactics to help the team was just not on. Maybe the Americans approached it that way to some extent. But they were the 'away' team. We were at home in front of our own fans. It was every man for himself.

Brands and Cadwell was one thing, but the bigger test for the Kawasaki and its new gearbox would come at the North West 200 in mid-May. A good friend and old racing buddy, Billy McCosh, always looked after me on my Irish trips. As usual, he picked me up at the airport, provided me with a free hire car and generally took care of me and Carol. As I was driving up to Coleraine I hoofed the renter past a long line of cars. To me there seemed to be plenty of room, but a bloke coming the other way obviously thought otherwise and ended up slewing to a halt almost in the ditch. There was no great harm done so I carried on my way, only to see a red Escort pull out of the line of cars I'd overtaken. More ominously, its driver looked a bit miffed as he jammed a peaked cap on his head.

Eventually, he pulled me over.

'What's your game?' he asked in broad Antrim.

'I'm on my way to the races.'

'Spectating?'

'No, riding.'

This seemed to interest him more than the chap in the ditch. Once he'd established who I was, the only ticket that interested him was one with my autograph.

The Kawasaki team was staying in the Carrick na Cull hotel by the harbour in Coleraine. These days it's an old folks' home, so maybe they'd still welcome me. That evening, chatting to Shenton and Ditch over dinner, I regaled them with the incident on the road.

Shenton thought I was bullshitting. 'Oh, yeah, oh yeah,' he said sceptically.

The following day I'm taking Shenton and Ditch – who'd never been to the North West before – for a lap of the circuit. Without doing anything daft I was using all the road where traffic permitted, just to show Ditch the racing line.

'Apex here ... aim for that ... watch that bump ...'
Next thing there's a flashing blue light in my mirror.
When we stop, a tubby little Ulster sergeant climbs out of
his big black police car and strolls towards us. Between
me and him, I can see Shenton's face in the mirror. 'Get
out of this, you clever sod,' his expression said.

'Mick,' began the bobby, slightly apologetically, 'hope
you don't mind me stopping you but I just wanted to
wish you the best for the race.' Stan was speechless. He
may not have understood me very well, but he obviously
didn't understand the Irish passion for racing, either.

Come the racing, and I couldn't have done any better if
I'd had a police escort all the way round – the bikes were
that good. The 500cc race was hard work, since the triple
was only barely quicker than a good TZ. But the big race
was a cakewalk on the new triple. After years of groaning
about MV's dominance at the TT, now I had an inkling of
how Ago must have felt. Naturally, I loved every minute
of it. The KR750 became the first bike to lap the NW200
course in under five minutes, breaking the lap record by a
staggering 7mph and taking a comfortable win ahead of
Ditch. When I left the pits after refuelling, the second
man hadn't even come into sight.

Just a couple of weeks later, TT practice got off to a
similar flier. On a wildly overgeared 750, I lapped at
105mph first time out. By Wednesday I'd managed
106.95mph, my fastest-ever TT lap.

Although on paper it ought also to have been favourite
on the Island, the 500 wasn't so well sorted. For one
reason or another I didn't get in much practice on it,
despite the best efforts of Nigel and Rod Scivyer. At the
time the ACU, God bless 'em, were still behaving as
though all race engines were air-cooled, despite the fact
that ours and most others were by now water-cooled. So
the rule still was that you had to kill your engines 20
minutes before the start of the race. This meant that the
liquid-cooled bikes were stone cold when they set off, and

didn't reach working temperature for several miles. It was plain dangerous, just asking for seizures.

Sure enough, when the Senior got under way late in dodgy weather, as soon as I rolled off the throttle for Quarter Bridge, the triple locked up solid. Rats! There goes the race. I let it coast with the clutch out for a little way then, just on the off-chance, let out the clutch to see if it would re-start. It burped and rattled, but to my surprise eventually started running on about 2½ cylinders. That still didn't make it a potential race-winner, but the bike had caused such interest that I thought I ought to try to put in one lap, so at least the fans would get to see it and hear it – even if it did sound like a bucketful of rusty nuts. So on I went.

It was a typical Manx day – not actually pouring down, but dreary and damp. Normally the triple revved to around 11,000rpm, but in deference to it being so poorly – and this, after all, was still in my mind a parade lap – I revved to it around 8,500rpm, which was only just in the powerband. I was still planning on pulling in after one lap, but my signals told me I was on the leaderboard. I half suspected someone was taking the piss, but thought I'd better keep going. Four laps later and the damn thing's still rattling along. I decided that if it wasn't run-in now, it never would be, and finally started giving it some stick. After five laps, I get a signal telling me I'm leading by 4 seconds. Unknown to me, lots of the other top guys were having their own problems so, amazingly, it not only lasted the six-lap distance, but won, 30 seconds ahead of John Williams. Although by this time the TT was a grand prix in name only, it was only Kawasaki's second win in 500cc grand prix, a tally they never added to until the MotoGP era, and then only just.

There was another lucky postscript to that Senior win. Six months later the Senior trophy was on display at Denis Parkinson's bike shop in Wakefield when Yorkshire's most short-sighted burglars broke into the place. Although they stole £700 from the safe, they evidently failed to notice a four-foot tall, solid silver trophy stood next to it. The pot, first awarded in 1907, used to have a pretty risky existence. At least once I've taken it to the Post-TT meeting at Mallory, where it sat around in the paddock all weekend. I don't suppose its other winners were any more careful. Now it's insured for half a million quid or something, never leaves the Isle of Man, and doesn't go anywhere without an armed guard.

During TT practice week I'd done a few course-learning laps in the car with my old mate Billy McCosh. We'd stop here and there, discussing lines, how to miss the worst bumps, all the rest of it. At the top of Barregarrow he insisted the technique was to cog down.

'No,' I said, 'on a 350 it's top gear.'

'Not at all,' he said, 'not at all.' He just didn't believe me.

Since I was riding for Kawasaki, I had no bike for the Junior. Billy and I ended up watching the 350cc race at the same place, Barregarrow Top. Charlie Williams was supposed to be first away, but because of some last-minute problem had to start from the back of the grid. So the first guys through were the likes of Rutter or Derek Chatterton, who were taking the bend in top, but definitely rolling the throttle. From there the field got slower and slower, going down one and even two gears as Billy suggested. He wasn't saying anything, but I could tell he was giving me sidelong 'I told you so' glances. Then came Charlie, who we'd practically forgotten about – absolutely pinned in top, flat behind the screen. Now it was my turn to look smug.

When I was at my best around the Island, if I was off line by more than a couple of feet twice in any lap, I'd notice and remember it. I always followed Geoff Duke's admonition to 'go in slow and come out fast', which he didn't actually quite mean. He meant go in fast – but not quite on the limit – and come out as fast as you can. It's a technique you can get away with on the Island, as opposed to short circuits, because you're rarely having to defend against someone trying to dive up the inside.

Friday's Open Classic was the other way round from the Senior: a faultless start then a broken chain whilst leading at the Gooseneck on lap three. Yet even that had its funny side. As I stomped down the hill to the marshals' post I heard a scream behind me: a fan had hopped over the wall to pick up the broken chain as a souvenir, only to discover it was red hot. John Williams won the race, but I got most of the headlines. My second lap was a new outright record, 109.82 mph. At the time that seemed to mean more to everyone else than to me. I'd known from the start that in order to beat the Yamahas, which needed one fuel stop to my two, something over 108mph would be needed. As usual, my main emotion was bitter disappointment at losing a race that had been there for the taking, especially as first place meant the richest prize in TT history, £1500.

CHAPTER 10

MIKE THE BIKE AND BARRY THE SHEENE

Many years later I learned that someone else was also gutted on the day of the 1975 Open Classic. The record I broke, of course, was Mike Hailwood's, which had stood since 1967. Apparently Hailwood was in the press room with Ted McCauley, the journalist who wrote his biography. As I screamed down Bray Hill, Peter Kneale broke the news over the tannoy: 'History has been made today, Mick Grant lapping at 109.82mph to break Mike Hailwood's lap record.'

Mike turned to Ted, grimaced and grunted 'the bastard!' I've been lucky enough to enjoy many accolades, before that day and since, but that's the one of which I'm proudest. At the time I'd met Mike but couldn't say I knew him. At heart I was still the bike-mad student who, like most racing fans, had read all about his exploits and regarded him as a near-god. I felt as though Zeus had stepped down from Mount Olympus, just to say I was a twat – which had to be a major compliment, however back-handed.

The lap itself I was less smug about. Yes, it was special to be the fastest man ever around the Mountain Course which, despite all the criticism it's endured in recent years, was still the most hallowed stretch of tarmac in motorcycling history. But the truth was that Mike had done his lap eight years before on treaded tyres and drum brakes on a 500 he didn't even like, whilst I had 750cc, slicks, discs and a bike I loved to bits. In other words, this was a milestone which ought to have been broken much sooner, which only went to show what a special rider Hailwood was.

I'd first bumped into him in 1973 or '74 when he had a one-off ride in the 350cc British Grand Prix. At the time I was so much into my own thing that I barely gave a thought to racing against such a legend. Then, come the race, I'm hacking round in around eighth place, when another 350 comes ripping past me into a corner. 'Mmm, he's a bit good,' I thought. It was Hailwood.

As my results got better I developed a bit of an affinity with the man. Whenever I took a long-standing lap record – at Oulton and elsewhere, as well as the Isle of Man – it always seemed to be Hailwood I was displacing. Over the following years we'd bump into each other now and again, but I didn't get to know him well until his TT comeback in '78.

Meanwhile, back in Team Green, I'd nothing against Ditch, but Rule One in racing is always beat your team-mate. Since he wasn't a TT regular, I had a massive edge on the Island. He'd raced there in '68 – actually before me – and again in 1970. But compared to me that was no experience at all and he was struggling to learn his way round. Taking him for a couple of tutorial laps in the van couldn't do much to bridge such a huge gap. In the Senior he finished 20th – not shabby, but 11 minutes adrift – and never raced the TT again.

On the shorts he was obviously a far tougher customer, but I felt that I had the beating of him and that was the way it turned out. By season's end I took the *MCN* Superbike championship by 18 points from him. Mind you, it could have ended differently. Competing in the Champion Classic at Ontario, my back tyre exploded, chucking me off at 140mph. It was almost an exact replica of Sheene's Daytona crash. The difference was that it didn't make me world famous, but it didn't smash my leg to bits, either. As I flew through the air I could see my Superbike championship disappearing but all I suffered were bumps and bruises.

The upshot of such a successful season was that I was indisputably the team's number one rider. At least, that's how I saw it and how the big-shots in Japan seemed to regard it, too. As a result I usually got first go at any new trick bits from the factory. I suspect this used to brass off Ditch a little, but in fact it was a mixed blessing for me. Sure, if the new part was better, it gave me an advantage. But often I'd be using up valuable practice time on something that didn't work. Aluminium rear disc rotors were a case in point. Ordinarily aluminium melts far too readily to be any use for brake discs. But these were plasma-sprayed, supposedly very space-age, and offered an obvious saving in unsprung weight. But somebody hadn't done their sums very well. I used to like trailing the back brake out of corners, so I was probably harder on them than some riders. Whatever the cause, I pitted after a session at Daytona complaining that the back brake seemed to have gone off. It had gone off all right – completely melted and disappeared from the back wheel.

By this time I'd become a bit of a name – second in the *Motor Cycle News* 'Man of the Year' poll (behind Sheene, inevitably) and now with my own column, *Grant's Graffiti* in the rival *Motor Cycle* newspaper. When news is short during the winter, the comics are apt to dream up daft stories. Often, you go along with them, if only to keep the sponsor's name (and your own) up in lights. One such brainwave was probably the highlight of my career as far as my family was concerned.

If dad had a passion, it definitely wasn't for bikes. He was far keener on horses, and although I had a bit of interest, only my sister really followed in his shoes. Cheryl never rode competitively, but from as early as I can remember she's been as mad keen on four hooves as I was on two wheels. In time her daughters caught the same horsey bug.

That being so, the stand-out event in my career – for them, if not for me – was the day Harvey Smith gave me a riding lesson. At the time *Motor Cycle News* was running a series in which various bike celebrities tried their hand at some other professional's sport. They gave me the choice of jumping out of an aeroplane, which didn't seem such a good idea, or riding a horse over a few poles. Since I'd ridden horses a bit, that seemed the better idea.

And who better to put me through my horsey paces than another Yorkshireman, and a gritty one at that? So off we went up to Harvey Smith's farm near Bingley. At the time Harvey was best known for giving two fingers to the judges after winning the British show jumping derby at Hickstead in 1971, a gesture that almost instantly became known as 'a Harvey Smith'. He put me on 'Milwaukee', one of his best showjumpers which, after riding my dad's hacks around the field, seemed like a factory machine – so well balanced you felt you couldn't fall off. If only.

Harvey started me off by walking the horse round a circular course over low poles. This was fairly boring for both of us, so after a few laps he told me to start trotting. Every time I came round he'd put the bar six inches higher. Eventually it reached about 4'6", at which point I went tits-up. True, it was better than nose-diving to earth from 10,000 feet, but it hurt. I'd not long before crashed out of the Austrian GP at Salzburg, knocking my ankle about pretty badly. So naturally I broke my fall by landing on the same ankle. As I lay on the floor groaning, Harvey's in my face telling me I should get back in the saddle at once. He looked a bit fierce, so I did.

Harvey wasn't the only fierce customer getting in my face. There was the tax man, too. It had begun not long after the farce with the TZ700's back wheel and dragged on and on. I don't know whether Customs had a quiet word with the Revenue, or whether the Revenue decided on their own that I looked dodgy enough for a closer look, but for the next two years I was repeatedly pressed about a bank account I hadn't declared.

Each time I was asked, the reply was the same. No, there's no such account.

If you've ever been at the wrong end of the tax man's telescope, you'll know you can't out-last them. They have all the time in the world and will chase you to doomsday if they think they have a case. And even by Revenue standards my persecutor was especially relentless and vindictive. I can't say that the experience affected my riding, but it did wear me down.

Eventually – thank God – Mr Relentless was moved to another office and his replacement had at least a veneer of humanity. At our first meeting he announced that this charade had been going on too long – the first official pronouncement I'd agreed with in two years.

'You have an undeclared account at the Midland Bank in Wakefield,' he announced.

It was news to me. 'I do?'

I was none the wiser but the penny dropped for Carol. She'd had a something-and-nothing account there which she'd closed a couple of years earlier. It was of no consequence but the previous bloke was probably going on about it in the hope that I'd finally cop to another account with a bit more wedge in it. The end result was a £500 fine, presumably in lieu of allowing the vindictive sods to sink their fangs into my neck.

It was a traumatic but valuable lesson. In the Seventies there was more folding money floating about the sport than there is now. Prize money was usually in cash and brown envelopes full of start money weren't uncommon. You'd be a more saintly man than me if you weren't sometimes tempted to just trouser the cash and keep it to yourself, but throughout my career I had good advice and sharp accountants who knew about the risks.

I once received a letter from a personal sponsor – Shell – warning me that the Revenue had demanded information from them on all their sponsorship payments. That was good of them. They'd had no option but to comply, and you didn't need to be a financial genius to see how it would go from there. It would be simple enough for the tax man to check who hadn't declared. He probably wouldn't even jump on them right away, but eventually that would become a lever to wring more admissions out of the culprits further down the line.

The problem with the Revenue is that they're perfectly happy to bide their time. They'll keep their eye on you and grab you when it's worth their while. You'll probably get away with fiddling the books for a couple or three years, but when they eventually catch up with you it really hurts – even if you don't end up in gaol. I've had a few friends in racing, including Joey Dunlop, who had major problems through being too slack with their accounts. Rossi and Haga probably thought the same. Yet with recent money-laundering regulations, the reach of the Revenue is longer than ever before. I remember a guy on the telly who said his ambition was to pay £500,000 per year in tax. You should be so lucky. That's the way to look at it.

By any standards '75 had been a good year. In Britain the KR750 had taken all before it. With a winter's extra development, '76 ought to have brought more of the same, but it began in the worst possible way. A chronic spares shortage – or so it was claimed – meant we couldn't even compete at the two big season-openers, at Daytona and Venezuela. At the time the world was still deep in the oil crisis depression. The bike press even speculated that Kawasaki might not race at all, although I don't recall there being any doubt within the team.

Things could only improve from there, or so we thought. Then came a double disaster at Imola and Paul Ricard when between us Ditch and me struggled to finish a single race. The 750 was forever seizing and I didn't do the 250's prospects much good when I threw it away at

120mph in practice on the French circuit. Luckily, I suffered no more than a bruised backside.

Imola's disasters weren't all on the track. Ditch and I had driven there with Stan who had the peculiarly British habit of thinking that if he talked loudly in fake German, everyone would understand. 'Fillen de tanken' usually left gas station attendants perplexed, but had Ditch and I in stitches.

That was the only fun on a 17-hour drive which left us knackered and famished when we arrived at our hotel in Castel san Pietro. All I wanted was a snack and a bed. Stan must have been livelier, or perhaps just out for revenge, and unscrewed the top of the pepper. When I came to use it, I dumped the lot in my soup. Stan thought this was hilarious, until I leaped to my feet and pinned him by the throat against the wall. Trouble was, being a wimp who didn't go in for fighting, I'd no idea what to do next – until I noticed his electric shaver peeking out of his bag. Two seconds later ... bzzz, bzzz ... he was missing his left sideburn.

At the Easter Transatlantic series Ditch and I helped the Brits to beat the Yanks by 412 points to 384. All season long in the domestic Superbike series Sheene and I had our usual head-to-heads. In other words, if our results showed a major weakness it was in long races like the Imola 200. Typically, we'd be competitive for 80 miles of a 100-mile race, then the crank would pack in. If that broken chain hadn't given the engine a let-off the previous year, the same might well have happened in the Classic TT. Apart from the expense, it was demoralising to travel halfway across Europe, or across the Atlantic, to contest a race you knew for sure you weren't going to finish. May's Belgian round of the FIM Formula 750 series at Nivelles was a rare success, when I won the second race. Even that was a mixed bag for the team: in the first race I'd retired when the chain jumped the sprockets. Ditch had been miles in the lead when his crank broke, yet again.

In its first season we'd run the KR750 engine to 11,000rpm. Since most of the breakdowns were big-end or main bearing failures, it was obvious that the crankshaft just couldn't take this sort of punishment. So for 1976 Kawasaki revised the porting and brought the rev ceiling down to 9,500rpm. Even with this, the engines still weren't brilliantly reliable, but they were much more dependable than before.

The 750 arrived from the factory in a basic trim, but could be raced in any of three stages of tune. For the top tune you took 4mm off the inlet skirt, changed the exhaust pipes and revised the jetting and ignition timing. This made it an absolute missile with a crazy, wild powerband. It was a set-up I only used once, for a race at Mettet in Belgium, a staggeringly fast circuit where horsepower was everything. In that tune it was a lot quicker than even a good 750 Yamaha, but you simply couldn't get the power to the ground out of corners. By the time you were upright on the next straight, the Yamahas had gone. The bike broke its crank crossing the finishing line, which was actually a long, fast curve. Heaven knows how I stayed on the thing. My legs were flapping about so much I tore the heel clean off a boot. Oddly enough, I never ran that state of tune again.

The rest of the time I ran the middle stage of tune. Only once, at Mallory Park for an *MCN* series round, did we use the slowest state of tune. This was a race into which Sheene had drafted a couple of Suzuki America team-mates – Dave Aldana and Gary Nixon – to try to put them between him and me to help him in the championship points standings. The plan had a couple of shortcomings. Aldana seemed to be on a bit of a mission and actually rammed Barry's Suzuki at the hairpin – I remember it well because Barry actually turned round and laughed.

Their other problem was that my Kawasaki turned out to be perfect for the Mallory track. It had no top-end and felt really flat, but supremely manageable. I could give it full throttle halfway round Gerrards Corner and it would dig in and accelerate hard under complete control – so much so that I could overtake Sheene on the following straight even though, on the dyno, his bike that day certainly had more top-end than mine. Ironically, Barry became convinced that I was running a big engine and even considered an official protest, when in fact I probably had ten horsepower fewer than him. It was a valuable lesson. Peak power isn't everything.

Sheene got the wrong end of the stick that day, but he didn't usually. As a rider he was always a very fair, safe opponent. Some riders you would only dare pass on the inside, because if you tried to nip by on the outside they'd think nothing of shoving you on to the grass. With Barry, there was never any likelihood of that. You always knew you were in for a hard race, but a fair one.

Whenever the two of us went to Scarborough on factory bikes, it was obvious that, barring mishap, the race was going to be between the two of us. The press would be flagging a big North v South grudge match and most of the fans would be Yorkshiremen who'd probably have cheered for me even if I'd run off with their missus. To Barry and me the hype was all bluster and bullshit. We'd get together after practice and do a deal – put on a show for most of the race, then go gloves off for the final three laps. And Barry would always stick to it. Once or twice he even waited for me when I'd had a bad start and been held up.

There were no fiddles. We never, ever, threw a result. We just preferred not to have a complete ding-dong for the full race distance, especially at a circuit as unforgiving as Scarborough. Occasionally, though, someone else would inadvertently mess up the plan. One day, it was Geoff Barry. Now Geoff was a fine rider, but he was on a Commando with maybe 40 horsepower less than us. But he was dicing with us – or thought he was, because we were still half touring. He was having a cracking ride but riding really wild, scuttling up the inside and tripping us up. At Mountside hairpin after a couple of laps of this, Barry looked at me and I looked at him. We nodded, and both pulled the pin early, going three seconds a lap quicker. Geoff must have wondered what the hell was going on.

Not that we always got things our own way. A similar thing happened with a young Ron Haslam at Cadwell Park. The main contenders that day were Read, Sheene and me, and the three of us thought it was going to be the usual story. Then suddenly this young tear-arse with shaggy sideburns appeared on a Pharaoh Yamaha. Generally, he was off the bike more than on it, but he was as quick as he was wild. Getting past him was going to require a bit of do-or-die, especially as his lines were all over the place and you never knew from one lap to the next which bit of track he'd be on. I more or less decided to chicken out of the whole enterprise. Barry didn't – but even so Ron held him off for the win.

During the mid-Seventies, Barry and I were probably the biggest double act in British racing. He achieved a lot more, certainly – not least, two world titles. But in superbike meetings at home, it was usually between me and him. During practice it'd be his times I'd be most concerned with, and I'm sure he felt the same about me. Apparently he knew of me before I recognised him, because in his biography he refers to 'an old guy with a red beard' slithering up the inside of him in a meeting at Croft. This was probably during practice in May 1971. Later that day he won the 125cc race on his ex-factory Suzuki on the way to running away with the British championship.

Since he'd also won the 125cc championship the year before, aged just 20, I'd probably heard of him, but he wasn't riding in my class so at the time he'd be just another face in the paddock. I probably also heard about his antics a month later on the Isle of Man, when he fell off his 125 at Quarter Bridge whilst lying second to Chas Mortimer in the 1971 TT.

So at the time, I can't imagine that I thought very much about Barry Sheene at all. If I did, I probably resented him a little. After all, there was me struggling along with an antique Beezer with help from hardly anyone, and he's got it on a plate: a dad, dear old Franco, who knew stacks of influential people in the sport; and Stuart Graham's ex-works twin-cylinder 125cc Suzuki which, although it was six years old, was as quick as anything on the grid. He'd done his first grand prix in '70 and had his first win at Spa in '71 on his way to finishing second to Angel Nieto in the world championship. If there was anything else to resent, other than his piss-taking, it was his sheer talent. He was so obviously a complete 'natural', like Phil Read. And unlike me. In contrast I always saw myself as a bit of a scratcher who had to work that much harder at his game.

All through my career I've seen lots of people embark on the grand prix route, get their arses slapped and come back in a worse state mentally and financially than when they'd set off. Barry was one of the few young British riders able to do it properly. For the rest of his career he always seemed to have a competitive bike under him. If there was a secret to his success, that was it. That, and being just a bit good. For the same reasons, if you did get the edge on him – like winning Man of the Meeting at Snetterton in '72 – it tasted that much better.

Like any racer, if Barry's bike wasn't as good as he thought it ought to be, he could get into a right old strop. Some years later when I was riding for Honda, I had a brand-new but completely over-the-counter RG500 (a strange state of affairs that I'll explain later). I can vividly remember the aftermath of one race when Barry was absolutely livid, because my bike was every bit as quick as his factory RG. But in the *MCN* series in the mid-70s it was different. My Kawasaki definitely had the edge on

Sheene's 750cc Suzuki in speed, weight and handling, although the Suzuki was probably a bit more reliable.

By the time I was dicing with him on the factory Kawasaki, to his factory Suzuki, we were pretty familiar with each other. I was six years older than him, so he probably thought me a bit of a Northern fogey whilst I positively knew he was every bit as much a Southern smart-arse. I don't think he once called me 'Mick' – it was always either 'Michaelmas', or 'Grar-nty', but it was all light-hearted. As competitors we were respectful friends. Occasionally we'd go out together, but were never social pals.

Other than the British grand prix the highlight of each season was usually the Gold Cup meeting at Scarborough, which always drew a crowd of 30,000 or 40,000. With so many people crammed on to the hillside at Oliver's Mount, the atmosphere was electric, and Barry and me would take the piss out of all the daft North v South hype. Apart from anything else, there were better things to write about – or on.

Each year Peter Hillaby, the event promoter, would hire Scarborough's Spa Ballroom for a race party on the Saturday night. The place would be packed with riders, fans – and their girlfriends. In short order, Barry and me would be signing birds' arms and T-shirts and, as the evening wore on, more intimate bits. Inevitably, one daring lass would unveil her knockers for the same treatment. Barry would hold one tit, while I signed it, then I'd reciprocate with the other. Normally, you scribble your signature as quickly as possible, but on these occasions neither of us would be in any great rush. With the bar now set at chest height, most of the other lasses would follow suit. And, since most of them only had two boobs, we made sure no other riders got a look-in. It was bizarre. In what other circumstances would a perfect stranger whip out her knockers to be pawed by someone they'd never met? Yet it happened year after year.

As well as being one of the characters amongst British racing's promoters, Hillaby was one of the easiest to agree start money with. A quick phone call and a verbal 'hand shake' was all it took. At the time my typical start money for a big meeting was maybe £3k. Sheene would be on maybe £4k or £5k. Another who was a joy to deal with was Chris Lowe, who ran Motor Circuit Developments. A call, a few pleasantries, and in no time we'd agree a flat rate for all his international meetings the following season. Barry preferred to negotiate a meeting-by-meeting deal.

Cadwell's Charlie Wilkinson was one of the worst payers for any UK international meeting. He had a book of what he thought riders were worth, in his own special code. After the best part of an hour's haggling we once agreed on £2k, and after we shook hands his face dissolved into a smile. Back at Cadwell a couple of months later, after the meeting in question, he consulted his code book.

'Hi Mick. £1750, wasn't it?'

'No Charlie. £2,000.'

He'd already bundled up the £1,750 and pushed it across the table to me. I pushed it back. He pushed it my way again. After a bit more to-and-fro he finally agreed to £2k. Charlie eventually came up with a formula: a proportion of the gate money. Trustful as ever, Barry and I put some guys on the gate to double-check his 'official' figures. Or maybe we just told him that's what we'd be doing.

Even Charlie was by no means the worst to deal with. With most of the rest, there was no such thing as a gentleman's agreement. If you didn't have it in writing, you could forget it – and nowhere more so than when dealing with ACU boss Vernon Cooper about the TT.

When Donington Park opened in 1977, circuit manager Peter Gaydon offered three times as much as anywhere else. It was obviously unsustainable and, after someone sensible did the sums, Tom Wheatcroft came pleading for us to take less, which I think everyone did. But that seemed to be the beginning of the end for start money on

UK short circuits. By 1980 it was beginning to dry up. The money used to come from somewhere, so heaven knows who gets it now, although circuit costs have risen immensely. There are no longer many venues with just a bit of tarmac, a dirt paddock, a shed and a bar. Far more expensive infrastructure is expected. At that time you could hire a circuit for maybe £125 per day. Now Silverstone asks more like £25k.

Beating Sheene in 1976 was a tougher proposition than the year before. By degrees the 750cc Suzuki was pensioned off, replaced by the RG500 Barry was racing in grands prix. This in turn grew as time went by, first to 560 and eventually to 680cc. From what I remember the 560 had about the same speed as the now-detuned KR750, although it probably stopped and handled a little better. Certainly we'd lost the edge we'd enjoyed the previous year.

I've ridden the 680 since and it was horrible. For a start, it looked like an oil refinery … pipes everywhere and nowhere to put your feet. Unlike the 500, its power came in with a huge rush. Barry seemed to be the only bloke who could ride it. Both Tom Herron and Noddy Newbold also tried it, but both fell off and never seemed to get on with it. When he'd first got on it Tom expected it to be a one-way ticket to the top of the rostrum and was stricken by the experience. Sheene's secret, if he had one, was that he was always a particularly smooth rider, like Read and, maybe, like me.

Despite this, there were still wins to be had, though. Even Sheene wasn't infallible. In June for the King of Brands meeting, he finished an uncharacteristic fourth whilst me and Ditch gave Kawasaki a one–two. Not long later at Snetterton on his 500, in a meeting where we shared a new lap record, Sheene seemed to be trying to get round the outside of me at Sears – an odd manoeuvre – before disappearing into a field. When the bike was carted back to the paddock, the entire front end was covered in carrots. Apparently, he'd come past me nanoseconds after his brake pads fell out. After incidents like that I was happy to be called Michaelmas from here to … well, Michaelmas.

Yet Sheene continued to edge ahead in the *MCN* championship. By mid-August, he led me by 83 points to 61. Reliability, as much as speed, was our problem and if it wasn't crankshafts it was something to do with the chain. A week or two later at Silverstone for the World Formula 750 round I'd no sooner shared a new lap record with Steve Baker than the Regina chain snapped. We reckoned the fault was caused by the rear chain adjuster slipping, so took the rather drastic step of bronze-welding the spindle into place. With a lap to go in the second leg, I led by a distance when I felt the rear end wobbling with what turned out to be a puncture. Although I hung on to win fairly comfortably, as I waved to the crowd at Stowe on the slowing-down lap the tyre decided to jump off the rim altogether, and down I went. I picked myself up and took a bow to the crowd, which they loved. Well, they would. It was only later that I realised my leathers were split from chest to crotch.

The other trouble was that there was still the 1,000cc support race to go. Unknown to me, Nigel had already whizzed to Stowe, nicked the good exhaust and carbs, and put them on the spare bike which was ready to go. As I stepped off the rostrum, he's already brandishing a roll of duct tape and spun me round half a dozen times to tape up my leathers. I was still dizzy by the time I climbed on the bike, but it didn't do much harm – I won the race from Sheene.

Buoyed by that, at Oulton I reversed the trend in the Superbike series. Now the gap was down to 17 points. At Scarborough a week later, we shared a win apiece, but Sheene's win was in the non-championship race. This was the notorious weekend when a huge crowd got a bit unpleasant. Yorkshire fans were actually throwing rocks at

Barry. After his win, I joined him in the parade car in the hope that accidentally hitting me wasn't worth the risk.

Rocks or not, Sheene wasn't making it easy. At Mallory he won once more, then again at Cadwell after a brilliant five-man dice. Going into the final round at Brands, it was a long-shot: I had to win and set fastest lap to have any chance of retaining the Superbike title. In the end, it didn't matter. Sheene narrowly won on the RG560 to take the series, ahead of me and Ditch. The same meeting was notable for witnessing what the press described as the 'Last race of Read's career'. Unfortunately it was never going to be his last finish, for he crashed at Druids, breaking a collarbone whilst leading by seven seconds from Sheene. A few months later in a jokey column in *Motor Cycle* I offered odds of 2:1 in favour of Ready changing his mind about retiring. For once I got it right.

Not so in the World Formula 750 series, long a lost cause for both Ditch and me. For the final round at Hockenheim all I could do was help Gary Nixon win the title for Kawasaki America ahead of Yamaha's Victor Palomo. Noddy Newbold took the first leg, Nixon the second, but Victor won overall to become champion. My contribution was a third in the first race after a shambles of a fuel stop, and a didn't-even-start in the second because of an unbalanced tyre.

The one place I didn't have to worry about Sheene was the Isle of Man. The previous TT had got off to a literal flyer when John Cooper flew Ditch and I to the Island in his light plane, straight from the airstrip at Brands where we'd been riding in the bank holiday meeting. For '76, we had a similar plan, but this time Coop could only fly us the few miles from Brands to Biggin Hill, where we'd hop on to a larger plane. As we sat on the grass strip waiting to leave Brands, Phil Read was just executing a perfect take-off.

Coop was obviously keen to follow suit, but as he trundled along next to the fence line there was a deafening bang as a neat dent the shape of a fence-pole appeared in the starboard wing. Ditch and I clambered out and manhandled the plane round the offending pole. We climbed back in, but now it wouldn't move at all. Coop muttered something about 'overweight', so out again – and push. The weight problem solved itself when he remembered to let off the handbrake.

Aeroplane problems on the ground I'm pretty cool about. Being 'up there' is what scares me. Once we missed – but only barely – the hedge at the end of the strip, it was only about a ten minute hop to Biggin Hill. So after 20 I'm a bit concerned to hear Coop on the radio asking if anyone can tell us where we are. Evidently, somewhere near Dover. Coop eventually got his bearings and made a perfect touch-down in a horrible cross-wind. After that, what could possibly go wrong at the TT?

Well lots, actually. The fortnight was even more disappointing than the previous year. True, there was more opposition – notably John Williams on 500 and 750cc factory Suzukis. And the fortnight began well enough, when I topped the practice leaderboard with the first 110mph lap, 17 seconds ahead of John. Later I upped that to 112mph. The still under-developed KR500 finished practice only fourth in the standings, but I was optimistic enough. In fact the only cloud on the practice horizon was another half-baked attempt by the ACU to turn back the clock. They were seriously proposing to ban slicks on the Island, despite the fact that treads simply couldn't cope with the power and speed of the big bikes.

In the Senior, both John and I struggled. I seized near Black Hut and toured in to retire. John, meanwhile, was flying. From a standing start he broke the outright lap record, went faster still (112.27mph) on the second lap, and after almost six laps led by five minutes, despite riding with no clutch for much of the race. Then, in the slow turn into Governor's bridge, his RG500 ran out of petrol. With the grandstands (and me) baying encouragement he pushed to the line in seventh place. Tom Herron took the win by just three seconds from Ian Richards.

Barring mishaps, the Open Classic seemed like a done deal. All I had to do to win was go the distance – which I missed out on by only the odd 226 miles when the KR's clutch broke up on the line. John scored the win his Senior efforts deserved. I had to settle for a £100 Bulova watch for being the 12,000th rider to start a TT. It didn't get much better from there. The following day at the Mallory post-TT meeting, I threw the same bike away at Gerrards, smashing it to bits. Well, it deserved it.

At around the same time Carol and I moved from Crigglestone to Lepton Grange on the outskirts of Huddersfield. It sounds fancy, but had originally been three modest-sized cottages a developer had knocked into one big house. In many ways it was a crazy idea. My first house had cost less than £5000, and within a couple of years I'd bought this monstrosity with 15 acres of land for ten times as much. I must have had delusions of becoming a country squire. Still, it had stacks of workshops and garages, so was ideal from a racing viewpoint. Coming from a little two-up, two-down, it must have taken us a couple of years to accumulate enough furniture to fill it, and even then we rattled around in the place.

In the autumn of '76 Sheene and I had another tussle when I was nominated to replace him as the ACU's FIM riders' rep. At the time Sheene and Kenny Roberts were actively campaigning for better circuit safety and prize money, and my nomination caused a bit of friction between us. Although I largely agreed with their aims, I thought their plan for achieving them was too confrontational to succeed. All things considered, it was a reluctant and unhappy foray into the politics of racing, which has never been my strong suit. It didn't take long, after consulting other riders whose views I respected, for me to withdraw from the nomination.

The episode did, however, give me a new insight into racing's power structure. As riders-rep-to-be, I attended two or three ACU meetings, presented what I thought were sensible ideas, and simply got blocked. Vernon Cooper, the ACU's boss, ran the whole show like his own private fiefdom. He once confided that the perfect size for any committee was 'an odd number less than three'. That's certainly a recipe for getting things done, but in whose interests? Any rider was just pissing into the wind against this sort of dictatorial attitude.

After the highs of '75, 1976 was a bitter disappointment for me and Kawasaki. I'd had a lousy TT, lost the *Motor Cycle News* Superbike crown, been a complete also-ran in Formula 750, and Kawasaki's best prospect, the KR250, remained a mirage. But at least I was holding to rule one of racing: I was still beating my team-mate.

Although I'm usually associated with the racing number '10', I didn't really make this my own until the start of the '77 season. Previously I'd had all sorts of numbers, at the TT and on the shorts: 2, 3, 4, 5, 12, you name it. I'd no doubt ridden '10' before, although not always successfully. At Mallory the previous September, I'd literally thrown the number (and the bike) away.

I've never been particularly superstitious, although there was a bit of a connection with my birthday, 10 July. Mainly it was an identity thing, which played a large part in popularity and start money – as Barry fully recognised when he made '7' his own.

With the staggered starting of the TT, numbers have a more tactical ring. Starting at 14 or 15 meant you had to pass so many slower riders ahead of you that you'd inevitably lose time. On the other hand, few of us wanted to get away first, partly because you had no-one to pace yourself against until it was too late, partly because the information reaching your signallers would be poorer. For me, 6 to 10 was the happy medium.

The number that probably mattered most that year, though, was 31 – as in OW31, Yamaha's latest four-cylinder 750. This was the full factory version of the

TZ750, ridden by the likes of Baker and Roberts. It had first appeared the previous year but kept getting better season by season, and was the yardstick in the world Formula 750 series which Kawasaki had declared was their main goal.

Initially, we were confident. The latest 1977 KR750 looked impressive, and even began the season well. We didn't do Daytona, but after testing at Paul Ricard Ditch took the bike to a win at Nogaro after I pulled out with a sticking throttle. Then we journeyed across Italy to Imola full of confidence. It was a disaster. In practice I was two seconds off the pace of the Yamahas, an absolute age. For some reason that year's KR was equipped with dual-rate rear springs – 60/90, if I remember correctly. Nigel popped in a pair of straight 88lb springs, and that made up most of the difference. Ditch naturally asked what miracle we'd performed, tried the 88s in his KR, and actually went slower. None of this did either of us much good. In the first leg I was sidelined by ignition problems, in the second by a broken gear lever. Poor Ditch crashed out, cracking a bunch of ribs. We scarcely noticed, but the 250cc race was won by some bloke named Ballington.

From Imola it was straight to the Transatlantic series and another drubbing by the Yanks, who beat us 348 points to 311. This was the series in which they thrashed us in the wet at Mallory. Their performance there swung the whole series, although I had the satisfaction of a second and a fourth at Oulton.

After all that it was a relief to get back on the roads for the North West 200, although even there the Kawasaki's old edge was under threat. John Williams took both the 500cc and feature races. He also set the fastest lap – 123mph – in the 750cc race, which he led before running out of fuel almost within sight of the finish. (John obviously had a knack for this.) As I crossed the line to win, the guy with the chequered flag was taken by surprise because he expected to see John, rather than me. As I passed him, his flag barely twitched.

Had we finished? Had I won? I wasn't sure, so stopped at York hairpin, to ask a marshal. He wasn't sure, either. After another 15 seconds or so, no one had come past so I figured the race must be over, and set off through a housing estate for a shortcut to the pits. Unfortunately my visor was peppered with dead flies and I completely failed to notice a rope across the road – until it lassoed me round my throat. I flipped backwards, the bike flipped backwards on top of me, pulling the rope barriers on top of both of us. It was not dignified and I was not happy – very not happy. A few seconds later a sweet old lady trotted out from her house, peered into this mess and asked very nicely if I was all right. Whoever you are, I wish to apologise now for my reaction.

Next stop, the Isle of Man, and a memorable one it was, even if the events of the following year overshadowed it. My 2:1 bet on Ready's retirement came home by a length: he'd be riding. After his well-publicised criticism of the event, this was the biggest news in the run-up to the races. Lots of TT fans wanted to see him fall on his face. Some even threw rocks at him. But, as usual, he certainly pepped-up the publicity.

He rode well, too, winning both the Senior and, with a little help from the decision to shorten the race to four laps and save him a fuel stop, the Formula One TT. No one should have been surprised: Phil was a very class act.

For once, though, I was setting headlines myself with the big Kawasaki. This was the year the KR750 was clocked at 191mph, a truly startling speed at the time. Lots of people didn't believe it. Lots still don't. I'm in no position to say for sure but I think it's credible. The day before the figure was taken I'd been out to help journalist Ian Beecham move his speed trap to the fastest part of the drop to Brandish, just yards before the 200 yard marker. At that point, some riders would be off the gas,

153

but for me it was definitely the quickest place on the course. It was downhill, with a fairly strong tail wind. On the banking at Daytona we were regularly timed at over 180mph, so I've no reason to doubt that with the TT's higher gearing, 190mph was possible in those conditions.

Speed traps are one thing, wins another, and at the start of the week I had just two TT wins to my credit – plus lots of fastest laps, and lots of retirements whilst leading, but they don't pay the rent. This time, at least, we had the 250. In practice we worked hard on set-up, and had it running well. A win seemed a distinct possibility, only for it to spring a coolant leak minutes before the start. Although the leak was hurriedly fixed, this meant I had to start with a stone-cold engine. The bike spluttered down Bray Hill on one cylinder. Stopping at Braddan to check the plug leads made no difference and although it cleared by Ballacraine, by the Bungalow my signals told me I was already 90 seconds down on Charlie Williams. Charlie went on to win, with me in a disappointing seventh place.

Much was made in the early Seventies of tyres not being able to cope with the sheer power of the new breed of big two-strokes. It wasn't half so dangerous, but the same was true – and for much longer – of chains. They, too, struggled to cope with 100-plus horsepower over long races. So in the Classic TT any problem was likely to be with the chain, which had sidelined us in both previous years. True enough, despite adjusting it during both pit stops, by the final lap it was jumping the sprockets again.

It was an anxious lap, but by then all I needed to do was finish. The race was in the bag. My biggest moment had actually come on the opening lap when the rear brake disappeared going into Ballacraine and I almost joined Tommy Robb in the commentary box. Luckily the brake came back, allowing me to lead from start to finish, with a new race record, 110.76mph. Along the way I'd broken the outright lap record on the opening lap, extending it to

112.77mph on the second. Chain worries aside it was a textbook race. And comfortable: Charlie placed second, 3½ minutes behind.

It was a pretty good cashbook race, too. One of the effects of the TT losing its GP status was that, at long last, the organisers had to find another reason for persuading riders to go to the Island. The obvious answer was money, which even the dimmest jockey can understand. Yet although being paid what you considered your worth was important to all the top TT riders, money was never the motivation during a race. Winning was. That year, though, there was a subtle difference, since a new prize money formula paid us for our position at the end of each lap, rather than in the final results.

So every time I passed the pits I thought, 'Ching! ... that's another £1,000. Nice.' I was almost disappointed when the chequered flag went out and the gravy train came to an end – except that I ended the race £6,000 better off. I'd have cashed it in, though (well, maybe some of it) for a 250cc win. I still thought the little tandem twin was Kawasaki's best shot.

CHAPTER 11

CAN YOU
RIDE TANDEM?

Other than the odd outing, one item consistently absent from the Kawasaki equation so far was their 250cc tandem twin. Prior to baling off the 750 at Ontario in 1975, I'd ridden the KR250 in one of the support races. It was no surprise to finish behind local hot-shots Roberts and Duhamel. But third ahead of Villa and a host of other grand prix regulars spoke volumes. Despite little in the way of race development it was instantly obvious that the bike had huge potential, yet all the emphasis seemed to go on the 750 and very rarely did we race the tandem twin. Kawasaki had actually said we'd be riding them at the 1975 TT, but the bikes never even turned up. Then, despite an announcement in December 1975 that 'following the encouraging performance at Ontario' the 250 would race 'in selected events including some grands prix' in 1976, again it never seemed to happen. For too long the 250 appeared to be Kawasaki's version of Honda's 'Never Ready'. It was always about to happen ... but *mañana*, or the Japanese equivalent.

Whenever the chance arose, I'd press Kawasaki to give the bike a proper campaign. As you'll know, eventually the project did come good, because by 1978 the bike had clicked with Greg Hansford and even more so with Kork Ballington, who won back-to-back 250 and 350cc world titles on the twin. But before that it was hard to understand why Kawasaki had even built it at all. Why bother if they weren't going to give it a proper run? I suspect there must have been some political conflict high up in the company, because there's no doubt at all that it could have been dominating world championships two years earlier than it did.

The 1975 250's main problem was that its pistons were 180 degrees out on its two geared crankshafts, which caused the most horrendous vibration. By the time it made its belated grand prix appearance two years later, the pistons rose and fell together and it was an altogether smoother and better engine. The 500, on the other hand, was always pretty hopeless. It was significantly heavier than a Yamaha twin and didn't handle half so well, yet despite an extra 150cc it seemed to have only a marginal speed advantage.

I'd made my name on 250s and 350s and always loved the feeling of precision you get with the smaller bikes. Ditch didn't seem particularly interested in the 250, but for me that was the way to go – especially as the writing was on the wall for the 750cc two-strokes after the oil crisis following the Yom Kippur war. So I never passed up an opportunity to press the 250's case to the Japanese or to John Norman, then head of Kawasaki in the UK.

Yet when Kawasaki finally decided to give the revised 250 a run for a full season of grand prix in 1977, they came up with the oddest plan. Ditch, it was decided, would ride it for the first half of the season, whilst I'd do the second half (which wasn't exactly how it worked out). A pair of Japanese riders, Kiyo Kiyohara and Matsuhiro Wada would also be doing selected races. From any standpoint, it just didn't make sense: with such a bitty approach Kawasaki might have had an outside chance to win the manufacturers' championship, but however well we went, none of us could win the riders' title. To my mind, it was nothing but a lose–lose strategy. I made my objections pretty clear at the time, but corporate minds seemed to be made up.

I already had the feeling the Kawasaki playing field wasn't entirely level. Although I'd always got a fair crack of the whip with the 750, Ditch seemed to be the blue-eyed boy as far as the 250 went. He and I weren't friendly enough to be drinking buddies – he was a Southerner, after all. But we generally got on well enough, which is the case with most team-mates. But there was a problem. Although there wasn't much between Barry and I in terms of age, from Stan's point of view I suspect that I was the established professional, able to stand on his own two feet, whilst Barry seemed very much to be his personal protégé. This even seemed to be reflected in the reports going back to Kawasaki. When I crashed it was generally 'rider error'; when Ditch stepped off there was something wrong with the bike.

Whatever the reason, over the previous season or so it had led to some pretty mystifying team decisions. For instance, despite the fact that I finished the '75 season as *MCN* Superbike champion – ostensibly Kawasaki's main objective – I discovered much later that for the following season Ditch was on almost twice as big a retainer as me.

This wasn't the only financial oddball. My original deal was to be paid a retainer by Kawasaki, in addition to any prize money I won, plus start money which I negotiated myself with the circuits. Although I obviously wasn't such a big draw as Sheene, by that time world 500 champion and a national hero, it was a substantial amount of money, certainly far more than my team-mate was getting. However, for '77 Kawasaki proposed adding to my retainer a fee in lieu of this start money, which they would negotiate on my behalf and keep for themselves. I went along with it – stupidly, as it turned out, for they weren't likely to bargain as hard for me as I would myself.

Ditch first rode the 250 at the German GP, finishing tenth, followed by third in Italy, eighth in Spain and a few DNFs. He had a bit of bad luck, once sliding off on another rider's broken screen. I didn't get to ride the bike until the French grand prix in mid-season, by which time another bike somehow turned up out of thin air, allowing Ditch to carry on almost for the full series. It didn't help my sense of fairness that, prior to that, I'd been doing meetings in the UK which Ditch, absent with the 250 at grands prix, hadn't been able to do, so my appearance money had effectively been pumping money into the same Kawasaki budget, which was allowing my team-mate to compete in the very races I most wanted to do.

At Paul Ricard I felt immediately at home on the bike, despite throwing it away at 120mph in practice, when I reckoned that getting through the fast chicane would put me on pole – or my arse. When the arse option won, I qualified about third, with Ditch on pole, but in the race the clutch slipped from the start and I had to retire. The clutch had been put together incorrectly. Ditch also retired. Team coordinator Ken Suzuki responded to this with his usual mixed-up English. 'It is very easy,' he said, 'to find a good rider, but difficult to find a good mechanic'. This had me totally baffled until I worked out that it was obvious from just looking, let alone timing, who could ride fast. Spotting a good mechanic wasn't so quick or easy.

I wasn't too chuffed to miss the next grand prix, the Yugoslavian at Opatija, through being on superbike duty at home. But after that came Assen, lovely old Assen, in late June. Practice produced another third place on the grid – thanks to the same Mr Yashida you last met trying to resuscitate Cadbury's gearboxes at Daytona.

Yashida-san was never without a big file full of data and tables – his bible – a thermometer, hygrometer and whatever else it took to set up each bike. Yet – and this will surprise anyone who's ever raced two-strokes – he never once asked us to do a plug chop. In fact I never once saw him even inspect a spark plug. Instead, on the morning of the race he'd consult his instruments, pore over his tables, then carefully place two sets of jets and two spark plugs on the seat of each race bike. To my knowledge he never got it wrong. The result was always like tearing calico – the engines were as crisp as could be. Usually he was content to leave it at this, but on a couple of occasions he strolled up and started fiddling with the carbs on the start line. With anyone else, even Nigel, I'd have physically beat him off, but such was my faith in this man that I let him carry on with whatever he was doing.

For no obvious reason I'd had the feeling almost as soon as I got to Assen that I was going to win. This wasn't the sort of self-confidence mind-game that the likes of Fogarty used to specialise in. In fact it was a sense I had before big races only a handful of times in my entire career. But from somewhere came a conviction so intense that I told John Norman we were going to put his bike on top of the rostrum. His reply was something to the effect of 'Yeah, yeah, we've heard that before', which only made me even more determined to pull it off.

Later, I got an even bigger incentive. On the eve of the race I sat down to dinner with Ditch, Shenton and the Japanese technicians in our digs at the Erklands Hotel in Rolde. Over a beer in the bar afterwards I told Dunlop's tyre man, Bucky, that I was going to go hard early on, build up a seven-second lead, then ease back and maintain that to the finish. I wasn't bullshitting, I really meant it, but with precisely zero Continental grand prix wins to my credit so far I could tell that Bucky also thought I was talking out of my backside. A few minutes later Shenton wandered by on his way to a conference with the Japanese.

Twenty minutes later, as Nigel and I were passing Shenton's room, we heard my name mentioned. We couldn't resist eavesdropping, but could barely believe what we overheard. It was along the lines of me crashing a lot and Ditch being the main man who already had championship points in the bag, so the team needed to get its signals sorted to get Barry in front of me. This was of more than passing interest to the Japanese, not only because to win was their obvious ambition, but because it had been decreed by their bosses that they couldn't go home until after the 250's first GP win. So far they hadn't even come close to a reunion with their families.

I was livid and spent all night fuming rather than sleeping and emerged for breakfast more determined than ever to win. I told Nigel to make sure the handlebars were tight because I planned on push-starting hard enough to break them.

At the time I was as fit as I'd ever been, running seven or eight miles every day. But in long races I always had a problem with cramp. It wasn't until I discovered quinine tablets a year or two later that I found a fix. In the meantime, I took salt tablets, which were about the size of a 10p piece. Before the race Carol passed me one with a glass of water and down it went. Mr Yashida was standing nearby, and evidently noticed, but said nothing. I think he thought it was some sort of go-faster pill.

When the flag dropped I was still raging and pushed away like a man possessed. Pure anger got me away at the head of the pack. The track was slightly damp, but drying, so I had a slick rear tyre and an intermediate front. Halfway round the first lap the bike slid completely sideways and for an instant I could see a wall of pain – and Shenton and Norman grinning around my hospital bed. I've never had a bigger motivation to get a bike straightened out.

At Assen the circuit loops back close behind the pits. Kawasaki were the only team to take full advantage of this, using walkie-talkies to get information from a timing crew on the back straight to the signallers on the pit wall. This meant that whilst every other team's signals were a full lap out of date, ours were a half-lap more current. In other words, along with Ditch I should have had a better idea than anyone else how the race stood. That wasn't how it worked out.

After one lap, my signals said 'P1' – which was pretty obvious since I could see no one ahead – '+4'. Four seconds ahead of the field. This was looking good. A lap later, 'P1 +7', then '+11'. Eventually, with four or so laps to go it was '+23'. Then it started spitting with rain and I knocked it off a bit. A lap later my board was still telling me '+23', so I eased off a bit more. Still '+23'. Next lap, going even slower, still '+23'.

By this time I'm thinking something isn't quite right, a feeling horrifyingly confirmed as I started my last lap and read 'P1 +7' – and that was already half a lap out of date. I fell apart. I lost the back end, the front end, and if I'd had a third wheel I'd have lost that, too. How I didn't crash, I don't know. But somehow I got to the finish line having pulled out another couple of seconds on the man behind, who turned out to be Franco Uncini. I've rarely had such an intense mix of emotions: relief, bafflement – and joy at my first grand prix win.

The Japanese flocked around me, delighted with both the win and their ticket home. Nigel was there, and Carol, beaming for all they were worth, but Stan seemed conspicuous by his absence. After the back-patting and hugging I turned to Nigel to ask what the hell had been going on. Apparently Shenton had been concentrating on Ditchburn to try to get him on to the rostrum (he eventually finished third), ignoring my progress and just passing old times to Nigel, who could only put on the board what he'd been given. It wasn't until the final lap that Nigel, who could clearly see my lead evaporating, took it upon himself to pass the news to me. Ironically Nigel later married Stan's niece.

It was Kawasaki's first GP win since Dave Simmonds' at Jarama six years earlier and their first ever in the 250cc class. You'd have thought it might be something to celebrate. Yet unaccountably Shenton was absent from the prize-giving. One man who was there – ominously, as it turned out – was the winner of the 350cc race on a Yamaha, Kork Ballington.

This wasn't my first experience of signalling problems. Years earlier Billy McCosh and I had entered an international event at Tilburg – he on his Suzuki twin and me on a Yamaha. The race was likely to be between me and Dieter Braun, who was a bit handy because he'd have been 250cc world champ at the time. For most of the race we were together, but at about half distance Dieter put his foot down and cleared off. I couldn't stay with him but had a useful lead on the guy lying third, Jack Machin. Every time I went past the pits, Carol leaned out with her chalkboard to let me know how I stood. Then it started to rain.

Within a lap her chalk marks telling her how many laps there were to go had run into a puddle under her feet. She asked the woman next to her, who happened to be signalling for Dieter, how many were left.

On the next lap, the answer – three – reached me as I passed the pits. Good-o, three laps to go and 15 seconds in hand. I can afford to ease off. Trouble was, this was rampant bollocks. There were at least six laps to go. Two laps later I got the last lap signal, then again, then again. I beat Jack over the line by about half a machine length. When I got back to the pit Carol had the good sense to disappear for a while – and never use a chalk board again.

Years later the signal wobbles resurfaced at Brands, in a race against Wayne Gardner. For the first few laps I pulled away from him without too much trouble. When it started to drizzle I had a lead of about three seconds, but decided to keep the hammer down for another lap before easing off. Obviously there's only room for so much information on a pit board. And equally there's a limit to how much you can take in as you howl past. This means your signaller has to convey a lot with a little, and over time you get to interpret what they're trying to tell you. Or not.

On this occasion they were giving me 'plus 3', then the same again after the rain began. So as far as I knew I still couldn't afford to ease the pace. In actual fact I'd gained another second on Wayne, which I only discovered as I slid down Graham Hill on my backside and he came into view, still some distance behind, out of Druids.

Back with the grand prix circus, Kawasaki's next outing was Sweden in late July, when I won fairly comfortably on a drying track. A week later we were in Finland. Imatra, a fast road circuit not unlike the North West 200, was right up my street – and the KR's. After muffing a pretty frantic start I took the lead from Mario Lega's Morbidelli on lap six. I was pulling away from him when on the last lap Walter Villa's Harley-Davidson caught me up and passed me easily on sheer power down the back straight – which no other 250 had come anywhere close to doing. I rode the wheels off the KR trying to keep up, losing out by just 0.3 seconds over the line. The Harley looked distinctly dodgy and I wasn't altogether surprised when his bike didn't appear in the parc fermé for post-race inspection after the race. It had allegedly run out of petrol halfway round the slowing-down lap.

Mario had been a mate since my first grand prix five years before. At the next grand prix at Brno, the two of us were chatting to Franco Uncini. Even though Franco was Villa's team-mate, the two Italians were convinced Walter had been using a 350 in the 250cc class and decided to protest Villa's bike if it looked as dodgy as it had at Imatra. Come the race I retired with a brake problem, but again Villa's Harley looked suspiciously quick. I was just revving myself up to put in a protest when Mario strolled across and asked me not to. He'd just wrapped up the 250cc championship that day (from Franco, ironically: Walter was third), and didn't want it marred by controversy. To my mind either Walter was cheating or they'd done something brilliant to the engine that they never passed on to Franco's bike. We never got to find out which.

With Mario the main compensation was the near-legendary Crocodile Club, a bunch of fairly loony fans who'd follow him from meeting to meeting. It scarcely seemed to take them ten minutes to erect a restaurant, barbecue and bar, and another ten to be half-cut. Racing certainly didn't spend a fraction on hospitality then that it does now, but I doubt that any paddock has bettered the Club's party set-up. If nothing else, my crew usually knew where to find me.

Any controversy for the next grand prix at Silverstone was largely self-inflicted. Practice had been a disaster, with no less than five seizures, but by race day I'd put myself third on the grid and was fairly optimistic. Then, as Ditch and I arrived in the holding area ten minutes before the scheduled start, the last bike was literally 50 yards away, already leaving for the grid. Our way was barred by an ACU official, Colin Armes. Eventually we were allowed on to the grid but with no time for a warm-up lap.

If this had been Mugello and my name Agostini, I don't think there's much doubt what would have happened. But the English way is always to bend over backwards to make sure overseas riders get the fairest crack of the whip. OK, being late was our fault, not Colin's. But the KR always needed a good blast to clear it before a race, and starting on cold tyres didn't do us any favours. After a cautious start I worked my way up to seventh place before losing the front and dumping the twin at Becketts. By then it wasn't much consolation when the ACU's Ken Shierson said he could see no reason why we'd been denied a warm-up lap.

It was a disappointing end to a curious season. Yet I managed 42 points from just three finishes, compared to Mario's 85 from a full season. Ditch's total was 27. I'm convinced to this day that if I'd had a full crack at the 250cc championship I could have won it. Kawasaki did, however, take the manufacturers' title – which only went to show that the rider's title was there for the taking, too.

It wasn't just that I won a couple of grands prix, but I regard '77 as the year I was at the peak of my game. I had stacks of experience but was still aggressive and pretty fearless, could work out a race on the go, and knew how to set a bike up. What added to the disappointment of the crazy way the grand prix campaign was arranged was that the KR750 was now well past its best. By now even a good TZ750, let alone an OW31, had the edge on it. If we rode hard, Ditch and I were definitely competitive, but it was more of a struggle than ever before.

Going into the World Formula 750 round at Brands in July, Yamaha were romping away with the series whilst we couldn't muster a single point. After the race, I still couldn't: with Baker pulling away in the lead, I took a big lunge inside Christian Sarron at Dingle Dell. For an instant it looked like working until I lost the front, but luckily didn't collect Christian in the process.

Next month, Silverstone: five seizures. Race of Aces: two thirds as Pat Hennen took a brace of wins. On the 750 I'd forgotten what winning felt like. Roll on Scarborough: 'Grant sizzles as Sheene fades' said the paper after two wins. Oulton, back to the usual, sliding off whilst chasing Hennen.

British racing lore had it that the most important meeting of the year was the last, which was usually the big Powerbike meeting at Brands. Results there set you up very nicely for negotiating deals for the following year, with all the woes that preceded it forgotten. Whatever the reason, I pumped myself up to finish the season on a high, winning the Superbike race by half a wheel from Dave Potter. Ditch, too: he won the feature race. For good measure a few weeks later at Macau, according to *Motor Cycle*, I 'completely dominated the meeting', lapping everyone except Stan Woods.

By then my talks with Kawasaki were well advanced and a few days later *Motor Cycle* announced that Grant 'looks certain to head a Kawasaki onslaught on the 250 and 350 world championships next year with major sponsorship from Life Helmets'. The article went on to say I'd probably be paired with Kork Ballington.

And that's how it proved to be. Shenton was still running the show but Ditch was out and Kork and I would be mounting a full grand prix assault, with the UK 750cc series playing second fiddle. I'd first met Kork in South Africa in 1973. He'd impressed me then, and since, we'd always got on well and have remained firm friends. After the pair of us tested the new bikes – even lighter and faster than before – in Japan in December, we were raring to go.

After the ups and downs of the previous year, the contract took a lot of wrangling, especially as Honda also had an offer on the table. Money was only partly the sticking point, but above all I wanted firm assurances that I'd be racing in all the grands prix. Then there was the helmet issue. Kawasaki had a deal that we'd wear Life lids. Trouble was, I already had a good deal with Nava helmets, and it wasn't just about cash. I always took the view that helmets were about rider preference and no one else's. After all, they're our heads, and I'd never been comfortable with Life lids. Naturally I said this, long and loud, but to no avail. Ironically, to the best of my knowledge, Life never paid for the deal they'd signed.

Even then, personal sponsorship was no small deal. The Nava job alone would have been worth maybe £10k per year. To that you can add leathers, bonuses from oil and tyre companies, and even Sonic Intercoms, then making their way but now very big in the field. At the time I wore Interstate leathers, dealing with Martin Pell. He was a lovely man who'd promise you a fortune you never saw, but was at least reliable – which is more than you could say for my previous supplier, TT Leathers. Altogether, this amounted to a big part of your annual income, although start and contract money were by far the biggest chunks. Apart from the TT, prize money was almost negligible in comparison.

My thoughts, as ever, were with number one, but I felt sorry for Ditch. He was a nice guy and at his best as good as anyone, but inconsistent. For sheer talent I'm sure he was every bit as good as me, but didn't have the same mental toughness I'd accumulated. I suspect that the pressure of riding in a works team was sometimes too much for him. He showed this early the following year by becoming second top scorer behind Potter as we beat the Yanks 361 to 318. Sheene was third, with me fourth. Being a top privateer seemed to suit him.

My 1978 season began with an eye-opening trip to South America for the Venezuelan grand prix. We arrived there ten days early, which was just as well. First of all, it was blisteringly hot and humid, to which we needed to acclimatise. Then it took fully two days to find the bikes and get them through customs. Teams which had arrived late through doing Daytona the week before didn't get their bikes until halfway through practice. Then there were the riots, twitchy armed soldiers roaming everywhere, roads on fire from petrol bombs, rocks flying through the air. At times we had to turn off the hire car's air-conditioning to stop tear gas from coming in. It was chaos.

The heat played hell with the jetting, which during practice was far too rich to get a good grid position. It was even tougher on riders, so I came up with the clever idea of taping a drinking bottle next to the rev counter. Like an idiot, I was so sure it would work that I didn't test it in practice.

Being a clever idiot rather than just your regular idiot, I'd gone to the trouble of fitting a one-way valve in the drinking tube. When I took my first suck the bottle began to siphon and just wouldn't stop. Hard as I tried, I couldn't get it out of my mouth so for next three laps almost became the first grand prix rider in history to die from drowning.

I finally fixed this by sliding off on the infield, landing on a pile of rough earth. I was knocked about and winded, but generally unhurt. I was just thinking about strolling back to the pits when a bunch of medics picked me up and threw me in the back of a pick-up truck. They'd probably been waiting since the previous grand prix for a hair-raising ride to hospital, which is where I was going whether I wanted to or not. Halfway there, I asked for a drink. They offered whisky.

After stripping me out of my leathers they finally gave me water at the hospital, then buggered off, leaving me to do a runner. I jumped into a passing ambulance heading back to the circuit to watch Sheene and Roberts battle it out in the 500 race. Oddly enough, that morning, well dressed and with all the right passes, I'd had a devil of a job getting into the track. By mid-afternoon, sweaty, dusty and in my underwear, I had no bother. And I never saw my leathers again.

Venezuela wasn't the only place with heat and mayhem. For the Paul Ricard Formula 750 round most of the teams were staying at a swanky hotel, Pied dans l'Eau in Bandol. Also there was Sheene and his mate, George Harrison. The rest of us were used to them making a din. It wasn't a bad din – he was a Beatle, after all – but it tended to keep us awake. On the night before the race I'm lying in bed, a bit mangled and swathed in bandages from a practice crash, when we hear screaming and banging from outside.

'I can smell burning,' says Carol.

Without even raising my head I replied with something supportive, like 'It's that bloody Beatle. Shut up and go to sleep.'

The commotion continues. Carol gets up, opens the door, finds the corridor's full of thick black smoke. The screaming doesn't sound like *My Sweet Lord* any more.

Between us we throw some kit into a suitcase, throw it out of the window on to a garage roof, followed by Carol in her bra and panties, and eventually make it to the beach. The scene behind us is straight out of a disaster movie – flames, smoke, sheets tied together dangling from balconies, half-clad folk milling about in shock.

Luckily, everyone has made it to the beach. Except Chris Carter, standing on his balcony looking very large and very forlorn, and completely unable to climb over the railings. Ditch and a couple of others rushed about, found an RSJ and propped it against his balcony. Still he wouldn't budge. Eventually someone shouted that the place was about to explode. At this he leaped on to the girder and slid down to the sand. Unfortunately, his pants did not and it was the night of a very bright moon – or two. I shouted that I'd pay any price for a camera, but there was none to be had.

The rest of the sparks that year, of course, were Kork's. He won four 250cc grands prix, six on the 350, and finished with world titles in both classes. I was just as consistent, placing 14th in both, with a best finish of third on the 350 at Silverstone. Greg Hansford finished second in the 250cc standings, third in the 350.

Pathetic, yes? Anything I say now might be seen as making excuses. But whether I could have beaten Kork or not, there were reasons I was so far behind. The most obvious is that Kork finished 21 races to my 6. True, I sat out a few after breaking an ankle in Austria, but it begs an obvious question about reliability – and I don't think I'm particularly brutal on machinery.

To be honest, at the time I was as baffled as you might be – until the penny dropped near the end of the season. For all the grands prix my Kawasaki mechanic was a Canadian named Jim Fitzgerald. Nigel stayed back home at Lepton to look after the KR750. The only Japanese technical guy was team coordinator Ken Suzuki, who rarely laid hands on the bikes.

For race after race, my bikes just weren't reliable. At Assen, a sprocket actually fell off. And not once did we get the carburetion right – a far cry from the days of Yashida-san and his tables. Kork, on other hand, always had a great set-up thanks to his brother, Dozy. As he went from strength to strength, we went round in ever-decreasing circles. Eventually I'd had enough of it and told Stan I wanted a change of mechanic. He wouldn't hear of it. On we plugged.

At Donington in late September, by which time Kork was already double world champion, it was still the same old story. The 350 seized going down Craner Curves, whilst the 250 was forever jumping out of gear – typical of what had been happening all year. I was so brassed-off I told Ken I wanted an independent engineer to look at the bike. And I meant it.

Shortly after, Jim made a point of coming up to me.

'I've got a confession to make,' he said. 'I've been doing my own thing all year and not listening to what you've been telling me.' He added that he been told to work this way by Shenton himself. With that out in the open, he agreed to work my way for the last couple of internationals of the season. We won almost everything. At Mallory's Race of the Year meeting I beat Kork twice on the 350; at Brands I cleared off on both the 250 and 350, with lap records on each. That didn't necessarily mean I was better than Kork; but it certainly didn't mean I was 13 places worse.

Of course 1978 saw one of the most memorable TTs – the year of Mike Hailwood's comeback. He'd barely raced a bike for 11 years and had a bad limp from a car racing accident. Reaction to his return was either that he'd wobble round making a prat of himself, get badly hurt, or put all the younger pretenders – like me – in their place.

Of course I had an advantage most pundits lacked: I'd had a close look at his riding only four or five years earlier when he'd whipped past me at Silverstone. I hadn't the slightest doubt at all that he'd still be able to cut it around the Island and even predicted in print that he'd win at least one race. His main problems, as I saw it, would be changes to the course since he'd last ridden there, and improvements to machinery. So when I heard that he'd arrived in Douglas a week before practice to familiarise himself with the course, I hopped on a plane to see if I could help. Along with two newcomers – Jeff Sayle and Jim Scaybrook, who'd done endurance races with Mike – we managed six or seven laps in a car and loads of analysis (and drinking) into the small hours. Mike seemed delighted at the help and thoroughly serious about his comeback. He definitely wasn't there for a holiday.

After three days I left Mike to keep charging around on his Martini Yamaha while I raced at Aintree and Cadwell. Come practice week, although I was as excited as anyone else about Mike's return, my main focus, as always, was on my own racing. Then the great man dropped the bombshell: 'Do you mind if I come round with you for a lap in practice?' At the time I was lapping at about 113mph, with Mike maybe 3mph slower but improving rapidly. It didn't look as though he needed a lot of help, but when your idol asks, you jump. In fact I didn't so much jump as panic. This was like God asking for a bit of help interpreting the Ten Commandments.

Apart from anything else, it meant that Mike would learn my guilty secret. I was pretty OK on the Mountain Course from the start to Ramsey, but from there to the Bungalow – I've no idea why – I was still rubbish. So we set off together, Mike first on his Yamaha. The first time he went off-line was leaving Greeba Castle, failing to avoid a rough patch of tarmac which wouldn't have been there when he'd last done the TT. He was a touch off-line at one other spot, but overall, pretty impressive.

Then – approaching Ramsey Hairpin, inevitably – he turned round and waved me past. My mind went blank. I must have run wide at every other corner. Eventually we got back to the paddock and compared notes. I told him his corner speeds were bang-on and his lines perfect apart from a couple of places. His main issue was to do with the huge improvement in brakes since he'd last raced: he was braking 30 yards too early, not making the most of the twin discs he now had. Otherwise, there was very little wrong. Something must have rung true for him, because in his next session he was bang on the pace and – obviously – a threat.

As to my riding, he was impressed – in a backhanded sort of way. 'How the fuck you're getting round at those speeds, I'll never know, 'cos you were all over the shop.' But coming from him, any sort of compliment was special. From there it was a mixed TT – for both of us. Mike won the first race of the week, that brilliant Formula One TT for Ducati, after a stirring battle with his old sparring partner from the Sixties, Phil Read.

Machine troubles marred the rest of his week. Mind you, he didn't give up easily. In the Senior he limped home in 28th place, averaging 99.36mph – slower than he had when winning the same race on a Norton 17 years before. My week was the other way round, with two breakdowns followed by a win in the last race of the week, the Schweppes Classic. The 350 had simply seized but we were baffled when the 250 ran out of fuel on the Mountain on lap three, since that meant it was thirstier than the 750.

The Classic had been billed as a showdown between Mike and me and, although you generally ignore that sort of hype, I was as fascinated as anyone else by how we'd compare. At the time I had Brian Richards with a signal board at Laurel Bank, which allowed me to get my positions from the commentary post at Ballacraine (it later moved to Glen Helen). As I reached there on the first lap of the Classic, it read 'P1 +0' to Hailwood. Mmm … maybe I shouldn't have given him those lessons for it looked like becoming an interesting race. But by the time I received my next signal at Ballaugh, Mike's Yamaha had seized.

I knew that Nigel had worked out that a full tank was good for three laps, so I was looking to stop for fuel at half-distance. But it was equally clear that you could never fill the tank as much in the pits as on the line, so I'd intended also to stop for a quick splash after lap five. Before the race, I'd even asked Ian Cannell, the commentator at the Bungalow, to keep a close eye on me on lap five. If I made to look down at the engine, that was my signal to Nigel that I'd be pitting for a splash and dash.

Inevitably, early on the fifth lap, something went wrong. The back brake's master cylinder decided to fall off – ironically because for safety's sake we'd doubled up the rear engine mountings, which only caused more vibration to reach the frame. As I passed the Bungalow I signalled to Ian that I'd be stopping, word of which got back to Nigel.

Then I had second thoughts. If I stopped, the pit marshals were bound to spot the dangling master cylinder. They wouldn't let me re-start until it was fixed, which might even be impossible. So instead of pulling in, I howled past the pits as Nigel's jaw dropped in disbelief. Nursing the bike over the final lap allowed John Williams to take 20 seconds out of me, but I clung on to win by 50 seconds. It had been disappointing not to be able to pit myself against Mike for the full six laps, but it did cross my mind that being beaten by a bloke ten years out of the game might be a touch humiliating. As it was, my only embarrassment was dislocating a finger opening the victory champagne.

For once chain stretch hadn't been the problem we expected. Maybe Renolds had come up with something new. During practice I'd arranged with Renolds's Vic Doyle and Regina's Mr Villa to thrash both their products up and down Jurby airfield. For the race I'd use whichever brand stretched the least. I was gobsmacked when the Renolds didn't stretch at all – and still hadn't after six racing laps.

From the Island it was business as usual at the Mallory post-TT meeting, struggling to keep up with Sheene's Suzuki and the TZ750s of Ditch and Dave Potter. Then Donington … Snetterton … more of the same. I was usually in the top three or four, but now short-circuit wins were rare. It seemed that with each year that passed the KR750's competitive edge was fading.

The low point of the year, though, was nothing to do with machinery. I missed that year's Ulster grand prix and was at Martin Lampkin's house on the Sunday when someone rang with the news that John Williams was dead. This was a terrible shock. I already knew he'd only suffered a broken collarbone when he'd slid off the previous day, but apparently there'd been some complication with a thrombosis. This might be hard for a non-racer to comprehend, but I felt the blow all the more because, not being at the meeting, my guard was down. It may sound perverse, but being physically closer makes it less upsetting, because then you have your race-face on, your guard up, and are almost cushioned by your concerns about yourself. John was a great guy and a great racer.

CHAPTER 12

COMING READY
OR NOT

So for one reason or another my showings in grands prix had been pretty sorry. Due to injuries, breakdowns and get-offs I definitely didn't finish the year as Kawasaki's Number One man. Despite this, I was asked to stay with them to ride the tandem twins in 1979.

Unfortunately the experiences of '77 and '78 had left a nasty taste in my mouth. I knew that, whatever the results showed, I was still riding at world-class level. Whether I'd have beaten Kork I've no idea, but I never got the chance to find out. Not that there was ever a problem with Kork himself, or Dozy, his mechanic, who were both nothing but professional all year long.

By this time there was another offer on the table. At the last big meeting of the '78 season, the Brands Hatch Powerbike International on 1 November, Gerald Davison sounded me out about the prospect of joining Honda for the following year. (A *Motor Cycle Weekly* photographer caught us chatting, me with a guilty look on my face. Gerald just looked amused.) The deal was both to ride for Honda in the UK but mainly to help develop a new, experimental 500cc grand prix Honda. It was a hard offer to turn down. Like most bike-mad kids in the Sixties, I'd been glued to the radio listening to tales of Hailwood and company battling against the likes of Bill Ivy, Read and the MVs. In my imagination, Honda would be starting off where they left off when they pulled out of grands prix after '67, which was very much as top dog.

Although we didn't clinch a deal there and then, Gerald and I met again a few weeks later in a London hotel where I signed up for two contracts: one with Honda Britain to ride their Formula One bike, both on short circuits and the roads; and another with HIRCo – Honda International Racing Corporation, later to become HRC – to ride their new grand prix machine. Because Honda didn't expect to have their new machine race-ready until mid-season, to keep my hand in, my contract also encouraged me to race an RG500 Suzuki for Honda – in Honda red – for the first part of the season. The other HIRCo rider would be Takazumi Katayama – 'Zooming Taxi' – who a year earlier had become the first Japanese rider to win a world title, in the 350cc class. On 25 November the *Daily Telegraph* got wind of Honda's return to grands prix: 'Grant favourite to launch new Honda challenge'.

Soon after, yet another career option arrived. In December I took part as a guest showjumper in the Olympia Horse of the Year Show. Press reports mentioned 'a somewhat reluctant nag' which I think was a slight on the horse rather than me. Or maybe not.

Despite jumping ship, I came agonisingly close to getting an accidental farewell bonus from Kawasaki. The KR750s had spent the previous season at my home in Lepton, where Nigel had looked after them. At the end of the season Nigel took two of them down to Bromley in the van, telling the team he'd be back the following week with the other one.

'What other one?' they asked. If we'd kept our mouths shut we could have kept it and they'd have been none the wiser. Eventually I bought my 750 from Ditch, who returned to the Kawasaki team for 1979.

The two years of what would turn out to be the NR500 project were as exciting as any I've ever had. The official announcement of Honda's plans came from Kiyoshi Kawashima, who'd succeeded Soichiro Honda as company president four years earlier, during the CBX1000 press launch in December 1978. It almost went without saying that the bike would be a four-stroke, since that had always been Honda's code. The project's technical boss would be Shoichiro Irimajiri, creator of the legendary six-cylinder racers of the Sixties and now head of Honda R&D. The announcement, over a decade after Honda quit at the top of grand prix racing – thanks largely to Irimajiri's designs – came like a shot in the arm to Honda dealers world-wide. They'd become heartily sick of reading about Yamaha and Suzuki track successes.

Gerald Davison, head of Honda Britain and a founding director of HIRCo, would lead the new GP team. He was no Irimajiri, but he had a bit of a pedigree. A former racer from an engineering background, he'd set up Honda Britain Racing when the parent company had little enthusiasm for competition. By 1977, having had success in endurance, 125cc road racing and motocross, all with little direct help from the factory, he'd set his sights on the new Formula One series. Initially they'd used roadster-based engines – like the CB750 on which Phil Read won the 1977 Formula One TT. Later they'd adopted the RCB1000 engines produced by another Honda subsidiary trying to buck the corporate 'no racing' policy. This was Racing Service Centre (RSC), headed by Nichihiko Aika, a former mechanic who'd been grand prix team manager during the Sixties. Like Davison, Aika was a died-in-the-wool race fan who strongly supported the racing efforts of Honda Britain and Honda France.

At the time I'd little sense of all the politics that had put Honda on this route. All I knew – or cared – was that a bunch of stupendously brilliant people in the biggest bike company on earth were paying me serious wedge to ride their new bike. And, being a Honda, that bike couldn't fail to succeed. And along with chief mechanic Ken Hull, Shinichi Sugihara and ex-MV man Carlo Merelli, I'd be working with my regular mechanics, Nigel Everett and Paul Dallas. When I first joined Kawasaki,

Honda and later Suzuki, the first item on the agenda was always to make sure Nigel could come with me. This was partly out of loyalty, but very much out of self-interest, too, because we worked well together and I had the utmost faith in him. Not having a mechanic you gel with can be a major handicap, as I'd found to my cost in grands prix the previous year.

There: sorted. What could possibly go wrong?

At our first meeting Gerald had described some of the NR's technology which, even compared to the exotic machine the public first saw, was pretty staggering. It might be cooled, he said, not by air or water, but liquid nitrogen. There would be lots of ceramics and other cutting-edge materials, and all sorts of other fancy stuff. It all sounded a bit far-fetched, but having the name 'Honda' attached to it gave the bike invincible credibility.

With hindsight, this can't have been much more than 'blue sky' speculation by Honda's engineers. Engine development had begun the previous April, but it wasn't until days before my first chat with Gerald that the first eight-valve single-cylinder test engine had been run. The prototype four-cylinder unit, code-named '0X' wasn't up and running until April 1979.

From our point of view the first phase of the project was to pack Paul and Nigel off to Japan for ten weeks to learn about the engine already under development. Apparently HIRCo were trashing a few engines in the course of testing and needed the extra manpower, and the pair would need the experience to look after the engines when the bike finally raced. It was from ringing them that I got my first impressions of the NR – mainly that it kept blowing up.

Honda's original plan had been to debut the bike at Assen in early July, but I didn't even test the bike in Japan until mid-June. Honda offered me a swanky hotel, but I preferred to stay in the same down-market flea-pit as my mechanics, which was a mistake. The bedroom was exactly the size of a single mattress but, unlike Paul and Nigel, at least I didn't have to share it with anyone.

Being in Tokyo was like going on holiday with your parents as a kid: you were totally dependent on somebody else. Hardly anyone had a word of English and all the street names, obviously, were in Japanese, so a complete mystery to us. If you ever went anywhere, you'd have to get somebody Japanese to write down where you were going and where you wanted to get back to, and whatever else happened you clung on to this piece of paper – because if you lost it, you were totally buggered. All I needed was a marmalade sandwich and a map of darkest Peru and I'd have felt like Paddington Bear. We were offered hire cars, but there was no point, since every street looked like every other, and we'd no idea where we were going anyway.

The local bar culture was just as baffling. If you ordered a beer the practice was to keep topping up your glass whenever it got half empty, so you'd no idea how much you'd drunk until your legs started telling you it was time to go home. The NR experience was already feeling pretty weird and exotic even before I laid eyes on the bike.

Nor was the mystery just with street signs. Before my first visit to R&D I had to sign some sort of secrets document, and then they let me loose. But every Honda employee had on identical work clothes, with just a little name tag – in Japanese – to tell you, or not, who they were. So until we got to know the staff we never had a clue whether we were talking to the boss or the bloke who sweeps the floor. And asking the cleaner to put a couple more clicks on the compression damping doesn't do a right lot of good.

At last I was ushered into the race shop, with several NRs in various stages of construction and a band of white-gloved mechanics fettling away. Nigel introduced me to Norio-san, the chief mechanic, and the rest of the team. Whatever else was wrong with the project, it had a good atmosphere. Nigel had found a way of bridging the cultural divide with his shamelessly crude sense of humour. This had got him off to a rolling start with the Japanese, who seemed to enjoy the same brand of vulgarity.

The bikes looked good, too. The workshop was as surgically clean as any you'd ever seen. To one side was dyno room after dyno room for engine development. In total the project engaged something like 250 people. At the top of this pile but under Irimijiri was the NR's chief research engineer Takeo Fukui, who's now boss of the whole Honda corporation. His first task had been to come up with a design capable of challenging the disc- and reed-valve two-strokes of Suzuki and Yamaha. To even approach the power required it would need eight cylinders, but 500cc grand prix bikes had been limited to four for almost ten years. Honda's solution was a 100-degree V8 pretending to be a four. With oval-pistons, eight con-rods, eight spark plugs, four twin-choke carbs and 32 valves this gave the breathing and revability benefits of an eight whilst strictly still being a four. According to HIRCo's calculations, such an engine could reach 23,000rpm and put out 130 horsepower.

Nothing like it had been tried before, yet no one at Honda seemed to doubt they could succeed. After all, the company's entire history had been of pretty much uninterrupted innovation and success.

The overall impression was of serious 'can do' – and money. Lots and lots of money. Honda were already chucking cash at the project hand over fist. Parts of the engine cost astronomical sums, even just to make, let alone develop. A single crankshaft, for instance, came in at around £10,000. Nobody seemed unduly bothered when an engine went pop, other than for the fact that the resulting pile of scrap wasn't exactly running as they'd hoped. It was the exact opposite of any privateer team, where every blow-up and crash grabbed a chunk of your budget that simply couldn't be replaced. To that extent, we were living a money-no-object fantasy. When one engine went, a bloke with a wheelbarrow simply trundled it away as the mechanics set about bolting in the next.

As if the engine wasn't radical enough, the aluminium monocoque chassis – the engineers called it a 'shrimp shell' – which wrapped around the engine like a cocoon, was equally experimental. The aluminium 'fairing' was an integral part of the monocoque structure, actually welded on to the headstock.

Nigel liked working on the monocoque, which was 'dead easy' to take apart. To get at the engine you removed around a dozen 6mm bolts and the bike split in two: the engine, swing-arm and rear wheel formed one section, the fairing-cum-frame, headstock and front forks the other. The two sections slid on runners into each other. Like everything else on the bike it was all incredibly clever – which didn't necessarily make it work.

Then there were its 16-inch wheels – chosen, I think, to reduce weight and lower the bike's profile and wind resistance. Neither Katayama nor I, nor anyone else as far as I knew, had any experience of making tyres of this size work. Nor did Dunlop and Michelin, the tyre companies involved. In fact in the first months of development, they couldn't even supply treaded tyres, which meant we couldn't test in the wet. The wheels themselves had carbon-fibre rims and spokes – yet more novelty – with magnesium hubs. There were just too many unknowns piled into the one package.

I used the Dunlops, Takazumi the Michelins. Apart from making for lots of duplication of effort, having two tyre manufacturers on one project was tailor-made for industrial espionage. Naturally each company was keen to get the drop on the other, and even more to know what the other was up to. One day a Michelin was returned to the truck minus a large square chunk of tread. Our old friend Bucky denied chopping it out, but who else would have done it? Besides, it would have been better just to have taken the chunk and lobbed the rest of the tyre over a wall where it wouldn't be noticed.

So much for the theory. When I first rode the bike at Suzuka it was instantly obvious that something wasn't quite right. The bike wasn't much bigger than a 250. Unfortunately it was no quicker. And because the monocoque's aluminium alloy had to be soft enough to be formed into the elaborate shapes required, every few laps – if you got that far without the engine blowing up – you'd have to come in to get the headstock welded. Time after time, it cracked. I'd been involved in the typical stop–start of development before, so the hold-ups didn't particularly bother me – except to the extent that there seemed to be something fundamentally wrong with the bike.

At the time I had a column for *Motor Cycle Weekly*, dictated to Chris Carter. Whilst this meant that the paper's readers got the low-down on my experiences with the NR, I obviously had to be careful about what I said. Honda were my bosses and it wouldn't do to upset them. The project was very new and hugely ambitious, which had to be taken into account. And besides, we were all to a degree emotionally wrapped up in the project. Initially, at least, it wasn't easy to be objective. It can't have been. In late June I told *Motor Cycle Weekly*'s readers that the bike was 'very low and light … flickable … broad spread of power and easy to ride … no doubt at all that it will eventually succeed'. Looking at those words now, I'm baffled. Maybe my new Honda hat was too tight around my head. More likely, like almost everyone else, I couldn't countenance the thought that mighty Honda could drop a brick.

Nigel was obviously more tuned into the details of the project than me. He reckoned the engine was basically good – but had a huge problem with noise control. Un-silenced, as it usually was on the dyno, it produced around 110 – 115bhp, on a par with Suzuki's RG500. But bolting on the race silencers knocked that down to

100bhp or even less. At the time neither Honda nor anyone else had much background in four-stroke racing silencing. They hadn't needed it in the Sixties and didn't need it now on their F1 car engines. Silencing two-strokes was a doddle in comparison.

In the first year the engine had no flywheel effect at all. The pistons, although usually described as oval, were actually flat-sided – more like the shape of a sardine can than a true oval. Because of the flat sides, the rings couldn't seal very well and used to suffer from massive blow-by. This not only robbed horsepower, which it didn't have enough of to begin with, but was part of the reason the NR was such a bitch to start. And in those days all grands prix had bump-starts. The other difficulty was the fact that it wouldn't tick over at anything below 7,000rpm. Honda were making it hard for themselves – and for Katayama and me.

The whole point of the fake eight-cylinder layout was to give an ultra-short 36mm stroke and lots of revs. Power started at around 12,500rpm, then there was power of a kind until 17,500, after which it steadily went off all the way to the red line at 21,000. Although later engines produced power further up the rev range, in the early months you were wasting your time going past 18,000rpm.

Nigel's main job was engine building. Each one would take a solid week of 10-hour days. He'd finish one and they'd cart if off in a wheelbarrow to the dyno room, where they'd trash it and bring it back again. As one arrived back with a con-rod poking out of the crankcases, a Japanese technician bowed respectfully and said 'Good morning, con-rod' in Japanese. That didn't go down too well. They never saw him again. He's probably been designing Prelude bumpers ever since.

Being the rider I just jetted in and out of Never-Ready-Land whenever there was testing to be done. Nigel and Paul were there for months on end, so had a far better understanding of the project's details. So, whilst I tend to remember the times it blew up, Nigel recalls the engine as having a good service life. Most came back to the race shop worn out, rather than grenaded.

All the time the team was under pressure from upstairs for encouraging numbers. So the engine team would pass on the flattering unsilenced power figures. They'd even dyno-test the NR without oil until it destroyed itself – but at least they could report another three horsepower, or whatever it was. With eight con-rods and all the other related kit, there were so many moving parts in the engine that oil drag negated much of the theoretical power. Because of this a lot of work went into reducing internal friction, using new oils that seemed more like water than the stuff we were used to. Again, it was cutting-edge stuff but only added to the huge list of unknowns. And when an engine did let go, it would be spinning so fast that almost everything inside disintegrated. Nigel reckoned finding a piece as big as a cornflake was rare. Since analysing this scrap wasn't always very informative, they'd change components one at a time and dyno-test engines to destruction, just to find out what the weak bits were.

The best race-ready horsepower I ever heard of was about 104, which would have been seriously competitive when MV Agusta were winning grands prix. But not any more. Because Honda were paying me to ride a RG500 Suzuki, I had the perfect yardstick to measure the NR's progress. I had some cracking rides against Sheene in British meetings, and knew exactly how good the Suzuki was, and how easy it was to ride compared to the NR.

HIRCo also had an RG of their own for comparison purposes, which they told us made something like 102 horsepower, a number they quite liked for obvious reasons. 'No-no-no,' said Nigel, 'it's got to do more than that.' Eventually they let us play with the jetting and in no time at all we found another 10bhp. More would definitely have been there but Honda didn't really want to find out precisely how much the Suzuki could make – or, in other words, how far behind the game they were. This seemed baffling – uncannily like the sort of head-in-the-sand attitude that had wrecked the British bike industry. Yet this was Honda. How could it be?

The demoralising thing was that even if we could have brought the NR's power up to the level of the RG, the Suzuki would still have won every time. It handled better, had a broader spread of power and none of the Honda's hideous chatter into turns. It was simply so much easier to ride. HIRCo had gone to great lengths to put the swing-arm pivot and final drive sprocket on the same axis to help out the rear suspension, but any advantage gained was far outweighed by the extreme engine braking effects.

Tests were typically for three days. I was riding the bike well, I knew, but a mile off the pace at Suzuka – maybe five or six seconds off Roberts's lap record, which is a lifetime.

Mr Fukui came up to me looking deeply concerned.

'Mick-san, when are you going to go quick?'

'I'm going as quick as I can. There's not a lot left.'

He let out a low moan and looked downcast.

The trouble was that the people involved in the NR project seemed to think, as I had, that because it had the might of Honda behind it, someone would fix it. It's such a big company, with so little failure in its history, that the feeling's always about that someone would come up with an answer. But the NR team itself was who had to fix it – and if they didn't, no one else could. I certainly couldn't 'fix it' by riding it harder. No rider on earth could make up that sort of time, and all they'd achieve by trying was to add crash damage and broken bones to the rising pile of blown engines.

'How many rpm you use?' Mr Fukui asked.

'17,500.'

'Oh, must go to 21,000.'

I explained that there was no point in revving beyond 18,000, and we were already breaking cranks fairly often even at the lower revs, but he's the boss. So Mr Fukui jabbers to the mechanics and the gearing is changed to suit. I spent the rest of the afternoon razzing the motor to 21,000, which may have given the tachometer plenty of exercise but didn't make a bit of difference to the lap times.

The next day I arrived for testing and for some reason Katayama wasn't there. Apparently he'd been due to ride a 'special' bike. After a bit of tutting and head-scratching, I'm asked to test it instead. Our two bikes were as unlike as two NRs could be. I liked my suspension pretty firm, he liked his soft; he had a left-hand gearchange, mine was on the right; he used Michelins, I preferred Dunlops. By the time I'd got into my leathers the mechanics have changed the tyres, suspension and control linkages, and off I go. I was as keen as anyone to find out about this 'special' bike, although nobody thought to mention what was special about it.

Mmm ... this feels better. After a lap I'm feeling impressed. It's got more power than any NR I've sat on before. Maybe the boffins have found some sort of answer. So I get stuck in for another couple of laps, careful to rev it to 21,000 as I'd been instructed the day before: 21,000 ... 21,000 ... this isn't bad ... 21,000 ... bang! Going into the big bend before the start line, the whole thing shuddered sideways across the road as the engine let go – and anything spinning that fast doesn't let go in a small way. It was as though someone had exploded a grenade inside the crankcases – smoke, oil and shrapnel everywhere.

Luckily I stayed on and didn't have far to coast down the pit lane. Our base at Suzuka was an old Nissen hut, from which would periodically emerge an old guy in a white smock pushing a wheelbarrow. It was his job to cart the wrecked engines away. After a few test sessions he'd developed a sixth sense of where his labours were needed next, and he was already on his way with a new engine as I rolled by.

Ahead of him strode a worried-looking Mr Fukui.

'What happen, Mick-san?'

'I broke it.'

'Oh. How many revolutions?'

'21,000, like you said.'

'Oh, that was big engine. Only safe to 17,500.'

Apparently they'd developed a 560cc engine in order to push the chassis harder. If only someone had said.

At the end of every three-day session the whole crew would get together for a big debrief. There'd be dozens of us – riders, mechanics, Honda personnel, brake and suspension specialists, guys from Dunlop and Michelin – although not the chap with the wheelbarrow, who seemed to be doing most of the graft. At one debrief Mr Fukui stood by the blackboard and wrote at the top 2min 17.8, which was my best time around Suzuka, then a long chalk line to 2min 12.4 at the bottom, which was Roberts's lap record.

'Mick-san,' he said. 'How do we achieve?'

Right. First of all we need another ten horsepower. The clutch needs to be better, the carburetion, too. Then we need to fix the chatter, this from the tyres, that from the suspension, the other from the frame, which used to flex and break. With a bit here and a bit there, theoretically I reckoned we could get near the lap time we needed. It was all 'ifs' and 'buts', but to me it seemed realistic.

Katayama wasn't present, so they asked the same question of Yoicho Oguma, the local test rider. He was always a couple of seconds slower than me.

'Ah,' he said, '30 horsepower', bowed his head respectfully and sat down.

It was pure nonsense. The only way they were going to get another 30 horsepower was to run a 650, yet I had the distinct impression that his was the answer they preferred. It was easier to get their heads round than a redesign of the whole shooting match. The truth was that with the chassis problems we had, another 30 horsepower was probably the last thing we needed.

It also turned out to be the last thing Oguma needed. One day they sent him out with the big engine and he hadn't done a lap before disappearing in a cloud of dust at the Suzuka Esses.

The mechanics probably didn't need it, either. I've never known poor old Nigel graft so hard. HIRCo insisted that every time an engine ran it had to be stripped and all 32 valves re-ground. On a grand prix weekend that would mean lapping in something like 160. As if that weren't enough, Carlo made even more work for himself by insisting on polishing everything inside the engine, as he'd been trained to do in his MV days. Norio tried to dissuade him but he wouldn't budge. Finally, 'OK,' said Norio, 'polish one engine as much as you want, but if it doesn't give any more power on the dyno, do it our way – OK?' So Carlo polished to his heart's content, and it made not a blind bit of difference.

CHAPTER 13

PISSING INTO
THE WIND

The NR's race debut was delayed so often that the press
dubbed it the 'Never Ready'. (NR actually stood for
'New Racing'.) I wasn't overjoyed that they were taking
the piss out of the project, but they did have a point.
Eventually the bike made its debut at the penultimate
grand prix of the year in mid-August. I'd have preferred
somewhere quiet and remote, but unfortunately for me
this was the British grand prix at Silverstone. It was a case
of 'coming ready or not'.

Before Silverstone we'd tested at Donington and
Snetterton. My column of the time records that at
Donington, which isn't a power circuit, I was within two
seconds of Wil Hartog's lap record. But at Snetterton, a
horsepower circuit, we were miles off the pace. It didn't
look good for Silverstone, which was faster still.

There was huge media interest, and they must have
been impressed. We had the slowest bikes in the paddock,
but the best hospitality by miles. Charlie Williams's TZ250
Yamaha – good, but nothing special – was actually faster
down the back straight. Then when we got to the corners,
the TZ would go round like a roller skate, compared to
the jack-hammer I was trying to ride.

The rear wheel chatter was terrible. In those days
Woodcote was fast, a fifth-gear corner. Yet even at that
speed when you shut the NR's throttle, the rear wheel
would hop and chatter – like an MV might in *second* gear,
but at maybe 120mph. I didn't know the solution any

more than HIRCo did, but I could explain to them what it meant in practice. As a rider there were two ways to get round the problem: either blip the throttle to bring the rear wheel up to speed – in which case I missed the corner altogether – or slip the clutch on the over-run, which would probably wear it out. Failing that we needed some device that would do the job for us.

The device they came up with was the slipper clutch. These are now common even on sports road bikes, but then they were yet another unknown. Each mechanic had a box of colour-coded springs plus a chart with about 30 different spring combinations to vary the degree of slip, so it wasn't an easy thing to set up. Early versions had a habit of jamming their pawls and giving no drive at all – so you couldn't even bump-start the bike. Honda kept at it, and after I left the project they developed a slipper clutch that worked.

In the meanwhile we were pissing into the wind – in the presence of Soichiro Honda himself, who arrived for the meeting. Despite riding as hard as I ever had, Takazumi and I qualified the last two of 40 on the Silverstone grid. I'm pretty sure neither of us even started with enough fuel to finish. The race began with a bump start. Because of the massive blow-by the engine wouldn't run below 7,000rpm, so you had to be a bloody Olympian to start the thing. The technique was simple: you just had to run alongside at 70mph and drop the clutch. When the flag dropped Takazumi got it right, and I missed it.

Patter ... patter ... patter ... push ... push ... push. Takazumi was actually waiting for me, 'cos we knew we didn't have a cat in hell's chance of a result. After about four attempts a bit of the zing goes out of your stride and I was just about to collapse on the pit wall when the damn thing fired.

By this time my legs were totally gone and I sort of flopped on to the rear end of the seat. For the first time in its life the NR decided to wheelie ... first, second, third gear, all on the back wheel. If I hadn't been so knackered I might have thought it looked pretty impressive. But unknown to me, there was oil blathering on to the back tyre. Because of the piston blow-by, we'd always known that crankcase breathing was a big issue. What we didn't know, because the bloody thing had never done one before, was what a wheelie would do to the oil. I was about to find out.

The crankcase breather was enormous, and at that angle it was actually below the oil level, which could only lead to one thing. So I pitched the NR into Copse, the first corner ... and the rest, as they say, is history, because I had no more chance of getting round that corner than of winning the race. I ended up on the grass on my backside but the bike somehow parked itself against a bale and burst into flames. Takazumi lasted six laps before his ignition packed in.

From Silverstone we hopped across to Le Mans for the French grand prix. In the meantime the bikes were returned to Japan in disgrace and came back a little lighter and with more power. Good old Gerald made sure the team was looked after properly – smoked salmon, foie gras, the whole nine yards. Maybe we ate too much, for neither Takazumi nor I qualified – despite, I've heard since, running big engines. We were unlikely to be found out for two reasons. One, even if we finished, it wouldn't be anywhere near the front; and two, the scrutineers probably wouldn't have a clue how to measure an oval cylinder, anyway. I dare say there was lots of other illegal stuff going on. Plenty of factory bikes had illegal titanium wheel spindles with a little iron bung in the end just to confuse scrutineers' magnets.

The organisers said we could start only if someone else failed to, but we went to the line anyway and refused to move. Since half the crowd were there to see and hear the new four-stroke, a near-riot resulted as we were slung off the grid. But, compared to Silverstone, it was relatively

ABOVE: *Cute, wasn't I? It wouldn't last.*

ABOVE RIGHT: *On holiday at Morecambe, already fascinated by engines and wheels.*

RIGHT: *Mum and dad, Dora and Sammy, enjoying some typically British holiday weather at Blackpool.*

BELOW: *With all my surrogate 'parents' – Gran, Edie and Bill – outside Mr and Mrs Waller's boarding house in Scarborough.*

ABOVE: *Looking surprisingly cheerful at piano practice. I never mastered 'chopsticks' – then or years later in Japan.*

LEFT: *Me (left) and Chris Bradley, failing to get a tan at Scarborough, yet again. Billy, my dog, had no need of one.*

RIGHT: *Posing with sister Cheryl on dad's BSA Bantam, which I used to smuggle out to Coxley Wood. Note streamlined socks.*

RIGHT: *Move over Modigliani. An art school bronze – perhaps of the aftermath of a high-side in later life.*

ABOVE: *The real me, leaping Cadwell Mountain on my not-so-trusty Velocette with the Jim Lee frame and Eric Stanbra's trick front brake.*

LEFT: *Looking surprisingly purposeful on the Lee BSA Gold Star at Croft in 1970.*

BELOW: *Still bearded, on Jim Lee's spine-framed Yamaha TR2. It later sprouted a disc front brake. Me, Rex Butcher (number obscured), Ron Chandler (20) and Phil Read (2) at Druids, Brands Hatch, in 1971.*

ABOVE: *The new me: green leathers, clean-shaven, full-face helmet with 'JL' logo – on the Lee Commando at Quarter Bridge in 1971, just before I knocked off Keith Heckles.*

BELOW: *My first Kawasaki outing, taking the Padgett's H1 triple to third place in the 1972 senior behind the MVs of Agostini and Pagani.*

BELOW LEFT: *The factory JPS Norton on the way to second place behind Peter Williams in the 1973 Formula 750 TT.*

BELOW RIGHT: *The messy aftermath of my Norton debut the year before, when the flywheel exploded through the crankcase at Anderstorp.*

LEFT: *Testing the factory 750 Ducati at Imola in 1973. It would have made a great TT machine. I left my helmet in the hotel so am wearing Bruno Kneubühler's.*

RIGHT: *The guys who gave me my first TT win in 1974, dear old Les Williams and 'Slippery Sam'.*

BELOW: *My second Kawasaki TT outing, on the air-cooled 750cc triple, also in 1974. Commentator Geoff Cannell was seriously unimpressed by my front wheel landings.*

ABOVE: *Wheel-to-wheel with Barry Sheene at Brands in 1978. For a few years we were the top double act in UK motorcycle racing...*

LEFT: *...another double act that worked well for me: with a youthful Nigel Everett in 1977. He'd be my mechanic for the rest of my racing career.*

LEFT: *...and Carol, the best one of all.*

ABOVE: *Green and mean at last but still not number '10': on the Kawasaki 500 triple in 1975. The bike never received the development of the 250 and 750cc Kawasakis.*

RIGHT: *The KR750 Kawa at Silverstone in 1978. Many regarded it as brutal but, except in 'A' tune, it was a pussycat to ride.*

RIGHT: *I said I could do it! Top of the rostrum at Assen after my 250cc grand prix win in 1977.*

ABOVE LEFT: *The most expensive mistake in racing history? Honda's NR500 during practice at Silverstone in 1979...*

LEFT: *...and one of the most embarrassing clangers: me going tits-up at Copse. The bike caught fire.*

BELOW LEFT: *The NR crew at Silverstone for the same meeting. The chap in the white suit is Soichiro Honda, who founded the company. The European at the back is manic polisher Carlo Merelli, with crew chief Norio to his left.*

ABOVE: *On – but not for long – Honda's best 500, the RG500 Suzuki, at the NW200 in 1979. I only narrowly avoided taking out Tony Rutter (4) as Alex George sailed on oblivious.*

RIGHT: *Me and Crosby (no relation to Graeme). For once, the jockey looks less scared than his mount.*

ABOVE: *Riding pillion on Gerhard Kanehl's bike at Doran's during the 1982 Senior TT. The crash gave both of us plenty of grief.*

LEFT: *Another strange mount, on the Kawasaki Christmas card (from left): me, Barry Ditchburn, John Norman, and team boss Stan Shenton.*

BELOW: *Suzuki's XR69 Formula One bike in 1982. When the fairing wasn't falling off, it was a superb racing machine, giving Reg and me a definite edge over the Hondas.*

ABOVE: *My last TT finish and last win, leaping Ballaugh on the Suzuki GSX-R750 during the 1985 production race. A similar bike brought me the 1985 British Superstock title.*

RIGHT: *Less glorious was my playing foil to Miss Wet T-Shirt in the Miss Wet Lovely Legs competition at the Pace Lido, 1986 TT. I lost, but beat Charlie Williams's spindly pins.*

BELOW: *Just walking Max the dog, at home at Lepton, around 1980.*

ABOVE: *If Carlsberg made pre-1965 trials bikes... Looking as though I half-know what I'm doing on my cherished HT-5 Ariel in the late 1990s.*

BELOW LEFT: *Scarborough was the scene of so many great results. This was my last, acknowledging two second places in 1985.*

BELOW RIGHT: *Sharing a joke with James Whitham after the 2005 TT lap of honour. It wasn't quite so funny years before, when he used to trash Suzuki kit.* (Mac McDiarmid)

ABOVE: *Easier to bump than the NR500: taking off on a 1939 Tiger 100 for the brilliant centenary re-enactment at the 2007 TT. The roll-up was a period prop.* (Mac McDiarmid)

BELOW: *Tipping into the Bungalow during the TT 2007 parade lap on the best of the KR750s, the magnesium crankcased version on which I won the 1978 Classic TT.* (Mac McDiarmid)

ABOVE: *Trials was, and still is, my first love, if only I were better at it. Tackling the Lakes Two Days in 2010.* (Eric Kitchen)

BELOW: *'Laughing Boy' Steve Plater and me at the Swartkops circuit, South Africa, early in 2010. The bike is the MkVII Suzuki which Sheene rode in 1983 and on which I won the Macau GP a year later.* (Ian McLaren)

painless. Silverstone did, at least, get me the only trophy I ever achieved on the NR – a wooden spoon later presented by Barry Sheene on behalf of *Motorcycle Racing*. Later I got another pot, but that was plaster of Paris.

There was still no shortage of effort. There never was. I was in Japan for more testing in November, February and again in March when Ron Haslam joined the project, replacing Takazumi who'd dislocated a shoulder when the NR's front wheel locked on in the previous test. By now the bike was certainly better than it had been in 1979. A redesign of the oval piston rings largely eliminated blow-by, which not only gave more power but without any other changes allowed the engine to tick over at just 1,000rpm – compared to 7,000rpm the year before. It also made the bike a damn sight easier to start. And, mercifully, they'd at last given up on those 16-inch wheels.

By this time I'd resolved my own issues with the team. My contract was on a year-by-year basis, so I'd had the option of leaving at the end of '79 and only after hard thought stayed with them. My problem was that I could see 1980 as yet another development year for the bike, since there seemed little chance of making it competitive that season. And at my age – I'd be 36 in July – I wasn't sure I could afford another lost year. On the other hand, being involved at the sharp end of technology with Honda was a fabulous experience I couldn't have got anywhere else. And the money wasn't bad.

The March testing didn't do much for the NR's progress and it did even less for mine. For one session they put a new fairing on the bike and sent me out to try it. On the second lap, it dug in and down I went. By the time I'd stopped tumbling I had a broken ankle. I didn't ride the bike again until late June at Donington. It wasn't the ideal start to the season.

That crash may have been the death knell for the NR's monocoque frame. Previously the boffins still seemed utterly wedded to their beloved 'shrimp shell'. Changing Japanese minds on such a matter of pride was never going to be easy, but eventually HIRCo accepted the obvious – that a conventional chassis would halve their problems (and maybe give more ground clearance). So in late spring Maxton's Ron Williams joined the project. On his first look at the monocoque, he pointed and said, 'It'll crack here, here and here.' The Honda people looked at him like some kind of savant, for that was exactly where it had been breaking.

Later they flew an engine to the UK for Ron to design a more conventional tubular frame around. The engine had no internals but, even so, all the cases were welded up so no one could take a sneaky peek inside. With European kit like Brembo brakes and Marzocchi suspension, the new chassis may not have been as sexy as the original alloy tub, but took a huge bunch of unknowns out of the overall equation. If Honda had begun with a more conventional approach in the first place, and only resorted to novelty as it was needed, a lot of the embarrassments of the first season might have been avoided.

Even after my ankle healed, progress was still very stop–start. Just as the year before, the NR had to wait until the British grand prix – then the third from last – to make its season's debut. Takazumi was lapped but finished 15th. A few weeks later for the German grand prix, the team still didn't have sufficient kit for two bikes, so again only Takazumi rode, finishing 12th.

With the grand prix season over it was decided to race-test the bikes at selected British international meetings. Even having Ron Williams on board didn't prevent some whacky decisions. The HIRCo boys had evidently filed away their data about getting extra power by leaving out the oil, so in one such race at Donington they did the obvious and sent me and Ron out with just a few teaspoonfuls of the stuff. Now I'm a racer so I like horsepower. But I also like lubrication. When I found out – after the NR blew up – I was furious. As far as I was concerned they were endangering me just to save their faces.

Ironically I reckon the best lap I ever rode – on anything, anywhere – was to put the NR on the Donington front row alongside Sheene at that meeting. The NR was sliding everywhere but completely under control. At the time the lap record was maybe 1min 15sec. I went round in about 1min 17, which was a mark of just how far the NR had to go to be competitive.

Ron would have been 23 at the time, but a young 23 – confident on the track but very reserved and polite off it. He was a bit like Mez Mellor in that he preferred to agree or say nothing rather than risk upsetting anyone. Whilst this went down well in some quarters, it maybe wasn't the best of credentials for a test rider. I was 12 years older and a great deal more confident, which allowed me to be more direct. In fact, as I saw it, that was what I was paid to be – because how can you possibly develop a bike if you're not candid about where you're starting? Being Japanese, Takazumi wasn't much better than Ron. He could ride, that was for sure, but in testing I always regarded him as a bit of a joke. He'd come in from a session and ask for a click of damping here, half a turn of pre-load there. It was bullshit. No-one's that sensitive. Yet the Honda crew swallowed it whole and looked up to him.

The downside of my approach was that I probably put more corporate noses out of joint. Certainly Ron's was more in tune with the Japanese way, which always tries to avoid confrontation by dancing around the facts. It's a mystery to me how they've been so successful at developing bikes, which they so obviously have, because to me that approach just doesn't make sense.

What with lousy results and my usual charm offensive, as the season ebbed to a close my standing with Honda seemed to be on the wane. Then there was the unfortunate fact that at 36 I was obviously nearer the knacker's yard than grand prix success. The truth was that I took my racing as seriously as I ever had. I ran seven or eight hard miles every day and was as fit as I'd ever been. Unfortunately Gerald, like most of the Honda people, was looking for excuses for the NR's sorry performance, and got it into his head that my fitness, rather than the bike's, was at fault. At the Race of Aces meeting at Snetterton, he actually said so. Now I was never an athletic-looking will-o'-the-wisp character, but I was fit. What he was suggesting was ludicrous.

'You cheeky bastard,' I thought. 'Tell you what,' I said, 'I'll borrow a push bike and we'll have a race for a lap – me running, you pedalling.'

Gerald agreed, bless him, but just to be on the safe side I gave the bike's brakes a bit of a tweak so they dragged just enough to make pedalling hard work. By the time I was halfway down the back straight he was a gasping dot in the distance and I had to wait for him. I never heard any more complaints about my condition.

It was a small victory that didn't do me much good in the long run. From then on my part in the NR project seemed to peter out. They kept Katayama on it, but Ron gradually replaced me and by season's end I was out of it altogether. The following winter Freddie Spencer joined the gang.

In two seasons my best grand prix finish – and I had a few of them – was a DNF. I'd have been more competitive on my Velo. Takazumi, with two finishes and a best of 12th, hadn't much more to shout about. As the engine had progressed it had also become heavier, despite the use of lots of magnesium and titanium, largely to make it more reliable. For 1981 the V-angle was reduced to 90 degrees to make it more compact. I gather Honda were claiming something like 130bhp by mid-season, although I'd take that with a pinch of salt. The NR did achieve its one success, though, with victory for Kengo Kiyama in a 200km race at Suzuka, partly through needing fewer pit stops than the two-stroke opposition. Yet even with Freddie Spencer partnering Takazumi, the bike scored not a single grand prix point all year. Its best showing came at Silverstone, when Fast Freddie was lying fifth before the engine broke.

Sometimes I wondered just how serious they were about the grand prix project, as opposed to using it as some sort of advanced training facility. One day I spotted a Japanese fellow I hadn't seen before, working on the Nissin brake on Takazumi's bike. He had some English so we got chatting, and I asked him what he'd been doing before joining the NR project. It turned out that he'd spent his previous three years designing the Honda Accord's front bumper.

It was almost as though Honda had forgotten how to do it. Now they'll collect the best race engineers together to take on the likes of Yamaha and Ducati, but the plain fact was that it had been half a generation since their grand prix heyday and they simply didn't have a wealth of hands-on experience in HIRCo at the time. Yet, at the beginning at any rate, there was no obvious shortage of confidence. For the most part it seemed that simply having the Honda logo on their overalls gave them that – although they weren't above accepting a spot of metaphysical assistance, too. One day 35 core members of the team and a NR front wheel were bussed off for a blessing at a Shinto temple.

Nigel was in the workshop at the time. 'Where's everybody gone?' he asked.

'They've gone to pray for the bike.'

'Christ, we really are in the shit.'

That afternoon Takazumi threw the bike away at Spoon Curve and wrote off every part except – you guessed it – the front wheel. Don't knock it – nothing else had worked, and Takazumi himself wasn't above dangling good luck charms from various bits of the NR. But overall it seemed, as much as anything, to be a project to bring their engineers through the ranks. And it certainly didn't do Mr Fukui's career any harm.

The whole deal was so wide of the mark that my impression was that the main purpose must have been to train up engineers and bring on new technology rather than win races. Surely nothing else made sense … surely a company like Honda couldn't get their sums so badly wrong. Maybe that's what Honda would prefer us to think. Maybe that would be the least uncomfortable perspective. That's certainly Nigel's view and seems to be the prevailing opinion these days.

From speaking with him recently, I know that Gerald Davison has a very different view. And he, of all the Europeans on the project, was probably in the best position to know. To his mind, Honda both underestimated the scale of the challenge and overestimated their ability to meet it. The engineers who'd brought all that success in the Sixties had tubsful of theory, but grew up with the practical realities of racing, too. Their successors in 1979 had no such grounding. 'Honda enters, Honda wins', wasn't so much their creed as their myth. Irimajiri, the genius of the Hailwood years, was now way up in the ranks. His influence was spread too thinly to be of much use down on the ground. The rest was all theory. And it didn't work.

I'm not sure if it ever could have worked. By the end of the Seventies no four-stroke could compete with a two-stroke of similar capacity. To even try it had to be heavier, slower and probably less reliable – which pretty much sums up the NR. This was nothing to do with FIM regulations, the capabilities of Honda R&D, or the phase of the moon. It was just plain physics. Staggeringly, it now all makes sense: Honda's decision to return to grands prix with a four-stroke had nothing to do with the engineers. The decision was taken by the company's main board *without any research or discussion* and simply handed down to R&D to achieve. That left the poor sods in the front line with nowhere to go – not in this universe, at least.

Honda's original aim was to win the world title with the NR500 within three years. Yet long before that it must have been obvious that there was as much chance of me winning Wimbledon. Even if there were long-term

214

technology benefits, the entire 'Never Ready' programme was a huge embarrassment to Honda. It was even to me, although everyone could probably see that I was doing my level best to push shit uphill.

I gather that as early as the winter of 1979/80 Gerald discussed with Irimajiri the idea of Honda bailing out of the project. He was amazed to learn that Honda already had a part-developed alternative just lying around with nothing to do. This orphan was a spin-off from Honda's motocross programme – the only area in which two-strokes were tolerated in the Honda scheme of things. It was, of course, the reed-valve 500cc triple which became the NS500. The original design came from Shinichi Miyakoshi, who'd taken Honda from nowhere to motocross world titles in the late Seventies, so clearly Honda still had some engineers who could cut the mustard. After three fruitless years of Honda going nowhere with four-strokes, Freddie Spencer put it on the rostrum in its first grand prix in Argentina and went on to dominate the 500cc class. I rode a production NS for the first time a few months ago. It was a peach.

For all that, the NR fiasco was a wonderful experience, one I wouldn't have missed for the world, even though the bike was crap. It just didn't work and never would. Yet everyone involved never put in less than 110 per cent (except, on that one occasion, of oil). They just got it horribly wrong. Over the long run I've no doubt they learned a lot which was put to good use in later decades, but at the time all we wanted was a competitive race bike. And the NR was never that.

CHAPTER 14

YOU CAN'T BEAT
A GOOD BASH

In 'domestic' racing – in other words, not on the NR500 – 1979 began as not such a bad year. It started with a pole position on my lovely new Honda Red RG500 at Daytona, but not for long. The time brought a flurry of protests and was rightly overturned as a timekeeper's error. Dale Singleton won on a TZ750 ahead of a young Freddie Spencer. I was happy to settle for ninth place on the first 500 home. A week or so later in Venezuela, the RG burst a crank in practice.

Back at home, my Honda career was almost as slow to take off as it was on the NR. Honda's Formula One bikes took an age to arrive, so until the eve of the TT both me and my new team-mate, Ron Haslam, were riding two-stroke Hondas – mine the RG Suzuki, his a TZ750 Yamaha. I loved my 'Honda', and Ron seemed to get on with his. For the *Daily Mirror* Trophy at Donington in March I won the 500c race, and was second to Ron in the 750cc event. Ditch, newly reunited with Kawasaki, took both the 250 and 350cc races. At Cadwell Ron and I repeated the Donington results. Even the Transatlantic, in which we were soundly thrashed by Baldwin, Mamola and company, wasn't so bad, for I finished third in the UK points standings.

By the time of the North West 200, 'Honda' was dominant: Ron headed the Duckams Superbike championship, whilst I led the Shellsport 500cc series. Then it all went badly wrong.

On the eve of North West practice I'd done a course inspection with event organiser Billy Nutt. At York Hairpin he asked if a particular telephone box should have a straw bale around it. Trying to make such a place safe is almost impossible anyway, but the box must have been 40 yards from the action so I didn't regard it as a particular risk. Come race day, I'm sat comfortably in third behind Alex George and Tony Rutter when, going into the same corner, a chain adjuster broke, locking the wheel. Barring heavenly intervention there was only one thing to do, so after bouncing past Tony, down I went – smack into the very telephone box I'd pronounced safe. It was ironic, but a long way from being the most important news: Tom Herron and Brian Hamilton were both killed in the same meeting. Frank Kennedy later died from injuries received in a pile-up at University bend, which also finished the careers of Kevin Stowe and Warren Willing.

My phone box was relatively unscathed but the medics diagnosed a cracked pelvis and broken ribs, which hurt like hell. It wasn't until the following day as I lay in bed feeling sorry for myself that I heard the news about Tom. He was one of racing's true good guys, a twinkly-eyed Irishman who always seemed to have a smile on his face and a kind word for everyone. He'd been a good friend and his loss hurt all of us.

After a few days of being a crabby patient I discharged myself from Coleraine Hospital and eventually made my way to the Isle of Man for the TT. The ACU knew all about my crash and insisted that an orthopaedic surgeon, Mr Beetson, had to clear me to race. I clattered into his office on crutches to learn I was in no state to ride in the early part of practice week.

'Come back in a few days,' he said. 'If you can't do a few press-ups and squats by then, you won't be riding.'

It didn't look promising but luckily I had a couple of allies. Anne Bashforth was a physiotherapist at Nobles Hospital, whilst her husband, Adrian, taught at King

William's College near Castletown. So I began an intensive course of treatment, with physio every day followed by hours swimming in the school pool. God knows how, but halfway through practice week I threw away my crutches and did my squats and presses for Mr Beetson. I don't think he truly believed I was fit to ride, but having said he'd pass me if I managed his exercises, he'd backed himself into a corner.

To make quite sure, he said that he'd take a helicopter to the Bungalow in the next practice session, where he'd assess me once again. I still had to be physically lifted on to the bike, but once on it wasn't too bad – except that the damage was mostly to the right side of my hip and I had no power at all on that side. When I stopped at the Bungalow I pleaded with the marshals, for heaven's sake don't let me fall that way. Beetson turned up, asked me how I was, and naturally I lied that everything was tickety-boo. One more chat back at the Grandstand – Beetson was a fine doctor, but he'd never make the grade at MI6 – and that was me cleared to race.

Getting the go-ahead was one thing. Actually coping with full race distance was another. Honda's new Formula One bike was just too big and heavy for me to handle comfortably, so Alex George rode it instead – winning by almost a minute from Charlie Williams. This would turn out to be Alex's best TT.

My first race of the week was Monday's Senior on the RG500. Although I knew Hailwood and Alex – riding the Cagiva 500 – would be my biggest rivals, my main concern was me. I'd no idea whether I was fit enough to finish the race. By the second lap I was surprised to be leading. Then the suspension began to go off, and when the crank broke on the third lap on the drop down to Kate's Cottage, it was almost a relief. I was in too much pain to have kept up that pace for six laps, and doubt I'd have even been able to finish them at all. Most of the Island didn't care very much either way, since their idol, Hailwood, won. When Alex dropped out, he led Tony Rutter home by over two minutes. But for once I'd been on the right Honda, the ones made by Suzuki: RG500s took the first four places.

By Friday's Classic I was feeling a bit stronger. Unfortunately the 996 Honda wasn't, despite Alex's sterling efforts at running it in the previous Saturday. Barry Symmons was a brilliant team manager, but he did tend to have his favourites and Ron Haslam was one. Besides, I don't think he really liked the idea of me riding at all, crocked as I was. In practice Ron's bike had suffered a misfire, which they hadn't been able to fix. In the race the misfire mysteriously migrated to my bike, so I got another DNF. They'd switched ignitions, which pissed me off a bit.

It was a heavy year for Carol, too. Whenever Nigel and Paul were in Japan with the NR, Bob Cox worked on my bikes in the UK, whilst Carol drove the van. After driving all the way to Salzburg, she wasn't best pleased when Gerald Davison and I took ourselves off to the bar. A while later she stomped in to say so. Unfortunately we'd inherited about a dozen bottles from the table's previous occupants, the contents of which Carol instantly assumed were now inside us. I expected a public dressing down, but instead she decided that what was sauce for the gander entitled her to catch us up. I think we were on only our second drink as she slid under the table.

The year ended with Ron winning the British Formula One championship. After busting my hip I didn't win a round until Cadwell Park in September, finishing the series third behind a young Kiwi hot-shot named Graeme Crosby. It had been an interesting season, for sure, but not a memorable one for results.

After breaking an ankle testing at Suzuka, 1980 began in much the same way as the previous year. What the press dubbed my 'season of mediocrity' took a turn for the worse when I couldn't agree a start money package for the North West. To my surprise and delight a bunch of fans made a fund-raising effort that allowed me to race. Winning for them on the RG was something to savour.

A week later Honda finally made a decision which made sense – for them if not for me. On the run-up to the TT they wrote to say they'd prefer it if I didn't ride my Suzuki on the Island. Although this ruled out a shot at the Senior, it would allow me a full-on go at the Formula One and Classic events on the big Honda, so I wasn't too disappointed.

The opening race must have been one of the most controversial ever run – at least until the Black Protest a year later. *Motor Cycle News* hack Norrie Whyte described it as the 'most bitchy' TT he'd ever seen.

The fuss began 20 minutes before the start, when Suzuki's top man, Graeme Crosby, moved from third on the grid to 11th, meaning he'd be starting alongside me. This had been OK'd by the organisers, but Honda objected that he was simply trying to use me for a free tow. Croz was told to move forward but refused. This isn't what you need before a race like the TT and he must have been in a right old state.

After that kerfuffle, the race wasn't much better. Conditions weren't good – fog banks on the Mountain and damp patches here and there. The big Honda coughed and spluttered so badly I almost retired at Ballacraine. After one lap I was in fourth place, but the misfire slowly improved and after two I took the lead. But in only his second year on the Island Croz was flying. Only a second behind after two laps, he edged two seconds ahead at half distance, but by then the Honda was finally running well. On lap five I got my head down and opened the gap, hanging on to take the flag 11 seconds ahead of him.

Unfortunately in all the excitement I'd forgotten something important. The largest fuel tank allowed by the regulations was 24 litres. For reasons best known to themselves Honda had sent me out with a 27-litre tank, but with bottles inside to reduce the actual volume available for fuel. They'd done exactly the same thing the year before when Alex won. At the time, this was perfectly legal – or, at least, a grey area – but I don't know why a company like Honda couldn't simply have come up with a pukka 24-litre tank.

To be on the safe side I'd been told to give the tank a thump – denting it to reduce its capacity – on the last lap on the run through Governor's Bridge, where no one would be looking, but I forgot. After all, when you're razzing around the Island, restyling your bike on the move isn't uppermost in your mind. It wasn't until I was cruising up the pit lane that Nigel spotted the oversight and mouthed something like, 'the tank, you wanker!' Well, that's no bother, I thought, and raised my arms in a mock victory salute and whacked them on the tank on the way down. It was never going to win an Olivier award for acting, because even Nigel raised his eyes to heaven and looked embarrassed. Unfortunately he wasn't the only one to notice the bad acting. Someone from Suzuki spotted it and the balloon went up.

As far as I was concerned, we'd won fair and square. The big tank didn't save a pit stop, didn't give us any advantage whatsoever. Croz took a different view. First he protested, then withdrew his protest. Then Gordon Pantall protested on behalf of his rider, Alan Jackson, who'd finished fourth. The results were put on hold until the race jury met the following day. Then they decided they needed until Tuesday to hear Honda's side of the case. Eventually, the protest was overruled and the result stood. But from then on the tank capacity rules were tightened up. And I never won an Oscar.

Although there were always jokes about me being tight or being dodgy, I can say hand on heart that I've never outright cheated, although I've bent the rules as much as anyone else and maybe more. But, despite all the allegations, I've never run a big engine. In fact I bent a lot more rules as a team manager than I ever did when I was riding.

With hindsight I suppose I should have questioned the instructions to bash the tank, but at the time I was just doing as I was told. Croz, not surprisingly, wasn't at all happy. He even threatened to throw away his second-place laurels, and I can't say I altogether blame him.

Two years ago Croz and I were guests at a chat show in Ireland. Prior to that, whenever we were on stage together Croz would flog me with the tank-bashing episode, and always had the upper hand because I always felt myself to be guilty – because I was guilty, although not quite in the way Croz seemed to believe. This time, Billy McCosh, who was a good friend to the pair of us, took Croz aside and gave him the full background to the affair, which I'd never done because coming from me it would have just sounded like an excuse for the inexcusable. Suddenly there was a completely different atmosphere between us. It took almost 30 years but we cleared it up eventually.

A rivalry of a different sort also surfaced in the Classic race at that same TT. I knew a little of Joey Dunlop, mainly from the NW200, which was on his home turf and where he was already a tough customer. Of course he'd already beaten George Fogarty in the Schweppes Jubilee Classic race in 1977. But since none of the big names were in that event, the established guys didn't take it all that seriously. Maybe we should have. After all, he'd posted the third-fastest lap in TT history from a standing start on treaded tyres, which ought to have told us something about what was to come.

To be perfectly frank we were probably a bit dismissive about him, a bit smug. In practice he'd struggled to place sixth, with a best lap of 108mph. He just wasn't on my radar. What I didn't know was that for the whole of practice week his Yamaha's rear-wheel spacers were back-to-front, throwing out the wheel alignment. The bike must have handled like a pig.

Above all, we saw ourselves as a well-drilled, well-financed official factory squad, whilst Joey was practically skint – and looked it: scruffy, with equally scruffy crew who seemed to spend half their time pissed in the 'Irish Embassy', and not a corporate logo between them. And John Rea's 750 Yamaha looked as big a mess as he did. There was obviously no way he could be any sort of threat – which is probably what Custer said of Sitting Bull before Little Big Horn.

Even without Irish help, the 1980 TT turned out to be a bit of a nightmare for us. We always had incessant problems with the Formula One bike's carburetion, which in turn meant that we had difficulty setting up the gearing for the intermediate-gear corners, since it wouldn't drive cleanly through. Eventually, we got it something like – until the night before the race when, unknown to me, Honda's top technical man, Mr Ika, replaced the chain and sprockets with some new heavy-duty kit. It looked like something off a tractor but, more importantly, changed the overall gearing.

For the first couple of laps of the Classic race, I was all over the place. At corners like Ginger Hall second gear was too low, third too high, so it was a real struggle to get through fast. At first I thought the problem was me so I kept nagging at myself to calm down, but after a while realised I was fine – it was the bloody ratios that were wrong.

Meanwhile, Joey's making hay. While we had the most high-tech quickfillers in the pit lane, Joey's boys had bodged together the biggest fuel tank you've ever seen. It may have been ugly, but it held eight gallons and saved him a fuel stop – and the quickest fillers in existence can't beat that. Leaving Ballacraine for the last time, my signals said I was less than a second behind and I still thought I was in with a chance. But Joey's last lap was phenomenal – the first at 115mph – and he won by 20 seconds. So now it was my turn to mutter 'bastard', just as Hailwood had done to me five years before. For years Joey described this as the most satisfying of all his TT wins, being 'tickled pink because he'd out-witted all the factory boys' – as well as being able to dedicate it to the memory of his greatest racing friend, Merv Robinson, who'd been killed at the NW200 just the previous month. And you have to hand it to him and his crew: they turned us over, even though we gave them a bit of help.

Yet I still believe that I could have won that race if the bike had been set up as it had finished practice. I wasn't happy and told Mr Ika so. Ironically he was actually signalling for me on the approach to Ballacraine – another corner I couldn't get right. If I'd known at the time that the gear problem was his doing, I might have been tempted to stop and lamp him with his signal board.

I now knew Joey was someone to be taken seriously, even though he didn't seem to tick many of the usual boxes. My next encounter with him was a couple of months later at the Ulster Grand Prix, the last round of the new World Formula One championship. This was a series Joey would make his own for most of the Eighties, but in '80 it was a bit of a Mickey-Mouse affair over only two rounds. After that acrimonious Formula One TT result, the title was between me and Croz, meaning I stood a few points to the good. At the last minute Suzuki drafted in Joey to ride as Croz's team-mate. Their plan was that if Joey could ride shotgun to finish between Croz and me, Croz would take the title.

My chaperone was Ron Haslam, who was supposed to do the same job for me that Joey would be doing for Croz. As usual the big Honda had its chronic carb problems, which this time I managed to make even worse. We had a choice of big or small carburettors, and with the big ones there was such a huge flat-spot I just couldn't get it out of the Dundrod hairpin, even with lots of clutch abuse. So for the race I opted for the smaller carbs. Now it came out of the hairpin like a missile, but Croz and Joey just sailed past down the long straights. It must have been the first time in Joey's career that he'd ever been asked to lose a race, but he understood perfectly and did a great job. I'm not sure which set-up Ron used, but it did neither of us much good because Ron did everything he could before sliding off whilst trying to let me through at the hairpin. Although he remounted to finish fourth, the game was up. Joey crossed the line a bike-length behind his team-mate but 20 seconds ahead of me.

So Suzuki's plan worked perfectly. Left to his own devices Joey could have won easily, I've no doubt. But he rode to orders and let Croz take maximum points for the win, whilst my third place left me two points behind in the final world championship standings. Mind you, Suzuki dropped an even bigger clanger than I did. Having done everything right so far, they let Honda sign Joey from under their noses for the following season, a decision they had another 20 years to regret.

Joey was on fire that day, dominated practically every race as his Irish fans went nuts with delight. He'd kicked off by winning the 250 race from Donnie Robinson and Ray McCullough, then the Classic race from Roger Marshall's TZ750 with a record lap at 118.95mph. Droning around shepherding Croz must have seemed easy.

The thing I could never get my head round with Joey was that he was never a hit on short circuits. He obviously had all the ability but rarely put it together on purpose-built tracks. I sometimes wonder if he'd have gone better if they'd lined the track with stone-effect wallpaper, because the hairier it looked the better he seemed to ride. And it's true that he very rarely crashed. Ironically he sustained his worst injuries at 'safe' Brands Hatch in a crash that wasn't even his fault. The only short circuit I can remember having serious bother with him was at Aghadowy. I'd no idea why we even went there, and I wouldn't have bothered going if I'd known I was going to high-side trying to keep up with him.

Because riders start separately at the TT, you don't have the same sense of head-to-head racing as you do elsewhere. So many of my biggest battles with Joey were at the North

West 200, which does have a mass start. He was a tough rider, but he was fair and didn't take daft risks. And as he grew more experienced he developed a rare canniness that sometimes gave him wins against the odds.

On the roads, he was something else. After I retired my favourite spot for spectating was on the outside at Cronk-ny-Mona, a really fast, tricky long left-hander leading into a blind entry to Signpost Corner. For a few years Joey was head and shoulders above everyone else through there. On the first lap he'd have both wheels drifting, pull out his usual advantage, and just cruise in control for the remaining laps. It was impressive, but there was always the suspicion that he had the best backing and the best kit.

Then came the 2000 TT and his first Formula One win since '88. On race day morning I'd just come in from the old fart's parade lap when Joey wandered over to ask if there were any damp patches he needed to know of. There were just a couple, which I told him about before going up to watch at my usual spot. In the race, Joey was unreal. For lap after lap his two-wheeled slides shook me rigid. And this from a bloke of 48. I'd had a lot of respect for him before and had grown to be fond of the man. But on that day my admiration for him shot up 200 per cent because I knew that there was no way on earth I could have done anything like that.

When Rob McElnea first went to the TT with the Suzuki team in 1983, a reporter asked Joey if he was worried about Rob. He answered that he was more worried about me, which was pretty flattering because by then I was well past my best. Mind you, Joey may have regretted his words because over the next two years Rob gave him some of the toughest races he's ever had on the Island. One of the greatest TTs ever must have been that year's Senior Classic, which I think was the race that turned Steve Hislop on to the TT, with Rob, Joey and Norman Brown going at it hammer and tongs and Rob emerging on top with Norman setting a new outright record of 116mph.

A year later Rob and Joey were at it again, Rob taking two wins to Joey's one – not that I contributed much to the excitement, droning around with a wrist broken at Donington Park, although I did manage third place in the Classic race. I can vividly remember Rob passing me on the Mountain Mile as though he had another 20 horsepower. Both Rob and Joey lapped at 118mph, and since I rode an identical bike I know just how impressive Rob's performance was. Rob's last TT exploit wasn't quite so grand – slinging a bike up the road at Sarah's Cottage during the centenary parade lap in 2007. James Whitham, who came through a few seconds later, told me he knew right away it must have been burly Rob who'd come off because of the size of the hole in the hedge.

Compared to someone like Sheene, I suppose I wasn't perfect PR material, although I always recognised the importance of this part of the sport and did my best. Without happy sponsors, after all, you'd soon have no sponsors and be out of a job. But not Joey Dunlop. He regarded the press as only slightly preferable to bubonic plague and was never someone you could promote in the normal way, as Honda later found. And yet he had his own sort of grass-roots charisma and developed a huge following despite – or more likely, because of – being the opposite of every marketing man's dream. Today, half the world seems obsessed with celebrity. Joey thrived as the ultimate anti-celebrity.

Joey and I became quite good friends. As a rider he respected me, I think, and I certainly came to respect him. You couldn't help but warm to his unassuming nature, but he was very shy and private – not a bloke it was easy to know. In his early career, especially, he didn't say much and, because of his thick Ulster accent, what he did say you could barely understand. He loosened up a bit after a drink (which, come to think of it, was a lot of the time).

Yes, Joey liked a drink. Throughout the mid-Eighties, Vila Real in Portugal hosted a round of the Formula One world championship. Joey liked Vila Real – partly because he usually won there, partly because the event sponsor was a major wine manufacturer. One year the event happened to fall on my birthday, so I was enjoying a quiet celebratory drink outside a café with Carol and Nigel, when down the rode strolls Joey.

'What ye celebratin'?'

When I explained that it was my birthday, Joey needed no encouraging to join us and bought a round of local brandies. From there it was all downhill. Joey was no slouch with a bevvy and Nigel can drink for England, so the two of them went at it with tumbler after tumbler of brandy, while I poured most of mine into a nearby pot plant. Eventually, Carol and I left them to it.

They were still at it hours later when Joey decided this was the ideal opportunity to brush up on his circuit learning, which he preferred to do at night. Being the sort of bosom buddy only drunks can become, Nigel joined him as he slithered around the Vila Real circuit, fag in one hand, bottle in the other. At 11.00 the following morning we happened to pass Joey's hotel, which was hard to miss because a hire car with both front doors open was parked literally halfway up the front steps. When Joey finally did emerge he was not a well man – but the bastard still went on to win the race. They don't make them like Joey any more.

Back in Britain in 1980, my sights, and Honda's, were firmly on the British Formula One championship. Although I was still riding my RG500, and sometimes Syd Griffiths's TZ750, Formula One was definitely the priority. This was another series in which Suzuki were the big threat. Reg Marshall pushed me hard early on. Later in the series Croz and Graeme McGregor were drafted in to bolster the Suzuki team, but I got solid results all year and was odds-on to take the title.

In the penultimate round at Cadwell Alex George gave me the payback from 'borrowing' my bike to win the '79 TT. Alex was always a hard man and when on form, a real goer. We'd rubbed shoulders for much of the previous decade, starting on Yamaha twins when his dad, a raw Glaswegian who was even tougher, used to help him out at meetings. I'd never imagined he'd be the least bit superstitious, but as we lined up on the grid he sidled over to ask a favour. I'd qualified fifth, Alex fourth, a row ahead.

'Help me out here,' he said. 'I can't start number four, it's my unlucky number. Would you mind swapping places?' Was this really Alex George?

There was obviously only one answer. Whether gaining a row made a difference, I don't know. But it didn't do any harm. I finished third behind Croz and Noddy Newbold, giving me an unbeatable 20-point lead in the series. Croz won the final round at Brands Hatch to pip Reg for second place. Young Ron, who'd had some scintillating rides but was unlucky with breakdowns and too inconsistent, finished fourth.

CHAPTER 15

THE LOST YEAR

That 1980 Brands Powerbike meeting was more memorable for other reasons than the Formula One championship. For the previous couple of months rumours had been flying that my future with Honda was mainly in the past. At Brands they stopped being rumours. There was still nothing official from Honda, but Gerald had taken me aside – ironically on the second anniversary and at the very same circuit where he'd first offered me the Honda job. Apparently it was '90 per cent sure' my contract would not be renewed. Apparently I was past it.

It was maybe the bitterest pill I'd had to swallow in racing, but getting sacked is a fact of life, so I made as light of it as I could. My *Motor Cycle Weekly* column a week later was headed 'Santa comes early – with the sack'. But the news hit me hard. I'd won that year's TT for Honda, given them the British Formula One crown, and whoever was to blame for the NR500 fiasco, I was pretty sure it wasn't me.

Over the following weeks I had two or three offers for 1981 (there's nothing like a newspaper column for advertising your availability), although none was the complete package. After five years as a factory rider, becoming a privateer again wasn't my first choice. Kawasaki's Alec Wright and I had serious talks on three occasions, but the drawback was their lack of a Formula One bike. Eventually I settled on a fairly messy arrangement: I'd ride John Newbold's factory Formula One Suzuki and an RG500 at the TT (as team-mate to Croz, which could be interesting); for the rest of the season I'd arranged a 1,025cc F1 Harris Suzuki via David Dixon, the British Yoshimura importer, and Steve Harris. On the shorts I'd have Syd Griffiths' TZ750 Yamaha again, along with a 350 Granby Yamaha for the British George Beale series.

As for Honda, I'm still waiting to hear whether I got the sack, although I was offered a parting bonus from Gerald. One day he rang me, sounding pleased as punch. The gist of it was that I'd had a good run but it was time to pack in on a winning note – so he'd taken it upon himself to organise my retirement party. It was this that finally tipped me off that I probably wouldn't be Honda's star man for '81. That kept me going for the next five years. From then on, every time I beat a Honda would be a special bonus.

I'd been with Kawasaki for four years and Honda for two, with regular pay cheques from both. Then suddenly on 1 January there was no money at all coming in. Every racer must suffer reversals like this and maybe I should have seen it coming, but it was a major shock to the system and I was really down in the dumps.

Down as I was, I was still a long way from the knacker's yard. Gerald Davison may have had a bit of a point: my best days were behind me. My peak had probably been two or three years before in the Kawasaki years. But so what? I could still ride and I had stacks of experience. Maybe I was past my best but I hadn't the slightest doubt that I'd still be competitive, especially on the Isle of Man.

At least I knew I could rely on my mechanics – Nigel, as ever, and Bob Cox – even though I'd be paying them from my own pocket. In this and other ways, my factory years had spoiled me. As a works rider you simply climb on a bike someone else has bought, prepared by mechanics he's also underwriting, and pay for almost nothing bar the odd beer and meal out. Yet by the time I was halfway through my privateer season, I was reeling from the cost of it all.

After a frantic week or two throwing it together, we first tested the Yoshimura Suzuki at Donington in

February. It was bitterly cold and hard to evaluate the bike but, apart from a mid-range flat spot, I reckoned it could be pretty competitive and the easiest four-stroke I'd ever ridden. How wrong can you be?

At Daytona a flare-out from the tank turned the bike into a fireball at around 170mph on the banking. Plumes of flame were spewing around my backside and for about 50 yards behind me on the track. There was a stark choice between jumping off or becoming a toasted marshmallow, so I baled out pretty quickly. I wasn't badly hurt but damage to the bike saddled me with a £3,000 bill.

It was the only time all week I got even close to being on fire. Trying to compete with Daytona's hot-shots had shown up the Yoshi's faults. It was a big, ponderous lump with almost no feel. I'd have got more feedback from a brick.

Back in England it was no better. I failed to finish at all in the first leg at Cadwell in early April, struggling into sixth in the second behind Dave Potter. A spiky young Aussie named Wayne Gardner had won that first race. He, more than me, knew what it was to be a privateer. His only wheels were a battered Austin 1800 with bald tyres, which for a while he even used as a caravan. If nothing else, I suppose it was an incentive to do well. Adding insult to injury, I was dropped from the home team for the Easter Transatlantic series – which seemed a bit rich considering I was a reigning British champion. OK, I'd been a flop the previous year – but riding a bike I'd never sat on before, with a broken ankle.

The difference was that the Yoshi was a brick for which I was paying the bills, which gives you an altogether different attitude. The damage from Daytona was the worst all season, but there were plenty of other expensive episodes. I vividly remember chasing Sheene at Scarborough and falling off big-time near the café on top of the plateau. For the previous five years I wouldn't have cared less what damage the bike did to itself, just so long as I landed somewhere soft. Not this time. As I slid along on my arse watching the bike tumbling down the road, I was already doing the inventory in my head … fairing … ching! £80 … tank … ching! £120 … forks … ching! £500. Sliding along had never been so painful where it hurts a Yorkshireman the most – in the pocket. By the time I got to my feet I was groggy from all the mental arithmetic.

In contrast to the big Suzuki the 350 Yamaha was a gorgeous bike. It taught me so much about running two-strokes that, if I'd known the same eight years earlier, I'd have been streets ahead of the rest. We'd throw in new pistons for every race, then practise on the 'old' pistons and rings at the next meeting. From the start we used a German Hoeckle crankshaft, which is not only designed to be rebuilt but is also stronger and straighter than the standard item so the bike vibrates less. The three of us spent a lot of time lightening the bike, and Bob was brilliant at setting up its Powerjet carbs.

The 350cc Beale series was hot that year, with Graeme McGregor, Keith Huewen, Charlie Williams and Jeff Sayle all battling for honours. I opened my account by winning from Macca and Heuwen in the opening round at Donington before missing a few rounds and finishing fourth in the series. For reasons which escape me but probably had something to do with money, I was also riding a GSX1100 Suzuki in the Streetbike Challenge. This was even more futile than Formula One, since nobody got near Honda's CB1100R all year. I think my best finish was second.

Apart from the odd blip, my results on the big bike were pathetic – like a ninth at Donington in June. I couldn't remember the last time I'd finished so far down a domestic field. The only bright spot looked like being the TT – then still a big deal for the factories, especially Honda and Suzuki. As a proven TT runner it was always likely I'd be approached, much as the likes of John McGuinness and Guy Martin are now, and Suzuki signed me up for the fortnight – as team-mate to the same Croz I'd so brassed off the year before.

As well as Nigel, in my Suzuki GB crew was a huge bearded Aussie guy called Mick Smith who'd been with Croz the previous year. Naturally enough he felt more camaraderie to Croz than he did to me, so didn't object when they pinched a few bits from my bike for his. Maybe he'd been listening to Croz mouthing off the week before about Suzuki giving me too much support for the TT, although I'd always thought this was tongue-in-cheek. One of these bits was the petrol tank, which was wonderfully ironical considering the shindigs the previous year. No problem: I got a brand new one. Better still, my bike was a real peach – Randy Mamola's regular grand prix bike.

It was an astonishing tool. At Rhencullen, for instance, if you didn't make an exaggerated effort to take the jump absolutely dead straight and upright, most bikes would tie themselves in knots. But not this one. Whatever angle you took off at, it was like a dart, straight and true. When we'd first got it, it was way too rich and wouldn't pull top gear, but during practice week Mamola's mechanic, Gerry 'Blossom' Burgess, came over to set up the carburetion. By race day I knew that if I couldn't win on this, there was something wrong with me.

In the race I first noticed something wasn't quite right when I got to Quarter Bridge, grabbed a handful of front brake and got an electric shock. The new tank was shorting on the coils, which were mounted just beneath. Maybe it was some sort of factory aversion therapy. If I braked less, I'd lap faster – obviously. On the other hand, Pavlov's dogs never won a TT.

Braddan Bridge … ouch! It stung.

I tingled my way as far as Kirkmichael, by which time I'd had enough of getting belted every time I wanted to slow down. So I dropped into the Shell garage just before Rhencullen, borrowed a can of WD-40 and blathered everything I could with this stuff. It didn't make a blind bit of difference. Sparky the Battery Boy does the TT.

Before the race Carol and I had done a lap in the car. On the Mountain you could barely see the edge of the road for fog, and when I got back to the paddock I pleaded that conditions were too dangerous to race. When they started the race I assumed conditions must have got better. They hadn't. By the Mountain Mile I was back in the worst pea-souper I'd ever seen for a race. Whilst this at least meant I didn't have to use much in the way of brakes so wasn't getting so many belts, it was a ridiculous state of affairs. At the end of the lap I called into the pits, pulled off my helmet – my hair was probably still standing on end – and grabbed one of the old Bakelite pit telephones.

It must have looked an odd pit-stop. Nigel's jabbering 'what's happening, what's happening?' in one ear whilst I'm on the phone with the other trying to get Ken Shierson, the ACU secretary on the line.

'The coils ... the bloody coils ... they're shorting ...'

'... Oh, sorry Ken, I was talking to Nigel ...'

'... But if anyone's hurt in this race, it's down to you mate.'

Forget visibility for the helicopters – it's more fundamental than that. If each marshalling post can't see the next one, then how can you possibly race with any measure of safety? It astounds me. The TT authorities are paranoid about negative media coverage at the best of times, but heaven knows what Fleet Street would have made of a rider needlessly dying of injuries because no one had seen him crash. That's exactly the sort of publicity the TT doesn't need.

A few years later when Formula One went to 750cc, Suzuki's bike was seriously fragile. When I blew a crank just before the final right-hander on the Mountain Mile, the engine blathered most of its oil on to the road, so I ran back down the track to get an oil flag. The nearest marshal's post was a tiny speck in the distance, but the marshal spotted me waving – and waved back. Not 'til I'd stood jumping and yelling in the middle of the road for the best part of five minutes did the penny drop and out went the red and yellow flag.

The plain fact is that to marshal the TT course to the standard of a British Superbike meeting, where you practically slide into a medic every time you fall off, you'd need just about every spectator on the Island on marshal duty. It's simply not realistic. A rider has to accept it as it is, and decide – or not – whether to do it. But what absolutely isn't acceptable is for a fallen rider to be lying in a ditch and nobody knowing about it. Today, that probably couldn't happen. But for years, it certainly could.

Luckily this time no harm was done. In the 40 seconds or so it took me to get to Quarter Bridge, the red flags had gone out to stop the race. Chris Guy, who was leading at the time, must have been very browned off, but it simply wasn't safe to race. In Tuesday's re-run all the luck went my way. Poor Chris slid off at Braddan while lying fourth in tricky, damp conditions. Charlie Williams was the biggest threat until a handlebar fell off his YZ500 going into the 33rd, which probably beats even 5,000 volts as a wake-up call. Although I lost third gear halfway through the race and for a while doubted the 'box would last the distance, Donny Robinson, my closest challenger, was struggling with clutch slip and I won comfortably. As it was, the last lap and a half was dodgy enough, with rain showers and the back slick spinning up everywhere.

By this time Honda had got the major sulks. In Saturday's Formula One race my team-mate, Croz, had problems on the grid and dropped back down the line to be last away. The first I knew of this – or not, because the commentators seemed as baffled as anyone else – was a signal from Carol at the Gooseneck: 'Minus 7, Croz Out'. If I had any thought of capitalising on the information, they petered out a lap or two later when I missed a gear at the same spot and mangled a few of the Suzuki's valves.

But Croz wasn't out at all. He hammered through the field and from start to finish was two minutes faster than anyone else, averaging almost 112mph. Trouble was, this wasn't how the timekeepers saw it: they timed Croz from the moment he ought to have started, giving Honda's Ron Haslam the win.

I've no idea why it caused such confusion. It wasn't a new situation. Both me and Charlie Williams, and no doubt many others, had delayed our starts in the past for similar reasons, and were timed from when we actually crossed the start line, not when we should have set off. Not surprisingly, Suzuki's Martyn Ogborne put in a protest and after a tense delay the tie-and-blazer brigade declared Croz the winner. Job done. Good on yer, mate.

Yes, I felt sorry for Ron, who for 2½ hours had thought he'd won the race. But as far as I was concerned Croz hadn't cheated, hadn't gained any advantage – quite the opposite, since he'd had to carve through the entire field – and was the fastest man on the day. Honda didn't quite see it that way. They were fuming. There was talk of them pulling out of the rest of race week. Then rumours of protests began to drift around the Island.

Honda have always tended to over-react to situations like this, but we were all pretty gobsmacked at the form it took when they finally lined up for Friday's Classic TT. Honda Britain were always red, white and blue. But not any more. Today they were black – bikes, leathers, helmets, moods, the whole shooting match. If it hadn't been so funny (for obvious reasons I wasn't Honda's biggest fan at the time), it would have been pathetic. Barry Symmons's justification was along the lines that in 75 years of TT racing the organisers had got nowhere so Honda were wearing the livery they'd have worn then. Pathetic. Didn't he know that Scott riders wore purple back in 1911?

Joey, Ron and Alex, Honda's three riders, hated it. Alex has since told me it was his worst day in racing which, considering some of the get-offs he's had, says a lot. And

I didn't see how it could do any good. If Honda won in black, they'd look like a bunch of whingeing smart-arses; if they lost, they'd just look ridiculous. Above all I felt sorry for the riders – not least because I've never in my career raced in brand new, stiff leathers, especially for a two-hour race. It wasn't even safe. The TT is already one of the most pressurised races any rider could tackle, and to add to the stress in this way was plain daft. A sports psychologist was definitely not consulted.

On the start line neither Gerald nor Barry were to be seen.

'Where's Barry?' someone asked.

'Down at Quarter Bridge painting the white lines black,' claimed some wag.

Naturally – there is a god, even in racing – they lost.

Joey, bless him, just did what he did best – go for it. He was flying. After one lap he trailed Croz by five seconds. Next time around he broke his own lap record and finally overhauled Croz on lap three. But he must have been really caning the Honda because their fuel calculations went to pot and he ran out on the climb from Hillberry. Apparently at the moment he was eagerly expected at the pits I arrived down the Glencrutchery Road instead, to a general groan of disappointment from all the Joey fans in the grandstand. Me and Croz weren't groaning, though – we'd seen him pushing.

Somehow Joey part coasted, part pushed to the pits, took a swig of lemonade and charged off again full of red mist. I don't know what brand of pop it was, but I want some: from Ballacraine to Ballacraine he was timed at 19:22 – around 117mph, 2mph faster than his own record. Maybe he was pushing the bike too hard, because a lap later he retired at the Gooseneck with a broken cam chain. Honda's misery was completed when Ron retired with ignition trouble, leaving Alex the top Honda rider – in fact the only Honda in the top ten – in third place.

For the final lap Croz and I knew we had it in the bag and showboated around together for a Suzuki one–two. I'll never know whether I could have matched his pace that day, since a missed gear going over Ballaugh on lap one had taken the edge off my engine. But, all things considered, it was the sweetest second place I've ever had.

My next Suzuki duty came in August at the Ulster Grand Prix, the deciding round of the Formula One world championship. I didn't arrive in the best of shape. A couple of weeks before, I'd fallen off a Norton 500T trials bike practising in woods near home. It was a nothing accident – the bike rolled backwards on a steep climb, and I was actually laughing until my left shoulder hit a tree and popped out of its socket. The local farmer, Nick Stancliff, drove me to hospital in my Subaru pick-up. All I could say was 'morphine, morphine, please give me morphine'. Eventually they got sick of me and knocked me out altogether to put the shoulder back in. Along with the right shoulder, cracked at Beckett's a couple of years earlier, it's never been right since.

Going into the Ulster Grand Prix, Croz, Ron and Joey were all in with a shot at the world title. Amidst all the controversy, Joey's third place in the Formula One TT had almost been forgotten, but on home turf he was hot favourite. This year it was my turn to ride shotgun – for Croz – but I didn't do much of a job. In wet but drying conditions Ron cleared off, winning fairly easily from Croz, with me another ten seconds down in third. Joey, much to everyone's surprise, was a disappointing fifth. Although this tied Croz and Ron on 27 points, the result gave Croz the world title again, so for once I was in the party pit.

That's the trouble with the Irish: they party too well. At about 4.30 I dragged myself away from Hector Neill's Irish reels – and a few reels of my own – and staggered to my room. I can't have been under the covers for ten minutes before the group – led by Nigel, naturally – decided to move the party to my bed. I dimly remember an accordion and guitar and lots of leaping and yelling before the legs gave way. I woke up on the floor.

In my entire career I never won at Dundrod, and was never better than second best. For all that I was regarded as a road-race specialist, it's one of only two circuits I've never felt comfortable with, the other being the old Spa-Francorchamps. I never had much of an issue with Scarborough, the North West, or the TT, but the Ulster ... Going round places like Windmill Corner, which is completely blind yet fearfully quick, I always seemed to have half a mind wondering whether there was an accident in progress round the corner. I'd turned down Honda's offer of doing 24-hour races for the same reason. I couldn't hack the thought of all that potential oil from grenaded engines, invisible in the night.

My first outing at Dundrod was on my 250 and 350 Yamahas in '72 or '73. To be frank, by the time I'd scared myself half to death in practice I was only hanging around for the start money. I pulled in midway through the 350cc race claiming a misfire. On the 250 I rode the clutch every time I passed the pits and eventually pulled in with 'clutch slip'. I simply couldn't get my head round the place. I was freaked, I suppose – unlike Reg Marshall who loved the place every bit as much as Joey did. I can't account for it, because I always enjoyed the North West.

I regularly go to Spa now for their big classic meeting. Sometimes, I'll show people around the old circuit in the car. At balls-out corners like 'The Cocoas' – Burnenville – you'd be howling past houses, walls and Armco in a two-wheeled drift with half a dozen other nutters for company. Madness. How Sheene got round there at 137mph on an RG500 I've no idea. For anyone to suggest that the man had no bottle is ridiculous. Yet despite all those scary memories, the current Spa circuit is one of my favourites, anywhere.

By 1981 Spa was shorter and safer, and I very nearly rode there again. The Junior TT had been won by Steve Tonkin on a CCM/Armstrong, and there was talk of me backing up Clive Horton and Jeff Sayle on a similar bike in selected grands prix, as well as helping to set up the bike. We agreed that I'd ride Jon Ekerold's TT Armstrong at Spa, report my findings to CCM and take it from there for the rest of the season.

It was a major disappointment, 17kph down on the fastest bikes through the speed trap, and I struggled even to qualify. Swiss journalist Gunter Weissinger managed to wangle me an up-rated ignition from a pal in an Austrian team, but it made no difference. Once home, I put a proposal to CCM which would have helped my income, which by now had gone from plus to minus, but no deal followed. My final outing on the Armstrong was at the British Grand Prix at Silverstone, when I was having a great dice with Christian Estrosi until the engine lost power.

On the domestic Formula One front, if I wasn't exactly challenging lap records, at least I was getting nearer the action: a fourth and third at Snetterton in July, second at Mallory, rounding off the year with fourth in the Powerbike International. I finished the year about sixth in the championship, my worst performance for years.

I don't know who won the Formula One series – possibly Reg Marshall, possibly Gardner. It doesn't seem to matter because by then the man who had been leading the Superbike championship, Dave Potter, was dead after clouting the unprotected Armco at Oulton Park's Cascades. He'd won the Superbike title for the previous two years and on this day was as good as anyone in the UK – consistent, fast and safe. Ted Broad, his mentor and sponsor, always saw that his bikes were superbly prepared. Dave's death seemed to finish Ted with racing, for I don't think I've seen him from that day to this. Afterwards I happened to speak with the circuit doctor who attended Dave's crash. It put him off so much he said he'd never do a race meeting again.

Even without tragedies such as that, 1981 had proved a bitty and frustrating season. I can't remember a year in which I rode such a motley array of bikes – everything from the 250cc Armstrong to a lumbering GSX1100 Streetbike. Yet although I hadn't won anything of consequence, I'd had some good rides and still felt I had something to offer. If only I could find someone who'd foot the bills.

By mid-season I was about £26,000 out of pocket. As so often, it took a while for the penny to drop. In previous years I'd enjoyed a fairly pampered lifestyle without having to think about the cost. For the first half of the season I carried on much the same, until I realised I had to tighten my belt. From a money point of view, at least, my best years were over.

Unfortunately, ageism was also rearing its ugly head – not that I gave much thought to -isms at the time. By now I was 37 years old, which didn't bother me a great deal but seemed to bug everyone else. It seemed I could barely do an interview without questions being asked about being past it. Protesting that there was still life in the old dog yet only seemed to highlight the issue. It probably wasn't what potential employers wanted to read.

Still, largely thanks to the TT, I had a good 'in' with Suzuki, who would be expanding their race plans for 1982 under team boss Rex White. By November I had a pretty good idea I'd be included in their plans, and in December *Motor Cycle Weekly* splashed a picture of their new team across the entire front cover: Keith Huewen, Reg Marshall, Mark Boughton, Noddy Newbold, Paul Iddon … and Michael Grant.

I had one other thing to thank the press for – I think. Writing in the *Daily Express* on 17 June, John Parry had begun a news item about my TT performances with the magic words: 'Gritty Yorkshire motorcycle ace Mick Grant …'

So it was official. And pretty soon it caught on. Whatever else he was – tight-fisted, dodgy, past it – at long last the Gritty Tyke had arrived. And where there's grit, there's brass. Or so I hoped. Either way, it beat being called an old codger.

CHAPTER 16

'WE'VE COME TO GIVE
YOU PROTECTION'

For the past year or so the big talking point amongst top TT riders had been the ACU's new policy on start money, which they'd drastically reduced for regulars in order to entice new names to the Isle of Man. In 1981 there had been serious talk of five of us – Joey Dunlop, Alex George, Chas Mortimer, Charlie Williams and myself – boycotting the prizegiving ceremonies if a workable compromise couldn't be reached. I've no idea what the others were on, but I'd been promised £8,000 in '79, which Vernon Cooper tried to halve when I didn't finish a race. The word was that Jon Ekeröld, then 350cc world champion, had been offered £20k.

None of us had anything against talented newcomers, especially guys like Jon who were a credit to the event in every way. Jon was already a mate and, along with Takazumi, one of the TT newcomers who most impressed me over the years. Before the Senior I'd bet Jon £10 I'd make up ten seconds and catch him by Ballacraine on lap one. It was me who had to pay up.

Mind you, Jon wasn't typical. Sure, the races needed good new blood. But too many name riders were treating the handout as little more than a well-paid holiday. The 1981 event had also seen Boet van Dulmen get a pot of cash for two DNFs. Most notorious of all was America's Dale Singleton and his famous pet pig – which was only marginally slower than he was.

By the spring of '82 things were no better. It seemed almost unthinkable but in April I publicly threatened to miss the TT if the start money didn't improve. It wasn't something I wanted to do, but I had a living to earn and as far as I was concerned the ACU were taking the piss. The truth was that I could have earned more money doing international meetings on the Continent, and I'd had plenty of such offers. Amazingly, my hand was strengthened just a week later in a classic case of the right hand not knowing what the left was doing: the Isle of Man treasury invited me to a ceremony to introduce their commemorative 75th anniversary TT coins – and who's there on the back of the 50p piece, but me!

It wasn't enough. With the entry deadline looming, ACU boss Vernon Cooper announced that rebels like me had to enter, or get off the pot. I'm still not sure whether I'd been bluffing or not, but if I was, it was blown. So after Cooper promised that any money left in the pot after the races would come our way I sent off my TT entry. 'I'm a man of my word and Mick can take it from me that he will be looked after,' he told the *Daily Mirror*. I don't remember that amounting to very much, if anything.

The first big road meeting of the year, the North West 200, was one to forget. At Juniper Hill on the second lap of the Superbike race John Newbold clipped the back of my bike. In those days the bend was fast – the chicane wasn't put in until the following year – and poor Noddy didn't have a chance. Ron Haslam went on to win the race, not that any of us very much cared. Ron and Reg Marshall pulled out of the main NW200 race in sympathy. Both Joey and I rode after promising to donate our prize money to John's widow, Alison. Winning was hollow, but at least it did her a bit of good.

Both Reg and I knew we were in with a good chance at the TT. The new XR69 Formula One Suzukis were trick, super-quick and absolutely loaded with fancy factory bits. Unfortunately not all of them were suited to the lumps and jumps of the Mountain Course. I learned this going into Glentramman, when the new lightweight fairing fell off its mountings and jammed my hands against the clip-ons. Ahead of me was a line of ugly iron railings, which I was heading for at about 170mph on a bike I couldn't brake or steer. The bike slithered along in the gutter for maybe 300 yards, with me more passenger than rider. When I finally came to a halt I couldn't stop shaking. I don't think I've ever been so scared. Reg had exactly the same problem.

Otherwise practice went well, with me and Ron vying for the top of the leader board. So it was obvious where the challenge would come from, and I pushed as hard as I ever had from the start of the Formula One race. Even so, I was surprised to learn from my signals that I finished the lap with a new record, 20 seconds ahead of Joey, who was neck and neck with Ron. For a while it went perfectly. Then my brakes started to go off and an oil leak had me slithering about in the seat. I was still leading but Ron was gaining fast. Then the ignition packed in at Ramsey Hairpin. All I could do was take a seat in the sunshine and watch Ron take his first TT win. Joey, who'd had ignition problems of his own, came a distant second.

For Monday's Senior I had a standard Mk VII RG500 – nothing like as trick as the Mamola bike the year before, but definitely good enough. The first lap was a right ding-dong. At Ballacraine Charlie Williams and Jon Ekerold led, but by the Bungalow I'd eased narrowly ahead. First time past the pits the margin was a mere two seconds from Jon; Charlie, riding the ex-van Dulmen YZ500, had pulled out. By half distance I'd eked this out to 20 seconds, now from Dennis Ireland and Norman Brown. That was when it all went horribly wrong.

I'd recently done a piece in *Motor Cycle Weekly* saying the ACU should get their act together about the TT. Basically, they ought to decide whether it was a meeting for fast riders or slow riders, not both mixed together in one unholy mess as happened at the time. If they didn't, someone was going to get seriously hurt. This was an issue the ACU never did address – it wasn't until the Isle of Man itself took over the running of the event after 2002 that a concerted effort was made to weed out the wobblers.

Part of the ACU's problem was their desire to make the event look more international than it really was. British riders always had to reach a certain standard before they were allowed to compete in the TT, but many overseas federations were less demanding. As for the ACU, they didn't seem to care whether Joe Poloma was going round at walking pace, just so long as they could put Bolivia or Ulan Bator after his name in the programme. Even more recently, I know of one Antipodean rider who had never raced anywhere at all before his first TT. All he'd done was a few track days.

Over the years I'd had a few near-misses with much slower riders. It's hard to explain to the non-racer just how hairy it can be to hammer round a blind corner as fast as you can – so fast there simply is no physical possibility of changing line – when a much slower rider in front of you suddenly decides the line he's on is so much less attractive than the one ten feet to his left. At his speed, he can easily chop line, but if you're going 40mph faster, you simply can't. If his trajectory and yours coincide, there's precious little you can do to avoid a coming together which definitely won't do either of you any good.

I don't suppose I was thinking of this after three laps of the Senior. I'd have been aware that I had about 30 seconds lead, which meant that if I kept out of bother and made no mistakes, the race ought to be mine. Coming out of Ballacraine, by which time I was leading on the road, I saw a guy ahead of me going into Ballaspur. I remember being a bit puzzled – surely I couldn't have taken ten miles per lap out of anyone? Surely nobody's that slow? Oh yes they are.

Still, I knew he was there. Going into Doran's I gave him plenty of room and eased my pace a little. But I was still going 30 or 40mph quicker than him – when suddenly, for no apparent reason, he just turned left in front of me and I torpedoed the back of his bike. Photos later appeared of me literally riding pillion with him, with my Suzuki cartwheeling into the distance.

We weren't going anywhere like that, so down we both went, over the hedge and into the ditch on the other side of the road. I thought this must be it – the big one – but when I stopped tumbling I couldn't believe how lucky I was. My ribs were sore as hell but there wasn't much claret about – though the other guy was unconscious and seemed in a fairly bad way. In the air ambulance to Nobles Hospital I had to hold his drip to help keep him going.

I was still pretty furious about the whole business when I got back to the paddock and bumped into Vernon Cooper.

'I told you this was going to happen,' I said.

'What do you mean?'

'Well, I've just hit a bloke and for all I know he's dead. And it's your fault.'

He replied that it was the first time he'd heard of such a thing happening, just a one-off. It was yet another instance of the ACU's wishful thinking. If they crossed their fingers often enough, all the risks would just go away.

Afterwards I checked out the lap times. In the race I averaged 113mph. This guy's fastest lap was 85mph, a speed any half-competent rider could manage on a production 250 with 40bhp. He was riding an RG500 which, although it probably wasn't as well prepared as mine, would still have had at least 100 horsepower. Shamefully, it took another 20 years before the TT's organisers took the dangers inherent in these speed differentials seriously and barred the slowcoaches from the event.

Friday's Classic race rounded off a grotty week. I was still pretty sore from the Senior crash and struggled to get into a rhythm for the first lap, plodding around in sixth place. By then both Charlie and Ron had passed me on the road and any chance of a win seemed gone, although the second lap was better and I worked my way up to third – the perfect time for the Suzuki to lose a cylinder. Pulling off at Ballacraine to make what they used to call 'running repairs', I was fiddling with the plug leads when I noticed black smoke curling out of the exhaust. This seemed to be a hint that the bike was going nowhere of its own accord. A few minutes later I heard that Ron and Charlie were also out. The race had been there for the taking, and that's what Dennis Ireland did.

The guy I'd collided with – the German Gerhard Kanehl – had a fractured skull, some brain damage and was ill for months. I never went to see him – there was no point, he was unconscious. And, although to outsiders it might seem callous, reminding yourself of what can happen if things go pear-shaped isn't something many racers really want to do. Naturally I was upset that I hurt this guy, but angry, too, that such a situation had been allowed to happen – and glad I wasn't a privateer paying my own bills, for the bike was a total write-off.

Gerhard made some sort of recovery. He must have, because months later I got a threatening letter from him. If he hadn't been daft in the head before the crash, he certainly seemed to be now. Basically he was saying I'd deliberately tried to kill him. His logic, such as it was, was that I'd mistaken him for Jon Ekerold since they wore similar-coloured leathers.

Apparently I was so incensed about Jon's start money that I decided to bump him off, and the obvious way to do this was ride a bike into him at 120mph. The fact that Jon and I were mates, that my last reference to him in print was that 'He'll be one of the stars who'll earn his start money' evidently had nothing to do with it. Nor did the fact that I'd most likely get just as mangled as him.

Anyway, Gerhard's mad-cap theory made sense to him. But it needn't be a problem. The whole unfortunate business could be fixed amicably if I paid him umpteen thousand Deutschmarks to leave me alone. Alternatively, in his equally reasonable way, he'd bump me off. Rumour also seemed to have spread that Kanehl had actually been killed in the crash, so some of his compatriots were also joining in on the act. They were much more reasonable – they didn't want my money, just my head.

Unfortunately the German authorities were taking this crackpot's ravings seriously. I couldn't go to Germany for fear of arrest for attempted manslaughter or rape by motorcycle, or whatever charge they'd dreamed up. Not being able to race in the biggest country in western Europe could have been a bit of a problem for me and for Suzuki, so I asked the ACU, my own racing federation who're supposed to care for the interests of British riders, if they could get this idiot off my back.

Now anyone who's had dealings with them will know that the ACU was not the most 'can do' of organisations, so I can't say I was very surprised that they decided it was all my problem and nothing to do with them.

OK, I responded, I'll get my people to sort it out. And when we have, we'll sue you, because we have clear evidence that we warned you about this sort of tragedy before it happened and you did nothing at all about it.

That seemed to strike some sort of chord. About three days later a letter arrived saying they'd put their barristers on the case. Eventually it was sorted out.

At the end of the season Reg departed for Honda, to be replaced at Suzuki by a burly lad from Humberside who'd just turned 23: Rob McElnea. Fifteen years his senior, I was retained with the team for what the *Daily Mirror* described as my 'final fling'. My priority, yet again, was the World Formula One title. The joke in the paddock was that Suzuki were preparing a special bike for me, based on a Zimmer frame.

There was a funny old start to 1983. For more than a decade the traditional highlight of the early season was the Easter Match Race series against the USA. Three years earlier, I'd had what *Motor Cycle News* called a 'dismal' performance riding with a broken ankle, and hadn't made the team since. We'd all been trounced and for a time it bugged me that I seemed to have been made the scapegoat. Despite some misgivings about the event, there are few chances in bike racing to represent your country, and I'd been proud to do so.

Easter must have been late that year, since there was plenty of racing beforehand. I got off to such a flier that I was hard for the Match Race selectors to overlook. By winning first time out on the latest XR69 at Mallory, apparently I 'cocked a snook at the Match Race selectors', according to the press. At Donington the same month – Christ, was it cold? – I dead-heated with Reg Marshall for second place behind Gardner. At Brands for the Transnational series a couple of weeks later I was leading fairly comfortably before losing the front into Druids. Most of us were on slicks when it began to drizzle, so I wasn't the only one: by the end, Gardner was about the only man left standing.

A day later at Oulton I got my tyre choice right on a drying track and cleared off. Donington – better still: first from new team-mate Rob Mac. By the finish, only he, Gardner and Trev Nation were on the same lap. 'Grant blasts back!' screamed *Motor Cycle News*. It felt good, although to be honest I never thought I'd been away. Within days I was back in the Match Race team.

Then it all went pear-shaped. Two weeks later, at Donington again, I was leading the *MCN* Masters race when I slung it away at Coppice, which is never a small crash. I wasn't too badly knocked about, but fractured my left wrist. Although I practised at Oulton for the opening rounds of the Transatlantic series two weeks later, I was in too much pain to be competitive. If I'd been riding just for me, maybe I'd have toughed it out, but carrying a crocked rider wasn't fair to the team.

My disappointment was Rob Mac's big opportunity, for he was drafted into the squad instead. Not that it did him much good – he binned it, breaking some bone or other. That meant Suzuki GB's two front Formula One runners were both sidelined: at Oulton Sheene was hurriedly brought in to replace us on our bikes, his first four-stroke ride for five years.

There wasn't much chance of Barry doing the NW200, so I had to be fit. On the eve of the meeting I put the plaster in a vice, twisted it off and went for my pre-race medical. One firm handshake with the event doctor and I was pronounced fit to practise. I assumed that was that, and managed to put the Formula One bike third on the grid, but the organisers had obviously had a rethink. When Tom Herron was killed at Juniper Hill four years before, he'd also been nursing arm injuries from a crash at Jarama. Two hours before racing began, my permission to ride was withdrawn. I didn't like it – apart from anything else, it cost me my start money – but they were obviously playing safe.

So were the Manx authorities, although it wasn't my wrist they were bothered about. I'd hardly stepped off the plane at Ronaldsway airport before two sinister-looking guys in suits sidled up to me. I wasn't smuggling anything, so wondered what was up.

'Mr Grant?' they asked.

'Yes, that's me. What can I do for you?'

'We've come to give you protection.'

'Protection? From what?'

'We've had another letter from Germany threatening to kill you.' Apparently a bunch signing themselves '5 your TT visitors' were after me following the Kanehl incident the previous year.

I told them thanks, but it was all daft. If they'd been serious, it would already have happened by now.

In truth I never took the threats seriously, regarding the whole episode as more bizarre than dangerous. To the press I shrugged it off, saying they'd have to get past Carol first. But I could have done without it. There are enough risks in bike racing without worrying about spectators with a homicidal grudge. The most comical event in the whole saga came on my first practice lap. I was hammering the Suzuki flat stick up the hill from Union Mills when something walloped me on the shoulder hard enough to make me feel like throwing up. My first reaction was that Gerhard was in a hedge bottom throwing rocks at me. Then I remembered that rocks don't have blood and feathers the way this rock had – but seagulls do, and he was unlikely to be chucking them. Frozen chickens, maybe, but not herring gulls.

By and large, though, homicidal Germans are the least of your worries around the Mountain Course. Once you'd got a bit of a name there, one of the downsides came from the fact that even in practice you set off in pairs – and often there would be someone alongside you looking for a tow. With some riders, it wasn't so bad. But others would be so hyped-up they'd over-ride the bike, tie themselves in knots and trip you up.

There's no doubt that the quickest way to go round the Island is to feel you're *not* going at your quickest. That became clear to me in 1972, riding for Padgett's, when I was very much up-and-coming and by no means the finished article. In the 350 race, Ago led by a street, with me and Tony Rutter vying for the minor places. For the first three laps it was wet enough to be slippery all the way round. The previous year the fastest Junior lap in similar conditions was Phil Read at a shade over 100mph, and even Ago's fastest in the Senior was only 104mph. I was only seconds shy of 100mph – close, but no cigar.

I was racing, but cautiously, and as the roads began to dry in the last couple of laps I began to get hurry-up signals because I was losing time on Rutter. It was like flicking a switch marked 'banzai' and I went potty. I had my feet off the pegs at the bottom of Bray Hill, hit the bank at Laurel Bank and came off the jump at Ballaugh with my little legs flapping in all directions. And all that for a lap at 99mph. But at least I got away with it and learned a valuable lesson.

Dave Hiscock was one who tagged on to me in practice, but the most memorable was Klaus Klein, who was a lovely, lovely man but German, and therefore a bit odd. At the beginning of one session he just parked near the start line and refused all efforts to move him until I'd lined up for my practice lap. So I knew I was going to have company. The trick then, as now, is to brake early into all those three- and four-apex corners and get a strong drive all the way through. The opposite is to slither in short-circuit style, park the bike barely under control, get through the rest of the bend any-old-how and come out one gear lower and 15mph slower – precisely Klaus's approach. I'm sure he thought he was helping us both to put in a fast lap, because he was certainly trying … rushing up the inside and getting into all sorts of tangles.

Meanwhile, I'm spitting feathers at this Teutonic nitwit messing me about. By the time we got to Ramsey it was obvious – to me, at least – that the lap was a write-off. In Klaus's head the opposite was true: here he was overtaking the lap record holder at every other corner, so he must be on for a cracking time. For pride's sake as much as anything, by the top of the Mountain I'd decided to really put the hammer down for the dive down to Douglas and show him who was boss. But as it turned out it didn't matter. As we came out of the 32nd, my engine blew. Klaus must have been right behind me, because before I could pull over I covered him in oil. As I eased over to the gutter Klaus was still on his way to complete what he obviously thought was a blistering lap.

It was blistering, all right. As I free-wheeled through the 33rd Milestone, I noticed a pair of leathered knuckles, closely followed by Klaus's helmet, appearing over the grass bank – just where a set of new skid marks went in the opposite direction. I didn't stop, partly because I needed my momentum if I was to coast back to Douglas, and partly because I thought he might hit me.

He was certainly angry enough. He came up to me afterwards, absolutely livid, as though my engine blowing up was an act of sabotage.

'For God's sake, Klaus,' I told him, 'you'd seen me blow up but obviously tipped in with oil on your tyre. So whose fault was that – mine or yours?'

The other big learner that year was my team-mate, Rob McElnea. As a youngster Rob was fast but a bit flighty. He'd first raced on the Island in the 1979 Manx Grand Prix when he'd led the Junior Newcomers race by 30 seconds, only to fall off at Whitegates, climb back on, and finish second. By his TT debut three years later he was evidently a bit less brain-out and just ran out of fuel after forgetting his pit stop whilst lying third. In the first practice session we went round for a lap together and apart from nearly taking out Greeba Castle – well, he's a big bloke and it's a fairly small castle – seemed to have the job sorted.

I should say so, for he won the final race of the week, the Senior Classic. To be fair the rider of the day was Norman Brown, who took his RG500 away like a scalded cat and broke the outright lap record second time around before running out of fuel. With Joey suffering handling and carburettor problems, Rob took up the cudgels to win the fastest race in TT history, at 114.81mph. I went well early on, but my wrist was still weak and a few hairy slides on the last lap dented my confidence. Fifth place was my first finish off the rostrum since '74.

Prior to that I'd become the second man to finish a six-lap race in under two hours in the Formula One TT. Unfortunately nobody took much notice because the first man to do so – Joey – was in the same race. It was a good job the race didn't last longer, for it was a blistering hot day and by the finish both of us were dehydrated and heat-shocked. We agreed it was the toughest TT we'd ever ridden. But the effort was worth it: second place put my world Formula One ambitions right on track. Next stop, Assen.

I'd always loved Assen. Its fast, flowing curves seem to suit any rider who's handy on the Isle of Man. The XR69 was working perfectly, and I wasn't especially surprised to grab pole. Joey and Rob were within half a second, but the rest were well adrift.

For a while the race looked like going to the same agreeable plan. Joey hared off from the start, with Rob and me chasing. With a bit of unintentional help from backmarkers, we managed to catch the Honda and started to pull away. With two laps to go I'd settled for what seemed a safe second, which would put me at the top of the championship standings. That's when the Suzuki holed a piston. So instead, Joey led the series from Rob with me somewhere in the distance. The game was up. All that was left was to help Rob at Dundrod.

Being Ireland, it rained for the Ulster. More surprisingly, this came at the end of a long, dry spell so the roads were especially slick. Still, I don't mind the wet and everything looked peachy when the flag dropped and Rob and I shot into the lead. A kilometre later, we were still leading. Then came Rushyhill, a blindingly fast left-hander. Rob tipped in ... gently, for there was lots of standing water. I tipped in ... ditto. Suddenly there's a howl and a plume of spray and a Honda hurtles under the pair of us.

That was the last we saw of Joey. He was on it all weekend, wet or dry. In practice he'd put in the first 120mph lap at Dundrod, and in the wet he seemed happy to push it harder than we were prepared to risk. Rob never got the hang of the conditions and on the last lap waved me through to finish second, but there was nothing either of us could do to stop Joey wrapping up his second world Formula One crown.

This was the last year before the Formula One limit was dropped from 1,000 to 750cc. Suzuki carried on with the same XR69 as before. Honda had a mixed strategy, running both their old across-the-frame 998cc fours and, from mid-season, the V4 RS860. This would be the basis for the 750cc V4s they'd use the following year.

Although the RS had more ground clearance, stopped and handled better and had good top-end speed, it lacked the bigger engine's punch out of turns. So before it got into its stride, we definitely had the edge. As late as July at Donington, Rob and I posted a one–two, with a new lap record. Honda's new man Wayne Gardner, though, was never far behind, and as his crew got the hang of the V4, became harder and harder to beat. It made for some good racing. After a brilliant seven-man dice at Silverstone the following month, just 0.7 seconds covered the three of us, but Wayne came out on top.

For the next couple of months, if Wayne stayed on, the odds were that he'd win. Like so many Australians who race in Britain, he had a hunger that was hard to resist. Those days dossing in his Austin had done him no harm at all. At Donington in September he gave us a chink of light when he broke a few fingers and a collarbone, and I won. But even with Wayne absent, Reg was often favourite. Wayne hung on to take the Formula One series by 107 points to Rob's 97, with me third on 88.

Whether that made him British champion was another matter. At the time, it was hard to work out exactly who was top dog. As well as the Formula One series, there was the *World of Sport* Superbike championship, the *MCN* Masters and, for all I know, the Wheeltappers and Shunters, too. Keith Huewen ran away with the Masters series. Mind you, his hair was a different colour then.

Just a couple of weeks before Dundrod I'd broken a hand in practice at Snetterton. We'd just changed a wheel but the brake pads hadn't been pumped back on to the discs, so when I hammered into Riches, there was nowhere to go but the carrot field. At Norwich hospital they treated an old fracture but didn't notice the new one, so taped up two good fingers and left the broken one be.

There'd been earlier get-offs at Brands and Donington, the latter doing a wrist. Then Joey had beaten me fair and square at Dundrod – at least partly because he wanted it more than me. I was beginning to wonder if this was some sort of a sign. By now I was 39. Had the old edge gone? Was I past it?

And yet within the previous few weeks I'd set a new outright lap record at Donington, and come out of that Silverstone dice only half a second behind Gardner, who was definitely the fastest man on British short circuits. I wasn't sure what to think. Ever since I reached the big-time in racing, I was convinced that some people have massive ability and some have huge commitment, but only the guys with a helping of both consistently win. In fact I'd always privately thought that of the two I was thinnest on the natural talent front, but compensated for by determination and sheer graft. I was never an easy guy to beat.

And like all racers, I suspect, there were always two competing voices in my head. When I started racing, the aggressive fellow used to get all the say. For years the cautious little chap didn't get much of a look-in – but he didn't fall off much, either. Unfortunately that didn't often help, because he was rarely controlling the bike. The aggressive one always seemed to have hold of the twist grip.

Naturally, as time goes by the timid voice starts shouting louder. But experience counts for a lot. Your set-up's usually better and you're not so easily fazed by what everyone else is up to. So on an open track – say, in practice – you're still able to go as quickly as before. But come race day, you probably won't take the risks you did before. This is why emerging from that bun-fight at Silverstone was so satisfying: Gardner may have won, but I felt pretty good about toughing out Reg, Rob and Joey, none of whom would willingly give half an inch. Eventually, though, there must come a time when the cautious voice would prefer to spend his weekends watching the racing on the telly with a six-pack by his elbow. I kept it to myself, but I was already aware that if there were two or three guys ahead of me, but no gap, I'd leave them be. Ten years earlier, the cautious approach wouldn't have occurred to me: I'd have made a gap, whatever it took.

No matter how enthusiastic you are, eventually the more timid half of your head begins to take over. This was true even for someone like Joey, who sustained his aggression for far longer than most, but always balanced it with experience and canniness. I've an enormous amount of respect for Joey, but doubt that if his career had been based on short-circuit racing, he could have continued at the level he did for so many years. On the roads, and especially at the TT, experience is priceless – one of the reasons my career continued as long as it did. Even on the Island Joey won races he'd no right to on the basis of pure speed, but was lifted above younger, faster men by sheer racing cleverness and nous. Even so, his nerve and skill still managed to take my breath away during his last TT.

I wasn't the only one having similar thoughts about my competitiveness. Journalists can be a pain in the arse, putting labels on you which seem to stick long after they're true or even relevant. 'Gritty Yorkshireman' was lazy and daft, but it made me smile and there are less flattering clichés. By now I'd have happily stuck with it, since it wasn't long before the press got bored with that and 'evergreen veteran', became the favoured tag. I hated that – and 'Golden Oldie' even more. Once you've got that sort of crap on your CV, the job's as good as buggered.

CHAPTER 17

'WRITTEN OFF MORE TIMES THAN A SECOND-HAND STOCK CAR'

That headline is what the press thought in the autumn of 1983. My own take was that I couldn't see why I shouldn't be able to go on for a couple of years ... as soon as I stop enjoying racing, I'll know it's time to give up. Suzuki must have been thinking along the same lines, because in early November they signed me to partner Rob McElnea again. I was even recalled to the Match Race team, not that it did much good. I'd be riding mainly world and British Formula One races; Rob would have a busy year doing the same as well as 500cc grands prix.

Winning that elusive world Formula One title was still top of my personal priorities. On the shorts, Gardner was still the man to beat, winning the opening rounds at Cadwell and Thruxton. With a year's development already behind it as the RS860, the 750cc V4 Honda was always likely to be dominant, especially early in the season. Just how dominant, we'd no idea.

For the opening few meetings Rob and I raced a Formula One bike cobbled together in the UK. We couldn't wait for the proper factory job to arrive, which it belatedly did for the Transatlantic series at Donington. It was so new it wasn't even painted. The fairing was plain white. In the first race, in the wet, the gearbox jammed in fourth. For a couple of laps I managed to hang on to fourth place but overdid it at Park Chicane and high-sided on the way out.

259

So that was me out of my come-back series, knocked about and wincing with a dislocated collarbone. It hurt so much and took so long to heal I wished I'd broken it instead. Luckily I didn't leave the British team a man short: some American rookie called Wayne Rainey dumped it in practice and missed the races with a foot injury. All round it would have been a good Match Race to miss. Even without Rainey, the Yanks had the top four points scorers – the tasty quartet of Mamola, Lawson, Roberts and Spencer – and absolutely thrashed us, 259 to 136.

From then on it was the Gardner–Honda show. At Snetterton he led home Reg and Joey for a Honda clean sweep of the rostrum, a result repeated shortly after at Oulton. Even the bike press was beginning to notice we were pissing into the wind with our across-the-frame 750s against the V4. (We'd get an even bigger shock when the RVF750 appeared the following year.) It was slow and unreliable, forever breaking crankshafts, seizing or losing gears. So come the North West 200, we chose to use the RG500 instead. Rob was away on grand prix duty, so battling the Hondas was down to just me. What I didn't know was that Honda's new Formula One bikes were having problems of their own, mainly with carburetion flat spots. When they failed to fix these in official practice, Joey arranged some unofficial practice of his own – on the country road past his house near Ballymoney. No one was surprised when he cleared off in the wet *MCN* Masters race. I was battling for second when I slung away the RG at Dhu Varen in Portrush. Apparently I suffered 'bruises and a sore head' – probably from thinking too much.

In the main race, Joey retired and Graham Wood led from start to finish on a TZ750. It took me half the race to get over my sore head, by which time I was down in sixth, but managed a late charge to finish second after overhauling Barry Woodland and Steve Parrish on the last lap.

After the usual game of bluff and bluster about TT start money – Charlie Williams and I both threatened to miss it – practice went surprisingly well. I topped the Formula One leaderboard at 112.55mph, with Rob top 500 at 116.23. Mind you, we both suspected the Hondas were holding back for bets.

The Formula One race was strange. Honda tried desperately to lose it – both Reg and Joey had major exhaust and fuel problems – but luckily for them we tried even harder. My gearbox broke on the Mountain Mile on lap one; Rob lasted a bit longer before his steering damper packed in, then his engine seized. So Joey and Reg claimed an easy Honda one–two and, barring miracles, bang went any world title ambitions I might have had left.

The Senior was a stunning race for everyone but me. While I wobbled to sixth with a loose clip-on – I had to stop twice to tighten it – Joey was on a mission. He set a new lap record on every one of the first five laps, only to retire last time around at Mountain Box when he ran out of fuel. Rob, 40 seconds behind at the time, went on to win by over three minutes from Reg.

Rob's fastest lap, 118.23 – only two seconds outside Joey's new record – was staggering. He passed me coming out of the last kink on to the Mountain Mile, just beyond the white bridge, which I'd always considered one of the most important corners on the circuit – so I was trying. But he must have had seven mph on me, on an identical machine, and pulled away for the entire length of the Mountain Mile, which was pretty demoralising, especially behind someone who supposedly draughts like a truck.

After a pretty boring ride into sixth place on the GSX1100 production bike, Friday's Classic race was another cracker, with Rob, Joey and me swapping the lead for the entire six laps. Riding the Formula One bike with the previous year's 998cc engine, Rob edged out Joey's 920cc endurance-spec Honda fair and square by 14 seconds. Old man Grant didn't go too shabbily himself, leading after two laps with a personal best 116.71mph and just about finishing third despite the chain jumping the sprockets towards the end. The outright lap record didn't go that time, but such was the battle for the lead that the race was the fastest in TT history – over 116mph. Although most TT fans don't automatically think of Rob as one of the greats around the Mountain circuit, nobody in recent times has come close to his win ratio. If he'd kept at it for longer, heaven knows how many records he'd have broken.

Even without my disaster in the Formula One TT, it was obvious by now that we'd no chance for the world championship. The Hondas were just too good. In fact the only thing we seemed to have going for us was the mood in the opposing camp, which turned a mite poisonous. This was unexpected because Joey was generally an easy-going bloke and Reg was no prima donna, but for one reason or another they seemed to spend half the season at loggerheads.

It all started at Assen. Rob Mac was missing with torn ligaments from crashing out of the French grand prix at Paul Ricard, so all Suzuki's hopes rested with me – and I topped the non-Honda results with third place. Early in the piece I'd missed a gear and bent some valves, not that it made any difference, since by then Reg and Joey had already cleared off, with Reg winning. However, it later emerged that the difference was mainly in their pit stops, where Reg's engine had illegally kept running, while Joey's had not. Joey was livid, but team boss Barry Symmons wasn't about to protest his own man so after a bout of jiggery-pokery, Mile Pajic was persuaded to protest instead. By then the protest was conveniently out of time so Reg's win stood, tying him and Joey for the championship lead.

Reg won again in searing heat at Vila Real. Like me, he never looked like an athlete but training four days a week with Grimsby Town football club paid off and he won at a trot. By the time Joey's booze and fags aerobics brought him home a minute behind, he had to be lifted from his bike in a heat-stricken daze. My fitness wasn't a problem until I lost the front end and crashed out.

Joey was so out of it that Symmons actually took Joey's place on the rostrum, despite being the worse for wear himself. As Joey was about to pit midway through the race, a local rider was obstructing his way in. When Symmons threw a plastic water bottle at him, all hell broke loose. The Portuguese rider's crew knocked seven bells out of poor Barry. Later he hobbled to our pit and accosted Nigel.

'I thought you might have helped.'

'Didn't seem to be any need. I thought there were enough of them.'

There was even more heat for Barry at the Ulster. At Windmill Corner on the last lap, Joey dived under Marshall to take the lead and the win. Reg, who blamed Joey for forcing him into clouting the bank, demanded that Symmons protest his team-mate for dangerous riding. If he had, he'd probably have been lynched. Instead the Irish fans settled for vandalising the Honda truck and hurling abuse at Reg and poor Barry. I finished my customary third, too far behind to witness all the excitement at Windmill.

For the final round at Zolder I finally made my presence felt – by accident. It was a fraught race all round. The organisers threatened to chuck me out of the results for topping up the tank following the warm-up lap, which we absolutely needed to do to go the distance. The first we knew of this was when an immaculately dressed Belgian jobsworth tried to push Nigel away from the bike. I grabbed hold of his dapper lapels and physically lifted him from the grid. After the race I was brought up before stewards to answer for my crime, and lo and behold, the British ACU rep who'd been so conspicuous previously was nowhere to be found to defend me.

After the kerfuffle on the grid I was still pretty harassed when the flag dropped, getting a lousy start while Reg and Joey rocketed into the lead. Inevitably the Suzuki started to misfire. I pulled into the pit lane, saw Symmons waving madly and pulled into the Honda pit by mistake – just as Joey was trying to make his mid-race stop.

Adding insult to injury I stalled the bike, couldn't restart it and was stranded at the opposite end of the pit lane from my crew. It wasn't even slightly funny at the time and pretty much summed up a disastrous series. Luckily by this time Reg's Honda had already expired in a cloud of steam, so although Joey only placed second to Pajic – on a Kawasaki, of all things – at least no harm was done to his title prospects. Otherwise it might have been my turn to be lynched. Heaven knows how, but I was so wound up after my farcical pit stop that I set the fastest lap of the race – not much consolation for finishing fifth in the series.

The year had been a major struggle. Apart from the odd result on the RG500, I'd almost forgotten what it was like to win. Gardner took the British Formula One series at a canter, although Rob Mac did well to finish between him and Reg. I placed fourth. Beating Reg in both legs of the Macau Grand Prix was small consolation.

But if our Formula One Suzukis had been out-paced by the Hondas the previous year, in '85 it suddenly got a lot worse. The RVF750, maybe the best four-stroke racer ever built before the MotoGP era, made its first British outing at the North West 200 in May. It was an exquisite little thing that looked like a real racer – which it was – rather than something cobbled together from whatever happened to be lying around. In fact it was a huge effort all round – by Dunlop, Showa, everyone involved. We were jealous as hell – and with good reason. From the moment he first sat on it, Joey was unstoppable.

There was worse to come – or so I thought. When we'd agreed my contract for the season Suzuki boss Denys Rohan said I couldn't ride a 500 any more. Since this was the only bike I'd won on the previous year, the news was as welcome as bubonic plague. Instead, Denys wanted me to ride Suzuki's new Superstock bike. I wasn't at all happy about this in theory, and even less so after riding the bike. Going into Park Chicane at Donington in early season testing, the oil filter unscrewed itself and the bike spat me down the road. What had I got myself into?

I could not have been more wrong. Suzuki may have been out of the running in Formula One, but in production-based racing they were about to become supreme, for this was the year the GSX-R750 was introduced. Super-light and with a genuine 100 horsepower, it more or less invented modern race replicas. Being used to factory race bikes that were much trickier still, I don't suppose I was as impressed with the bike as the average road-riding punter. But it didn't take long to see that the bike had potential.

That Donington practice crash, it turned out, was my only off all year. By the time I'd won the first four rounds of the new Superstock series, Denys's plan didn't seem like such a bad idea.

With the costs of racing spiralling, Bruce Cox's 11-round Superstock series was billed as an attempt 'to give racing a shot in the arm and create a class that people can afford'. The series was televised, backed to the hilt by *Motor Cycle News*, and right from the go seemed to capture the public imagination. Better still, it attracted most of the top riders and manufacturers. This was the series in which Terry Rymer, James Whitham and several others would later make their names.

My bike was built around Suzuki's demonstrator, the first GSX-R to arrive in Europe. Fairly extensive chassis mods were allowed, although the engines were almost stock. With well over a decade's top-flight experience each, Nigel and I were as well placed as anyone to extract the most from the rules – not to mention Suzuki's spare stock of factory forks, brakes and wheels. And apart from a somewhat fragile gearbox, the GSX-R was probably the best starting point of the lot.

Those four wins produced fairly predictable headlines, although I definitely preferred 'Superstock Superstar' to 'Wily Veteran'. Best of all, they produced a massive series lead. It wasn't, though, a cakewalk. In the opening round at Brands I was just two seconds ahead of Reg's Honda; at Donington, I had to fight from behind to beat Steve Parrish's FZ750 Yamaha by just 1/100 second.

By the time of round three, where I edged out Reg, again, and Paul Iddon, tongues were already wagging about Granty's 'dodgy' GSX-R. By round four, another win from Reg, you could barely find anyone who didn't think we were cheating.

Bruce Cox, the series promoter, had said before the series that he'd have one bike checked every meeting to make sure it was pukka. As the rumours went into overdrive I asked if he was going to check mine. I really wanted him to, but he didn't. In the end I arranged for Rod Scivyer to tear down the engine and invited any interested parties to watch. The GSX-R was quick, yes. But it was also totally legit.

From then on I won only one more round. What happened, I think, was that when we'd first built the bike, Nigel, myself and the rest of the Suzuki boys had been a bit cannier and more imaginative than anyone else. But none of the rest were mugs. It was only a matter of time before they got the best out of their bikes, too – and that's precisely what they did. But by then, of course, they were taking points off each other as well as off me, so my championship lead was never really threatened.

As well as myself, Keith Huewen, Trevor Nation and Mark Salle all won rounds. Trevor, who'd been nowhere early season, won three of the last five. Stavros might have won one, too, if he hadn't been excluded from the results at Snetterton. After the final round at Brands, where I wobbled round in a safe seventh place, I led the standings by 127 points to 98. Second was Reg, after riding the wheels off what was probably the worst bike in the series, the VF750 Honda. Served him right for all the thrashings Honda's other V4 had given me in Formula One. Not surprisingly, the GSX-R750 was voted 'Machine of the Year' by *Motor Cycle News* readers. Unfortunately they didn't rate me quite so highly, putting me fifth in the 'Man of the Year' poll behind Dave Thorpe.

The same bike – or, rather, it's production cousin – also gave me my last TT win. We arrived on the Island via a disappointing North West 200. I managed third in the Superbike race behind Reg and Graham Wood, but the feature event was a disaster. Nobody saw which way Joey's RVF went. Mark Salle led the also-rans, then seized. Then it was my turn – until my crank broke. Then Macca's turn – until his chain snapped. The Formula One TT wasn't any better. I was lying second when my gearbox broke at Ballaugh. Macca also retired, whilst Joey buggered off on the RVF, leading from start to finish to beat Rutter by over five minutes.

The 750cc Production TT was only ever going to be between the GSX-R750s – if only we could get them to handle. In that first year the bike had a short swing-arm (for '86 they lengthened it an inch) and was wildly unstable on the Michelins we were running. It may not have had the power of the F1 bike, but attacking Sulby Straight flat-out was far more terrifying – and I've never been comfortable with a bike that loose.

The only guy who seemed happy with the handling was newcomer Glenn Williams who spent practice week grinning while Tony Rutter and I tottered about like shell-shocked wrecks. This may partly have been due to the fact that he raced a turbocharged Z1 Kawasaki on street circuits back home in New Zealand, so he was obviously fairly mad. On the other hand it may also have been due to the Metzeler tyres he was running. I was so convinced that these were the way to go that I actually offered to buy some. Michelin, naturally enough, weren't happy, but I figured that upsetting them was better than tank-slapping through a Manx hedge.

Starting the first lap I was still fairly paranoid about the handling, allowing Kevin Wilson to grab a narrow lead. But by Ramsey it was obvious the Metzelers had transformed the bike's stability, and from there on I got stuck in, beating Wilson by 13 seconds. It couldn't have been more different from the previous year, when I'd struggled with the bloody awful GSX11000 – a bus in comparison with the GSX-R – to finish seventh in the same race. That gave me only my second bronze replica, until Barry Woodland was thrown out of the results and I was moved up a place. This time around, the top four bikes were all Suzukis. It was a mark of how good the GSX-R was that the best lap, set by Glenn Williams, was faster than anyone managed in the 1300cc production class.

The odd thing was that Michelins had always enjoyed a good reputation for stability. Halfway through practice, Rex and I had met for a pow-wow with the top Michelin man. I told him I was sure their tyre was the problem and that unless we changed it we couldn't possibly win the race. If that was true, the best Michelin could hope for was a bad result and bad press. They reluctantly agreed, so off I went to buy some Metzelers. There was no point in rubbing anyone's nose in it. Whether or not they're vital components of the team, as tyre companies certainly are, you try to look after your sponsors. As it turned out Metzeler wouldn't take any money for their tyres, but we agreed quite clearly that if I won they wouldn't make any capital out of the result. In the next week's bike press who's featured in the Metzeler ad but me and the GSX-R?

That was my last win and what turned out to be my last TT finish. In the Senior the same afternoon I fell off the 500 at Black Dub – in a perfectly straight line. To this day I've no idea what went wrong, except that it was windy and maybe a gust got under the fairing, but as I slid down the road I wondered if this was the big one. Luckily, when I came to a halt in the gutter, all I had was a broken thumb – my only break in all those years on the Island. But as I sat on the bank waiting for the helicopter and nursing my bruises, I wondered if someone was trying to tell me something. Later in the same race Rob

Vine was killed at almost the same spot. That was the beginning of the end.

While Joey was doing his usual disappearing act – chased hard by Reg, the closest he ever came to a TT win – I was in Nobles Hospital with my old pal Mr Beeson, the same orthopaedic surgeon for whom I'd done my press ups a few years before. He asked when I needed to be fit to race again.

'Next Thursday practising for the Formula One race at Assen.'

'Right, we'd better put a pin in it.'

Mr Beeson was well up for this. 'Do you want to watch?' he chirped. So he numbed my hand and chatted away as he drilled and tapped. Other than the smell of bone it was just like being in my workshop at home. Mind you, the damn thing's never worked properly since.

In the event it wasn't my thumb but my brain that put the mockers on Assen. Just before the start the heavens opened, which was good news for anyone not riding an RVF, since this was probably the only chance anyone had of challenging Joey. It also meant that, if I went relatively steady early on, I could eke out my fuel and avoid a pit stop. At the same time, I'd be saving my tyres for a final push.

For a while it all went perfectly to plan. After his pit stop Joey was still 30 seconds ahead, but his tyres were shot and I was catching him by three or four seconds per lap. By the time I caught him it was obvious his rear wet was falling apart. I thought of nipping past him, but by this time my tyres were pretty ragged, too, so I decided instead to tag behind until the last lap. By this time both of us were slithering about, on and off the grass, but he held me off to win by a couple of bike lengths.

From then on we were nowhere. Vila Real: Joey by 20 seconds from Graeme McGregor, with me a distant third. The Ulster: Joey again by a mile, me second, Macca third. Hockenheim: Joey, with me a lowly fifth. Joey's RVF had won all six rounds of the world championship. I finished second –

my best-ever placing – but with just 40 points to his 90. Even between us, me and Macca wouldn't have won.

It was much the same story in British Formula One, except this time Reg was the problem. More often than not, he'd win and I'd be second or third. In fact my finest performance of the season came at the Silverstone round – in a charity running race. Eat your heart out, Gerald Davison: old man Grant was top racer in ninth, one ahead of Rob Mac. By the final round at Brands, Reg already had the title in his pocket. All I could do was keep Roger Burnett at bay to finish as runner-up. Reg won, as usual, but I came home on Burnett's heels to beat him by four points in the final standings.

A month later the 1985 Macau grand prix, it transpired, was my swansong. In six visits to the Portuguese enclave I'd picked up five wins, including the previous year. Then I'd held off Reg's three-cylinder NS500 Honda on the Mk7 RG500 Suzuki – to my mind the best RG they ever made. I was looking for more of the same, but all season Rob Mac had been riding the composite-framed Ciba-Geigy Skoal Bandit bike. For promotional reasons Suzuki insisted I use a similar machine at Macau. It was horrible, didn't carburete, wasn't set up – one of the worst bikes I ever rode. We had a harassing time trying to sort it out, but never did. The bike didn't finish either leg of the grand prix.

I'd made myself a promise several years before, that when I stopped enjoying racing, that's when I'd pack in. After pushing and free-wheeling this bloody Suzuki down the last straight to the pits, I handed it to Nigel and found myself saying 'That's it. That's me, finished.' It sounds fairly absolute and committed now, but even as I uttered the words I remember wondering, 'Who the hell said that?' Nigel was obviously shocked. So was I.

It was more instinct than decision. A lot of it had to do with the doubts I'd been having over the past couple of years about ... well, I suppose 'bottle' is the right word. The crash at Black Dub was certainly part of the process, too. I had several other things on the go, like building a new house to replace the monstrosity at Lepton Grange.

All things considered, 1985 had been a fairly good year. In both Formula One series – world and British – the best I could realistically expect was to finish second to the Hondas, and that I'd done. Better still, I'd wrapped up the high-profile *MCN* Superstock championship. Yet inside I knew it was all a bit of a con. I'd always been a tough rider but was definitely not as prepared to take a risk as I had been two or three years before – a fact it wouldn't take the opposition long to suss out. Yes, I could have carried on making a good living as a racer, especially at the TT, but my heart wasn't really in it anymore. I just didn't see myself as a jobbing racer collecting pay cheques in the minor points. So the more I thought about it, the more retirement seemed the right course. Yet for any professional racer, packing in is one of the hardest things they ever do. It's not the decision itself, hard though that is, so much as how you fill the void that racing leaves.

The evidence was right in my face, so I fudged it. I came home from Macau and told Carol that I'd give Denys Rohan, then in charge at Suzuki, a big wage demand for '86. If he agreed to it, which was unlikely, I'd carry on; if he didn't, that was me – done.

The fateful meeting with Denys arrived. 'Mick,' he began after the usual preliminaries, 'you've had a real good career. There's a contract there if you want to sign it. But I'd like to be the person who helps you to stop at the right time.'

'What do you have in mind?'

The idea was a new position which would allow me to do salaried promotion work, company car and all, then take over the race team two years down the line when Rex White retired. It scarcely needed thinking about, and I'll be forever grateful that Denys made a tricky choice so simple.

'You've got yourself a deal,' I said, and we shook hands. It was the best decision I ever made in racing.

CHAPTER 18

TEAM
HUDDERSFIELD

One of the best things about working for Suzuki was that they also imported Lancia cars – great things to drive but hideous rust-buckets to own, so a company one was perfect. Basically, my new job was to pull punters into dealers' showrooms. I spent two years whizzing around towing a trailer with my factory XR69 inside, video and TV facilities – a mobile motorcycle show. Each week I'd cover two or three dealers, arriving at five pm and leaving with the last punter. For the first year it was fun – helping sell seven bikes in an evening would give anyone a buzz – but it wasn't exactly high octane. Halfway through the second year I couldn't wait for it to end.

As well as glad-handing dealers, when I packed in racing I tested some of Suzuki's prototype road bikes. One, the FJ11000, I thought was a great piece of kit. It had a screen that could be electrically raised or lowered to reduce buffeting for the pillion, which worked quite well except that many testers thought the intention was to protect them, so left it on the highest setting.

Testing gave me an insight into the Japanese approach to development, which was in some ways as baffling as the NR500 project had been. It was obvious from the start that the bike's big issue was a high-speed weave. Because I was the racer amongst a pool of maybe half a dozen testers, I usually got to ride first – so I was first with news of the weave. But instead of trying to do something about it, they'd send the French guy out, the German, the Yank and the Japanese. Now if one person tells you it's pouring down outside, you'd still get as wet as if four folk give you the same tale. But by this time three hours have passed and they've only just got around to changing a tyre, suspension settings, or whatever. It was sorting a bike by committee – a very long-winded process. After three days we'd accomplished about six modifications.

When we first started, the Suzuki was nothing like as good as the FJ Yamaha, which we were also riding for comparison. After each test, we had to complete a form, rating everything from vibration and seat comfort to braking stability, all out of five. The policy was that if even one element failed to average 2.5, the bike couldn't be signed off for production. The weave meant that at least one score was always below that. It didn't help that the bike had a huge back tyre, which was only accentuating the stability problem. I was told we couldn't change that for marketing reasons: the Yamaha also had a huge tyre.

On the final day, in frustration, the project leader hefted some new forks out of the back of the garage, slid them into the bike and – hey presto! – the weave was gone. It was clear Suzuki knew all along they had a problem, but were presumably hoping to get by with a cheaper design of forks. With the more expensive ones, it was a superb machine.

When I got home I recommended to Steve Kenwood at Suzuki GB that he order stacks of the Suzuki FJ. I thought they were that good. Then, sure enough, at the press launch in the Lake District several months later, the bike handled like a tea-trolley again. Suzuki had switched back to the inferior forks. Even though it was none of my doing, I felt a right prat.

As promised, at the end of the 1987 race season Rex White retired and it was my turn to step into his shoes as boss of the Suzuki GB team. This wasn't an auspicious time for bike racing in the UK. In the previous two or three years, race costs had risen whilst bike sales had just as relentlessly declined from their peak in '81. Without an outside sponsor my budget from Suzuki would be slashed.

At first, that didn't seem to be a problem since Suzuki had provisionally agreed a deal with Old Holborn tobacco. The budget was enormous – £1 million over three years – and would have allowed us to do almost anything we wanted. By this time Reg Marshall had rejoined Suzuki, for whom he was off in Australia doing the Swann Series. As his soon-to-be boss I'd spoken to him before he'd left, when he'd insisted that, whatever else happened, he absolutely would not ride production-based bikes the following year. At the time that wasn't an issue since we seemed to have the budget to run a squad of pukka racing machines.

Then, out of the blue, I got a phone call announcing that the Old Holborn deal was off.

It turned out that a guy high up in the tobacco company had a history with another individual high up in Suzuki racing, and absolutely would not deal with him. They were adamant.

To me it was bad enough that Suzuki would be strapped for cash. Almost as big a tragedy was that a large sum of money that the beleaguered industry could badly do with was likely to go elsewhere. 'If you won't deal with Suzuki,' I asked, 'could you deal with another motorcycle company?'

They could, no problem. They seemed as keen as ever to promote their weed through bike racing.

I still had plenty of contacts from my days at Kawasaki so gave the nod to Alec Wright (father of current race team boss, Colin), who was then in overall charge of Kawasaki racing. Mind you, a spot of commission for my trouble wouldn't go amiss. Three years earlier I'd handed over my Senior TT-winning 500cc triple for display at Beaulieu Motorcycle museum. It was still there on loan from Kawasaki. Was there any chance of Kawasaki making that bike over to me? No problem.

I duly attended a meeting as a sort of intermediary between Old Holborn and Kawasaki. Everything seemed to be hunky-dory until they came to the last issue: the team's livery.

'Obviously,' said a tobacco man, 'it'll be orange and black', Old Holborn's corporate colours.

'No,' replied Alex, grimly, 'green. Kawasakis are always green.'

So the deal fell through and Old Holborn's dosh disappeared into cricket or snooker or tiddlywinks. And I never got my 500 Kwacker.

After our stab at the Old Holborn money fell apart, I was left with a budget of about tuppence-ha'penny to run the team. The old Heron Suzuki workshops in Crawley would be abandoned. Instead, I'd be running everything on a shoestring from home. It definitely wasn't the ideal way to start a career in race management, but I was itching to be getting back into racing.

Suzuki wasn't the only UK importer feeling the pinch. Everyone's sales had plummeted. Mainly to cut the spiralling cost of racing, the importers were keen to push the classes towards production-based machines – superbike, supersport and superstock, as we know them today.

Dealing with the ACU was always frustrating. On the manufacturers' committee was Colin Wright, Andy Smith, Barry Symmons, Dave Hancock and myself. We'd get together before each meeting with the ACU. Our rule was that a majority vote between the five of us dictated our policy towards the ACU. It worked solidly and well. Usually the ACU would take this on board for about a nanosecond before retiring to talk amongst themselves and coming up with something altogether different. As often as not, the first we knew of this was when we read it in the following week's bike paper. Naturally they smelled a rat where there wasn't one, thinking the motive behind production-based classes was solely to sell more road bikes – although why that should be in any way sinister, heaven only knows. It was a struggle, but eventually the manufacturers prevailed.

This left most people happy – except poor Reg, who'd gone out for the Swann Series thinking his future was assured with Suzuki. He still wanted nothing to do with anything resembling a road bike, which is all we had. There was also the small matter that I could only pay him peanuts when he'd been used to pistachios, at least. Ideally I'd have loved to keep him on, but it was impossible. Reg's other shock had come in the Swann Series itself. He'd finished third behind Kevin McGee and Mike Dowson's factory Yamahas. But what had impressed him more was a 'totally out-of-control wild thing' which went by the name of Mick Doohan.

As well as Reg, out went Nigel – someone else I could no longer afford. When I'd retired he'd worked for Chris Martin, then Neil 'Smutty' Robinson until he was killed at Scarborough late in 1986, before joining Reg. Like Reg, he'd arrived back from the Swann Series to find he was out of work.

If our miserable budget meant anything, it was that our riders had to be blokes I could get on the cheap, but they also had to be good. Phil 'Mez' Mellor I already knew pretty well. He was from Huddersfield, a strong runner, on the roads in particular, and although he generally rode in the smaller classes we'd raced against each other now and again. The previous season he'd had some support from Suzuki, so drafting him in was natural.

I'd actually managed Mez when standing in for Rex at the previous TT. He had a brilliant week, leading Joey in the Formula One race before finishing second. In the Senior the odds looked even better. Just before the start it poured down. We started him on intermediates and when I noticed that Joey was on slicks, I knew the race was ours and told Mez so. I should have kept my big mouth shut. He was leading when he slid off at the Nook. Joey won after a hairy ride of his own, including aquaplaning all the way down Bray Hill.

So Mez was an experienced, proven rider. What we needed to back him up was a young hot-shot – partly to bring along new talent, partly because he'd be cheap. Another Huddersfield lad was the obvious candidate: James Whitham.

I'd first met James in 1981 when I'd used his father's airfield at Crossland Moor to test some gearbox mods on the Harris Suzuki. Then, he'd struck me as an enthusiastic, cocky little kid, although a few months later when Carol and I took him to a meeting at Scarborough, he seemed almost paralysed with insecurity.

His dad, David, was a complete one-off and totally the opposite. Once when I was testing, Jamie Lodge was also there running his MBA125 up and down the airstrip, watched by his parents. They owned a couple of supermarkets in town, so were a bit up-market compared to David, whose tightness was legendary. He preferred to run about in rusty old vans rather than lash out on anything younger than he was and thought nothing of wearing cast-off clothes. The Lodges stood in the natural place to watch their lad put his bike through its paces – on the grass next to the runway. They weren't to know that the grass, once harvested, was as good as money to David. But they soon found out.

'Oi,' came a yell heard by half of Huddersfield. 'Get off the fucking grass. Get ... off ... the ... fucking ... grass.'

Mrs Lodge made a face like sucking lemons and was probably still wondering who this uncouth man could be when a few minutes later David emerged smiling from the 'pilot's lounge' – a battered caravan – with a mug of tea for each of them.

Having the airfield to test on, especially when I was a privateer, was a godsend. But it did have its distractions, since you always risked being roped into one of David's ideas. One day he encountered me nosing around the planes at the airfield. Apparently the one I was looking at, a little single-engined thing, was his.

'Come on,' he said, 'we'll have a fly around.'

Ten minutes later I'm several thousand feet above Huddersfield, being shown the sights. It was then that I noticed a little blue light flashing on the instrument panel.

'What's that?'

'Oh, nothing important. Just the fuel warning light.'

'For fuck's sake, David, get this thing on the ground.'

Although he was careful with his money, he did have the odd extravagance. Once, on a whim, he spent £22,000 on a microlight. A while later he rang me up to ask if I could weld up a broken bracket on the plane. No problem.

The bracket turned out to be an aluminium plate holding the HT coils for the Microlight's Rotax engine. Not high-tech, but fairly important. I looked it over, and it was obvious that however much weld I threw at it, it was going to break again in the same place. A better solution would be to make a new one.

'No, don't bother. I'm going to sell the thing, anyway.' He was crackers, but lovely with it.

A couple of years later James was about to start racing on an MT125 Honda, and turned up one day at Lepton Grange hoping for help getting cheap riding gear. I'd sent him away with my old Granby Yamaha leathers and arranged a free lid from Kiwi, my helmet sponsors. A year or two later we found ourselves racing at the same meeting at Cadwell Park and I made a point of watching him from the top of the Mountain on his new MBA125.

You'd have been impressed – but only if you sold MBA spare parts for a living. First time through the Hairpin, he scuttled in out of control and landed on his arse. After picking himself up he was even wilder – he seemed to go through Hall Bends sideways – took the lead at the Hairpin, and promptly fell off again coming out. In a little over a lap he'd led twice, fallen off as many times, and was now out of the race. He knew I'd been watching, but I thought it best for both of us to keep my impressions to myself.

James's career improved after that. After all, it couldn't get much worse. He started stringing together impressive results in national meetings. Some time in 1986 I suggested to him that if he wanted to make a living at racing he needed to move up to the Superstocks class, which I obviously knew something about. It was high-profile, really competitive, and relatively cheap – right up his street. Later I arranged through Rex White for Suzuki to supply him with a GSX-R750 and spares to do the series in '87.

Before that I arranged a one-off ride for him on a spare Superstock bike in October's Brands Hatch Powerbike International. At Druids hairpin he was running right to the kerbing on the exit, which might work on a 125 but on a 750 would definitely end in tears. Sure enough, on the next lap, I saw this elbow go from up there to down here as he cracked open the throttle … whee, bang … and he'd high-sided himself into the Armco. Undeterred, he picked himself up and in the race he diced all the way with Trevor Nation. For his first time out on a 750 that wasn't half bad.

Early in the New Year the two of us drove to Crawley, loaded a new GSX-750 and a pile of bits into the van, and James's Superstock career began. I helped him turn the bits into a racer but from there on was very much hands-off. It was his team, to run how he saw fit. He crashed lots in that first season, including writing the bike off at Scarborough. At Mallory after he trashed another GSX-R dicing with Reg Marshall and Fred Merkl, I persuaded Suzuki to lend him a spare bike for the Superstock event. When he won, they decided to keep him on the bike to help Mez in the championship.

The result was inevitable: next time out he threw the bike away at the bottom of Cadwell Mountain. Adding insult to injury, the bike cleared the fence before crashing down almost next to Suzuki's truck. With James it always seemed to be two steps forward, one backward, but it was obvious that he had something special. By this time I'd already decided he was my man for the following season, but if he kept trashing bikes at this rate Suzuki might not agree. 'All we need,' I implored him, 'is one good result before the end of the year.' He did himself proud, winning at Mallory, finishing second at Oulton, and rounding out the year with top spot at Brands.

'We can do summat now,' I told him, and he was in the team for 1988.

Unfortunately that 'summat' was on the cheap. Mez was fairly cheap, James even cheaper, they had me as a novice team manager and everyone knows I'm cheap. All of us used to cast jealous glances at the likes of Honda and Kawasaki, who did have a budget and were able to do a proper job. I didn't know it then, but the fact is I've never run a team which had a realistic budget. Mind you, budget wasn't everything, at least not back then. After all, the best financed team I've ever worked with – Honda's NR500 – came up with naff-all.

By this time Carol and I had abandoned the monstrosity at Lepton Grange and moved down the hill to a smaller house we'd built after the customary battle with the planning authority. I can't say they didn't have a sense of humour, because the man they'd programmed to say 'no' on their behalf was Mr Fussy. Apparently I could build anything I wanted – over his dead body. Tempting though this was, we appealed in the conventional way.

It's at times like this that a history of bending rules comes in handy. Before the appeals board visited the site, I took the precaution of tearing lumps out of it with a JCB. By the time I'd finished, Battersea Power Station would have been less of an eyesore, so after a few minor modifications, the plans were approved. As well as housing Carol and I, this would be the base for Team Suzuki.

In some respects having to get by on next-to-nothing probably made for a better team spirit. We couldn't buy our way out of problems, but hard work and enthusiasm don't cost a bean. It probably helped that what I'd achieved as a rider had been won by hard graft and commitment –

exactly the qualities we needed now. Between the two of them James and Mez wrapped up four or five British championships over the following seasons which was something to be proud of. Better still, we had a lot of fun.

One way or another I knew what I was getting into. Mez was experienced and pretty much the finished article, whilst James was young, green and daft. I expected to have to mother him a bit, with maybe the odd verbal kicking. My preference would have been to bring Nigel Everett into the team, but the budget wouldn't stretch to that, so in came Butch Cartwright, a mate of James who'd helped him the previous year. Mez also brought his regular mechanic, Malcolm. Of the two, I reckoned Butch would probably be busier – at least as far as replacing mangled bodywork was concerned.

In his own way Butch was as green as James, but more bolshie. He'd been used to doing things his own way, and I suspect resented me as a bit of an intrusion. At the time all the major teams had got together and agreed to park their race transporters in the same part of the paddock, mainly to put on a glossy, high-profile front. Our contribution would have been more impressive if we'd actually looked at all glossy – and if Butch had been singing from the same sheet. For the Knock Hill meeting, I arrived to find Honda, Yamaha and Kawasaki oozing glamour in one corner of the paddock, with Butch parked half a mile away. We had a bit of a set-to which cleared the air, and after that we got on well.

Butch had a talent for clearing things. One night he fell asleep whilst driving the team truck. Just ahead of him was a tragedy in the making – a Yorkshire bloke who'd been made redundant, gamely followed Norman Tebbitt's advice to 'get on his bike', scraped together what little money he had to buy a battered motorhome and headed south to find work. The first hiccup in his plan came when his motorhome ground to a halt on the hard shoulder; the second when Butch careered into the back of him and spread his dreams across three lanes of the M1. I guess it was sort of a Team

Grant tradition. Nigel had done much the same thing in a hire car in Finland a few years before, smacking into a local car and giving the driver a bad case of whiplash. The legals from that went on for quite a while.

When he wasn't asleep Butch, unlike me, had the most unbelievable memory. If we had a handling problem with the bike, I'd need to sit down with my data books and work out the problem in my head. As often as not, Butch would chirp up something like, 'It just needs a couple of clicks on the compression.'

'How'd you work that out so quickly?'

'Easy. Four meetings ago we had the same problem, and it fixed it.' This seemed miraculous to me, since I couldn't be relied upon to remember what had happened the previous day.

Like any mechanic, he dropped the occasional clanger, although considering how busy we kept him his record was remarkably good. We weren't always so lucky. When we ran the RGV250s in the Supersport 400 series, we were suddenly obliged to use unleaded pump fuel, which gave us massive detonation. Even running the smallest possible squish clearance, after just one meeting the pistons were trashed and the head needed re-machining. At the time we had three 250s, for James, Martin Jupp, and Chris Morley, which gave us plenty to do.

I set on a keen young kid to help out, showing him how to measure the combustion volume with a burette. While I'd be down in the machine shop trying to revitalise half-wrecked heads and barrels from one engine, he'd be upstairs measuring the volumes in a cylinder I'd just had on the milling machine.

'How's that one?' I'd shout upstairs.

'Bang-on,' came the reply.

That's lucky, it normally takes a few goes to get it that close.

When the second cylinder was equally 'bang-on', I began to get suspicious. A third 'bang-on' sealed it. I trotted upstairs and asked him to show me how he'd done it, then watched in amazement as he turned the tap on the burette – and left it turned on oblivious to the water running out of the plug hole and over the engine. I showed him again how to do it. Same result. He may as well have used his hat as a burette. I had to let him go.

When his RGV wasn't self-destructing, James had a brilliant season, winning the ACU 1300cc Production series – mostly riding the GSX-R750 – and finishing second to Darren Dixon in the Formula One championship. The big production class was perfect for us. It was cheap to run and our Suzukis were as competitive as anything on the track. The biggest struggle was with the 600 – then called 'seniorstock'. Every other manufacturer had a serious sports 600, whilst we were stuck with a bike for going to the shops – the GSX600. It even looked slow. The minute they saw it James and Butch christened it the 'Teapot'. Making it even half competitive was going to be difficult.

James is convinced that the GSX600 he raced was the dodgiest thing he ever sat on. The fact was it wasn't all that far from being legal. But it was the worst possible starting point. Our first job, like every rival teams', was to build it like it should have been built, 'blueprinting'. On the dyno it gave quite good power, and at Brands for one of its first meetings James and Mez were dicing with the leading bunch for two or three laps. Then – it was as if someone had flicked a switch – they both began to scythe their way backwards through the field. This became the pattern.

It didn't take a technical genius to suspect – shades of the old air-cooled Yamahas – that as the engine got hotter it was losing power. At the time we were contracted to Shell. I asked their technical people how hot the oil could get before we'd expect to lose significant power. Apparently there was almost no limit: as long as it ran more or less normally, the oil would continue to do its job.

Next we put a GSX on the dyno and ran it hard with the cooling fans turned off. The oil temperature soared even beyond what Shell said it would stand, yet the power dropped by less than one horsepower. Mmm. The problem clearly lay elsewhere, although surely it had to be heat-related. If it wasn't the engine running too hot, maybe it was the air entering the carburettors. If that became less dense, sure enough, power would fall off.

At about the same time Doug Polen had experienced a similar problem racing a 750 Suzuki in Mexico. The team's first reaction had been to pile on more and more oil coolers, and with every one the bike got slower still. Eventually the penny dropped that all these radiators in front of the engine were making it even harder for cool air to reach the carbs. So one of Jim Lee's chaps, Allan, came up with a clever system of NACA ducts. Based on aircraft technology, these create a vortex which forces fresh air into the ducts, which in turn feed it to the bike's airbox.

Bingo! After that, the power never dropped off. Even so, it never really had enough to begin with, so was never going to make a top runner. James placing third in the championship was nothing less than inspired. But other than the odd bit of gearbox bother, the engine was strong and never let us down. What it didn't have, and never would have without serious rule-breaking, was truly competitive horsepower. The ducting, as far as my reading of the rules went, was totally legal. True, the odd bit of titanium might have found its way on to it here and there, but nobody's perfect.

I've never been comfortable with the role of recruiting sponsors, or brown-nosing generally, but since we couldn't afford professional specialists, any backers we did get was almost entirely down to me. After dozens of fruitless approaches, I was leafing through the Yellow Pages early in '89 when I came across a listing for the British Rubber Company. They didn't make tyres, they made condoms, but maybe there was enough of a connection to dangle before them. By then I'd become thick-skinned enough not to mind being told to sod off. I made the call.

Eventually I'm put through to a chap called Euan Venters. After explaining who I was and what I wanted, he invited me along to London for a chat. An hour later we had Durex sponsorship. True, it was only around £20k per year, but that was 20,000 times more than our existing backing. Even today, a lot of teams look as though they have big-bucks sponsorship, and sometimes they have, but often only a fraction of it finds its way to the hardware. The branding often looks far more impressive than it actually is.

Team Durex Suzuki was launched at a posh hotel in London's St James, which Murray Walker kindly agreed to host. We had about four hectic days to get the bikes painted in their new livery, plus paddock jackets and shirts designed and printed. The St James do was followed by a track launch at Donington Park on the same May weekend as the North West 200 meeting, which caused us a few problems. Since we had to send six bikes to Donington as props for the launch, we were able to send only a skeleton crew to Ireland, just two GSX-R1100 production bikes for Mez and James, on which we planned to do both the proddy race and both legs of the feature event. James had a brilliant ride in the production race, just edging out Dave Leach's FZR1000 Yamaha on the final lap to take the win.

That wasn't the hairiest ride he had that day, for James still goes on about my drive to the airport for the dash to Donington. (In his book, *What a Good Do*, he's rather rude about my driving generally.) Literally as they finished the main race, he and Mez jumped into the back of my hire car. I went berserk, driving our little diesel Renault across pavements, over the floral displays in the middle of roundabouts, anywhere rather than being snarled-up in traffic. Eventually I got on a bit of open road and wound the Renault up to about 90mph, just in time to nearly impale us on a tractor trundling out of a drive. Mez and

James were in the back, still in racing leathers, but not saying much apart from the odd shriek. It was only a matter of time before the police stopped us, especially since a few of the cars we'd carved-up had reported the nutters in the Renault. Just outside Ballymena we were nicked. Luckily, most Irish cops are well into their road racing. So after getting a bollocking they gave us the full blues-and-twos escort to the airport.

At the time Durex had spent five times our budget on a promotional hot-air balloon, which wasn't even on the telly, whereas our British championship was. Because the basic spend was small, I persuaded Euan to give us an extra £2,000 per meeting if 'Durex' was mentioned on air. At the time the Beeb was notoriously shy of naming sponsors of any sort, but I had a chat with the commentator, Barry Nutley, explaining our predicament. He was as good as gold. We used to love listening to the recorded highlights … 'and that's the Durex Suzuki' … ching! – another two grand in our pitiful budget. It worked until halfway through the season when a new BBC producer put the mockers on Barry's help.

To add even more to the budget we went into the rag trade, selling Durex Suzuki merchandise at the circuits. James and Mez were too plug-ugly to be anybody's idea of catwalk models, so I can't imagine that punters actually wanted to look like them. Yet in the first season we grossed around £120,000, of which our cut was maybe ten per cent. It was hardly an adequate budget but added up to something we could work with.

Inevitably, because of the nature of the sponsor's product, there were plenty of lewd jokes around the paddock, although the only one that worried us was the thought of a race bike having a puncture. That would not be good for the idea of reliable birth control, although I'm not sure how the idea of Whitham flinging himself all over the countryside squared with carefully planned families, either. Luckily none of the bikes ever had a flat, but I hope James and Mez would have had the sense to pretend it was a mechanical problem if it had happened.

The 1988 TT had been a bit of a damp squib. We managed just two fourth places, Mez in the big proddy event on the GSX-R11000, James in the 750cc production on the smaller GSX-R. For '89, though, we were buzzing, fresh off a win at the North West and with a pocketful of new sponsorship. Ever since the arrival of the first GSX-R, Suzuki had enjoyed several good years on the Island. In 1986 they won every one of the four production races, through Barry Woodland, Gary Padgett, Mez and Trevor Nation. James didn't have a lot of TT experience, but the fourth place he'd had the previous year was in the best of company – only Steve Hislop, Brian Morrison and Geoff Johnson were ahead of him. With another year's experience under his belt, we reckoned a rostrum was on the cards. If nothing else, it was going to be hectic. We had something like 16 bikes to prepare.

James began the week with a good sixth in Formula One. Then came the 400cc proddy race and proof I'd never make a race mechanic. When I was riding, I was Joe Cool during pit stops. As a pit-man, I was a dead loss. When Macca McGregor came in for his stop, my only job was to take the key out of the RGV's ignition, unlock the filler cap, and step out of the way. After the fuel went in, all I had to do was the reverse. Simple. Or not.

Macca screeched to a stop, I put the ignition key in, pulled the cap off – and in horrible slow motion the key tinkled to the bottom of the fairing. To get it out we had to physically lift the bike vertical and shake it. Macca spat a few oaths at me before going on to second place.

In truth it was a miracle he even finished. The bikes were equipped with race kits designed for 100-plus octane blue gas. On ordinary Manx fuel they never managed a practice session without holing a piston. I told Macca he'd just have to go gentle for the race. This isn't the sort of thing a racer likes to hear.

'I'm going to rev the nuts off it,' he said. 'If it doesn't last, it doesn't last.' Luckily, it lasted. Amazingly, they both did. Eddie Laycock and Macca gave us a one–two. When James and Mez took their Teapots to third and fourth in the 600cc race, we were flying. And our best shot must surely come with the GSX-R1100 in the big production race.

On the second lap word came through that Mez was off at Doran's Bend. It was my first real taste of being on the tough side of the fence. When I'd been racing, the one place that Carol didn't like to go was the Isle of Man. On the lap after I broke the course record in 1975, as I was due to reach the Bungalow, Ian Cannell, the commentator there, said over the air: 'I can see a rider coming, that will be the new lap record holder …' After a pregnant pause, this was followed by news that, 'It's not Mick Grant.' It was another 20 minutes of torment before word reached Carol that I was fine, marooned at the Gooseneck with a broken chain. That's the sort of thing that all racing wives and girlfriends go through on the Island but I could only imagine how she must have felt as I sat at the side of the track cursing the bike for breaking down.

Now I was in a similar situation. I knew Mez was off, but had no idea whether he'd lost a bit of skin or something more serious. I was still no wiser when news arrived that James was off, too – at Quarry Bends, where there's no such thing as a small crash. I felt less like a team boss and more like a racing missus.

Next thing, word arrives that James is OK but Mez is being air-lifted to hospital. So off we set for Nobles, with Christine, Mez's wife, Malcolm, his mechanic, and Butch. Apparently he has severe internal bleeding which they have to stop to stabilise his condition. But, thank God, he's alive and so long as he is there must be hope. Twenty minutes later – it seemed like an eternity – the same doctor tells us they're struggling to stop the bleeding. I'm trying to console myself that if any hospital is used to dealing with this sort of stuff, it's Nobles. Mez was surely in good hands.

For everyone but the medics, who at least know what they're about, there are no scripts for this sort of situation. Anything you do feels clumsy and inept. I tried to console Christine, suggesting that at this time in his career Mez ought to be thinking about retirement, and when he pulled through we'd do what we could to pave the way, if that's what he wanted to do. Christine was livid and ripped into me. Five minutes later, her husband, one of racing's true Mr Nice Guys, was dead. I don't think she's spoken to me since.

James, at least, was fine, at least physically. He'd seen Mez's crash, knew that at the very least he was badly hurt, and his concentration went haywire. A few miles later he clipped the kerb at Quarry Bends. He'd just got to his feet when Steve Henshaw and Mike Seward arrived and piled into his debris. According to James, by the time he stood up, there was still no flag out, and that's one of the problems with the Isle of Man. If a flag had been out, that second crash might never have happened. That, more than any inherent flaws in production-bike handling, was the cause of Henshaw's death and Seward's injuries. But it was easier to make the bikes the scapegoats and almost immediately top-level production racing was abandoned – not just at the TT but on British short circuits as well. This just wasn't a logical response to the problem. It also lost some good, close racing which was popular with manufacturers because they saw it as a way of selling bikes.

Any circuit is there to be ridden. Whether a bike handles or not, you ride it within its limits. Riding any bike beyond that point is dodgy, whether it handles well or not. Although much has been said and written about the bikes or the tyres being at fault for Mez's crash, the truth is that he made a mistake and, tragically, paid the worst possible price. There are some excellent marshals on the Island, without doubt. And the standard today is higher than it was then. But ultimately you just have to accept that on a 38-mile circuit the quality can't be as good as at major short-circuit meetings.

Death is nothing new in racing. Most riders seem pretty thick-skinned about losing colleagues, at least on the surface: they have to be if they're ever going to get on a bike again. And as a rider you cling to the conviction that you – not fate, not someone else – are in control. For the most part that enables you to keep tragedy at a distance – unlike poor Marie Armes who for years had the appalling task of breaking the tragic news of TT death to families and dealing with the emotional aftermath.

It was the worst day I ever experienced in racing. As a team we were shattered. Nothing prepares you for episodes like that, but I've always had a clear view in my mind about the danger of circuits. Whether you're racing over the Mountain or at Mallory Park, bikes can bite. It's a dangerous business and it's delusional to believe otherwise. Whether that attitude was right or not doesn't much matter – it's just the position with which I approached racing. To my mind, it's the only honest one to have.

Most people who race the TT have a wonderful time and survive it, but not without an awareness of the risks. Whenever I travelled to race there, I used to silently tell myself for chrissakes don't come back in a wooden box. So the dangers were never far from my mind. And they're risks you must accept. You either piss or get off the pot. I'm sure Mez had much the same view.

Harrowing though 1989 was, since I'd never pretended that sort of thing couldn't happen, there was never any doubt in my mind that I'd be back the following year. To me, it just didn't make sense that it took a tragedy before you recognised that racing was dangerous. It always was, always will be, whatever measures are taken to make it less so. In that respect, being team manager was no different from being a rider, except that worrying for other people is always more wearing than worrying for yourself. If a rider chooses to take a risk, that's his risk. But no one back in the pits can take one for him, whether that's about machine preparation, strategy, tyres or set-up. However much a rider uses the heat of the moment to put the risks to the back of his mind, as a team boss you simply can't do the same, second-hand. You worry, almost as if you were normal – which you're obviously not because you used to be a racer, too.

Only two months later it was James's turn to find this out the hard way. At Dundrod for the Ulster GP the front brake rotor of his Formula One bike disintegrated going into Flow Bog Corner. He slid feet first into a bank at about 100mph, smashing his ankle to bits. At the time he was leading both the British Production and Formula One series. The crash wasn't his fault, but put him out for the rest of the season.

Later in the year came two significant phone calls, the first from James.

'Mick,' he began, 'I don't know how to tell you this but I've signed for Honda for next year.'

Shit!

I could hardly respond. I was gutted. But it got worse. Literally ten minutes later Heron Suzuki boss John Norman rang from Japan. Although he had nothing in particular against racing, he definitely didn't see it as a marketing tool. (Although he did later admit that when I took one to victory in the Senior TT in 1975 he'd sold a shedful of Kawasaki 500s which previously he could barely give away.) At least, that was his view when the racing budget came out of his bottom line. But this was different.

'I've got great news,' he began. 'I've got a deal for James to do World Superbikes on a Suzuki.'

When I told him about the earlier call, what little enthusiasm he'd had for racing seemed to disappear.

Luckily Steve Kenwood, Heron Suzuki's sales manager was still keen to carry on with the racing effort, despite the lack of support from upstairs. A small budget was cobbled together allowing me to run one rider, Roger Burnett. The bikes were the same old Formula One 750s that James, and before that Roger Marshall and Paul Iddon, had ridden. Because Butch had gone to Honda with James, for a while I had to farm out bike preparation to another dodgy Grant – Ron, from his workshop in London. 'RG' was a clever mechanic and a lovely man, but also a bit of a loose cannon. He'd recently left Honda under a bit of a cloud. Before that he'd been everywhere and done everything. Like everyone else in racing, I'd heard plenty of tales of his exploits in the States when he rode for Suzuki America – going the wrong way down freeways to escape the police, wrecking hire cars, all sorts of lurid stuff.

Our first meeting was the Jerez World Superbike round. James and Carl Fogarty were both there, on a high from Daytona, where both had led before crashing out. But in Spain they struggled. James qualified 21st, with Foggy not far ahead. Halfway through practice Butch sidled across to our garage.

'We've got a problem,' he said. Apparently the bike was doing this, that and the other and nothing they'd tried had made it any better.

I knew the probable answer, I liked Butch and liked James. But they were the opposition. They were being paid to beat my rider. I was being paid to do the same to them.

'Sorry, Butch. I just can't help you.' I felt awful.

I'd been shocked when James left for Honda, but not bitter. It wasn't a question of him making his bed and having to lie on it. No one knew better than me that you're only in racing for a few short years, and every race could be your last. If James felt he was bettering himself, and he clearly did, then he was right to make the move. And in fairness, all the time he was with us at Suzuki it was a bit of a Mickey Mouse effort. We never really had the budget to do a proper job, whereas at Honda he would have been well resourced and well paid. It was ironic that, for James, their bike just didn't work for him half as well as ours.

Come the TT, RG didn't seem to be making as much effort as I thought was needed. On the eve of the first race I came back from running errands, gave the supposedly race-ready bike a quick once-over, and found a couple of cracks, one on the chassis, another on the rev-counter bracket. In my book Ron was good enough to have spotted them, but evidently didn't. After putting a plea on Manx Radio for someone who could TIG-weld the frame up at short notice, I found myself at a workshop owned by a guy named Martin Lockwood, near Archalagan Plantation above Ballacraine. It was an utter tip, full of the sort of junk that's bound to come in useful one day, but never does, and in the meantime you're forever tripping over it. But underneath the rubbish was a beautiful little TIG-welder, and Martin knew how to use it. Job done.

What was also done was my working relationship with RG. You simply can't afford that sort of sloppy preparation at the TT at the best of times. We had to be even more careful since the Formula One chassis, although a lovely bit of kit, was by then four years old – a pensionable age for an aluminium racing chassis. I gave Ron his marching orders.

All in all, it wasn't a year to remember. Roger was without doubt a very talented rider but even allowing for our limited resources his results didn't reflect that talent. As well as being accustomed to riding for much better- resourced teams than ours, I don't think he had the hunger he once had, in stark contrast to James. Our best results all year were two third places, at Snetterton and Thruxton.

CHAPTER 19

A NARROW SQUEAK

James's disastrous year with Honda brought him to the brink of packing in. He'd crashed the RC30 so often that his confidence was at absolute rock bottom. In most of the crashes – over a dozen in all – he'd lost the front end and had no idea what he'd done wrong. Nothing his crew did seemed to make any difference. Even Foggy, his team-mate, had a pretty lacklustre year. After leaving us on a high after 1989, James finished the following season a quivering wreck.

James knew he'd dropped a clanger well before the season was over. One day he called round unannounced to say so. He wanted back with Suzuki for 1991. There was nothing formal, but after the year I'd been having I liked the idea. The truth was that by this time he probably wasn't at the top of any other team's shopping list. He'd struggled to get a ride elsewhere. But the talent and commitment he'd shown in '88 and '89 can't have just disappeared. I knew, probably more than anyone – probably more than James himself at the time – that he had lots left to offer. After all, he was still only 25.

On the other hand, a Suzuki squad with ancient bikes and almost no budget wasn't many riders' idea of a dream team. So Team Huddersfield got together again.

The Formula One bike may have been old, but it still had some life. Almost everything about the chassis was adjustable, so it could be tuned to suit any rider, any track. It had originally come with conventional factory forks. When upside-downers came on the scene, James and Butch were keen to get a pair of Öhlins. We simply didn't have that sort of money so stuck in a modified pair from a GSX-R1100 road bike. Once James got his head around the fact that they weren't Öhlins, they worked pretty well.

We were probably a little short of horsepower. Top speed was good, the bike just took a while to get there. Like the old Teapot, the engine had a knack of losing power as it got hot, so the previous year Allan, Jim Lee's sidekick, had knocked up a pair of feeds to the air-box. They looked like something off a Hoover, but did the trick, especially at high-speed circuits. In both 1990 and 1991 our best results came at speed bowls like Thruxton and Snetterton.

At the start of the season, tuning the bike was the least of our problems. It was James who needed fettling. It was obvious from what little pre-season testing we were able to do that he wasn't the rider who'd left us. Butch and I were still much as before, but James was reeling. We needed a way to get his confidence back in a hurry, so I came up with a dodgy plan.

Most of the top teams would be running 750s for the whole season – the limit then allowed by the Formula One/ Superbike rules. But at maybe half a dozen other meetings, such as Mallory Park's Race of the Year, we could run anything up to 1,300cc in the feature events. Since our aged 750 was likely to struggle, a big engine for these races seemed the obvious way to go. Butch and I first cobbled together a GSX-R1100 engine in an old factory chassis, but James hated it. Back to the drawing board.

Plan 'B' involved a set of big pistons from Cosworth to take the Formula One bike out to 888cc. The bike looked exactly like the Formula One, but was a missile. That gave me the idea for plan 'C'.

When we'd built the 888 there was never any intention to run it illegally, at least in British championship events. But the fact that we had it opened up another possibility.

Practically our first major meeting of the year was a big international at Donington Park. After wrestling with my conscience for at least a second, I asked Butch to slip the 888 engine in the bike. This wasn't to cheat, exactly, although it was obviously wildly illegal – but to give James a leg up and give him back some confidence. We were pretty sure that, whatever we'd done, he wasn't likely to trouble the top factory guys, which wasn't our aim. James, needless to say, hadn't a clue he was riding a dodgy bike. In essence, it was him, rather than the rest of the grid, that we were trying to con.

James got a solid result in both races, which did his confidence a power of good. The other good result was that we didn't get rumbled, which would have been a major embarrassment for Suzuki, quite apart from having God knows what effect on James. It was a calculated risk but worked a treat. From that point on his season really took off. And for all its problems, the Formula One bike seemed to be made for him. He could practically make it talk.

That year there was a daft set-up of two parallel British championships, each of six rounds. One was televised, the other not. In the first series, TT Supercup, James placed second to Rob McElnea. But all year his performances had been getting stronger, and by the last round of the TT Superbike championship at Brands, he and Rob stood neck and neck.

A betting man would definitely have had his money on Rob, who was a class act and hugely experienced. James careered round the paddock like a headless chicken. I took him aside and asked why he was racing at all. There was never any doubt about his answer: 'Cos I enjoy it. For fun.'

'Then just go out there and enjoy yourself.'

Whether that had any effect I don't know, but somehow he held it together in the first leg to finish second with Rob third, leaving them exactly equal on points with just one leg to go. If anything was going to test his mettle and confidence, this was it. It was a brilliant race, a brilliant end to the season. The pair of them were wheel to wheel for the whole 28 laps, with James just nipping ahead at Druids last time around and holding Rob off by inches, while Butch, me and Andrea, James's girlfriend, jumped around on the pit wall like demented things. James was British champion.

After the woes of 1990 it was probably the best day I had as a manager – and definitely the best in a while for James. We'd accomplished it on next to no budget on a bike that ought to have been retired at least two years earlier. Yet even though we still had naff-all money and the season had restored James's reputation, there never seemed to be a serious question of him going anywhere else for '92. He was probably the hottest young prospect in British racing and could have walked into any other team. But the last time he'd left, he'd got badly bitten. He wasn't about to do the same again.

I dare say James thought of going elsewhere. I knew that his ambition was a proper go at World Superbikes. So was mine. During the autumn positive noises had been coming out of Japan about Suzuki's new liquid-cooled 750, which helped keep both of us on the Suzuki script. The reality was a bitter disappointment. For marketing reasons we couldn't even use the old Formula One bike on which James had won in 1991. It had to be the new GSX-R Suzuki, which just wasn't up to scratch. Germany threw a fortune at Ernst Geschwender and Udo Mark's bikes, but they weren't a lot better. It wasn't just power that was lacking. Compared to the Formula One bike there was very little adjustment in the chassis, and all season long James struggled to get it into turns – so much so that we christened it the 'ironing board'. He literally had to leap head first into corners and drag the GSX-R around after him. It was this that gave him his infamous hang-off style.

We started the season with about £20,000, a pitiful sum compared to the likes of Kawasaki who would have been on at least ten times that. (They went on to win the championship through John Reynolds.) Our 'race transporter' was a solitary Renault Trafic van. For a while, we were reduced to using Reynolds' cast-off tyres for practice. During those two seasons most of our earnings – James's as well as mine – came from results bonuses, much of which was ploughed back into the team budget.

One other thing came from Kawasaki. Alec Wright, the Kawasaki team boss, gave me the idea of trawling around all the Suzuki dealers with one-off sponsorship deals – so that for a meeting at, say, Snetterton, a dealer in Norwich, the nearest large city, would pay £500 to have his name on the bike. In that way, we put another £11,000 into the pot. It was a struggle, not least for Butch who seemed to spend half the season changing stickers.

But as upbeat as we felt, it was damned hard work and worse seemed to lie ahead. Bike sales were at rock bottom and all the manufacturers were looking for ways of cutting back. I suspect there had been a bit of a power struggle between the two big wheels at Suzuki GB. Denys Rohan was generally pro-racing, whilst John Norman was largely anti-, and it seems that Norman's view came out on top. The upshot was that, although they were happy for me to continue to run the 'official' Suzuki race team, there was no budget and I was no longer even on their payroll. It seemed like a good time to cut and run.

From my racing days I'd always had a strong connection with South Africa, and for a time during the early part of '92 it looked as though a sponsorship deal for the following grand prix season might come from there, via the Nashua and Ricoh importers. The plan was to co-opt a small chunk of the promotional budget from each country that ran a grand prix meeting, and it very nearly worked. As a dry run we entered local rider Russell Woods on a Nashua Harris Yamaha at the Kyalami grand prix. I'd promised Nashua 12th place, and that's exactly what Russell achieved. It was looking good – until just one country put the mockers on the idea, which was enough to kill it for all the rest. It was all so tantalisingly close – even to running with a South African paddock theme, promoting Cape wines and other local products.

James didn't come close to retaining his championship, but 12 wins and 18 rostrums during the 1992 season wasn't at all shabby under the circumstances. As the season wore on, he began to get a little more distant, as though there was something on his mind. The last time he'd been like that, he jumped ship to Honda, so I was concerned. Eventually, he coughed. He'd been sworn to secrecy but, after a bit of prevaricating, told me of being approached by a would-be sponsor. The guy's name was John Stratton. He evidently had a chunk of money he wanted to put into running a race team. But don't tell anyone.

Fine. I just left it at that.

Next thing, I learn that this mysterious Stratton wants to speak with me, so we set up a meeting. I've always reckoned I can pick people: just look at their shoes. His were quality stuff, which said he was probably kosher. He also had a strange squeaky voice, which might have told me something else – like so has Mickey Mouse.

Looking back, there were other clues. He became quite a regular visitor to my house. I'd pick up him and his quality shoes from Huddersfield station. As we got more familiar he made the fundamental mistake of calling Carol 'Flo' which – whether a reference to Andy Capp's missus, or George Formby's in *No Limit* – didn't exactly endear him to her. Now Carol is nobody's mug. Apart from saying she'd top him if he ever called her that again, she decided he was a wrong 'un. 'That guy is bad news,' she said. I should have listened.

At Stratton's request I put together a detailed budget for a season of 500cc grand prix. To my mind, winning the world championship was fundamentally a question of money. Given an unlimited budget, you'd buy the best rider, best bikes, best crew, and if you know what you're doing, given enough time you can deliver a world title. The numbers Stratton was kicking about didn't reach that high. They'd buy a middling team with two high-calibre riders. And there was never any question of who they'd be: James and Carl Fogarty. I reckoned we could finish in the top dozen in our first season. That's the point at which you'd tell your sponsor that's what £x just did – now where do you want to finish next season? In other words, how much are you ready to spend?

For phase one, I reckoned that at a pinch we could do a full season for two riders for £500,000. I gave Stratton the news, half expecting him to keel over.

'Oh, that's no good,' he squeaked. 'You need £750,000.'

Now never in 20-odd years of racing had I known a sponsor volunteer to increase the budget, so that set bells ringing, too. On occasions Stratton would turn up to meetings sporting black eyes, which he always claimed were from falling down steps. I made a mental note never to send him up a ladder.

Stratton wanted to base the team workshop at some premises he owned – or said he did – near Mallory Park in Leicestershire. I insisted we'd be based around Huddersfield, either in our old Suzuki workshop or, if needed, somewhere bigger locally. He accepted this, but asked that I look at the Leicestershire set-up anyway. We drove into the cobbled courtyard of a grand country house, surrounded by stables, half of them occupied by vintage cars – dozens in total, each worth a mint. Stratton seemed completely at home. I was impressed, but still insisted on running the team from nearer home.

At this stage he openly admitted that he had no capital at the time, but kept mentioning a 'window of opportunity' coming up which would net him a cool million quid, and that was just the start. Naturally James, Foggy and I discussed our doubts time and again. On the day Stratton was due to arrive with the contracts, the three of us were chatting in my kitchen.

'I don't believe him,' said Foggy.

'Yes,' James chipped in. 'The only reason we're here now is because we're all bloody greedy.' By that he didn't mean we were craving for the money, just that the opportunity was too good to resist. Even if there was only a 20 per cent chance it was the real McCoy, we felt bound to follow it through. After all, other than time, what did we have to lose?

So what were we going to do? Every time I'd spoken to Stratton by phone he was in Enfield, with busy office noises in the background. Between the three of us we agreed that I'd press him for more concrete evidence of his ability to deliver on his promises.

Later, Stratton breezes into the house, greets 'Flo', and sits down.

'Look, John, we have a problem. We just don't believe what you're promising is going to happen.'

He was upset.

Would he mind if I rang his partner?

So in front of the others I rang his partner, also called John, in Enfield.

'Hi John, Mick Grant here. Can you help us feel a bit more at ease?'

'No problem. How can I help?'

'John's saying he's got a million quid arriving in September. Is that true?'

'Yes, cast iron. It's going to happen.'

Which of course told us no more than we already knew, just that one more John was playing to the same tune. Still we didn't believe it. And yet, what if it were true ..?

Part of the deal was that we'd all get a 3-Series BMW apiece. James and Carl did their own deals, but at the last minute Carl decided he wanted another £40k. That was all right by Stratton, too. We still weren't convinced, not by a long way, but on we carried with this absurd adventure, even meeting with IRTA to book the team's place on the grand prix grid for the following season.

The next piece of business was Macau, our first outing as Team Stratton – or Team Alice, as it might have been called. That's Alice as in 'Wonderland', not Casey Stoner's Ducati sponsor. Stratton provided us with graphics of the sponsor's livery, a new credit card which would soon be sweeping the Western world. A pair of four-cylinder Harris Yamahas were leased from Padgett's for £15,000, painted up, and shipped to the Far East.

A few days before we followed the bikes, I gave Stratton an ultimatum: quite apart from the lease, running the bikes was going to cost serious money, none of which was going to come from my pocket. So unless he put £2,000 in my hand, I wouldn't even board the flight. It happened – just. I was actually in the airport lounge when he trotted in and placed a bundle of readies in my mitt.

So we had our running costs, but Padgett's were still waiting for theirs. Clive was as excited as anyone about Carl and James riding the bikes. But naturally he'd like his money up-front, if you don't mind. All I could promise was to press Stratton as hard as I could, and that we wouldn't actually run the bikes until they were paid for.

On the morning of the first practice session, I rang Clive yet again: still no money. It seemed like the end of the line.

'Well, that's it then,' I told him. 'We'll not run the bikes.'

Clive was niceness itself. 'Look, you've gone so far. I'm not saying you can race but at least practise. We can try to sort the rest out as we go.'

Later that day I rang Clive again. He seemed a happy man. 'A transporter's arrived,' he explained, 'with a gull-wing Mercedes on it, collateral against the lease.' Since in anybody's money a gull-wing Merc is worth more than the lease arrangement, this seemed solid. Which was more than could be said for Stratton.

In the midst of this, the race almost seemed incidental. Foggy won, James was third, with Toshihiko Honma splitting them on a full factory YZF Yamaha.

By the time I got home I'd already told Stratton where he could shove his hare-brained deal. Then Clive rang. He sounded chastened.

'Don't tell anyone what I'm about to tell you,' he began. 'Yesterday a very big bloke arrived for the Merc.'

'Fine,' Clive had told him, 'just give me the 15 grand and it's yours.'

'You don't understand. My job is reclaiming things, and I'm reclaiming that Merc. Now.'

And he did. It hadn't been Stratton's to bargain with.

Although I was out of the deal, James and Carl clung on to it for a while longer, but Stratton soon fizzled from sight. A few years later Jamie Robinson, then a promising 250cc rider from Huddersfield, rang me out of the blue. Apparently a would-be sponsor had approached him, offering £85k for his next season's racing. He wondered if it could possibly be our old friend John Stratton. I suggested Jamie record his voice the next time he rang him. Two days later, he rang me back and played the tape. The squeak was unmistakable.

CHAPTER 20

SET A THIEF ...

For 1993 Suzuki's race budget shrank from not very much to nothing at all and I was out of a job. James moved on to ride for Fast Orange Yamaha under Rob McElnea. During my racing career I'd been able to put a fair bit of money aside, but it wouldn't last forever. Besides, I needed something to do, so helped ex-racer Wayne Mitchell to set up a UK dealer network for Spanish Derbi motorcycles. Glad-handing dealers didn't exactly give me the buzz that racing had done, but was enjoyable enough. Being well known in the trade usually gave instant entry into dealers' doors. I'm no salesman, but I like to think I was instrumental in shifting quite a few bikes in those years. The problem was – much like my promotional role at Suzuki in 1986 to 1987 – it was a bit too much like a proper job. Even though I was only expected to put in three days every two weeks, which most ordinary blokes could only dream about, my attention span wasn't up to it. If you've been as lucky as I had, working at something you'd almost do for nothing yet still getting paid pretty handsomely, anything else is an anticlimax.

In late '95 I was approached by Doug Barnfield of the Motorcycle Circuit Racing Control Board, the body responsible for running British championship road racing. They needed someone to police the technical rules, which seemed right up my street. Naturally, given my own dodgy reputation, there were lots of cracks about 'poacher-turned-gamekeeper'. Even Carol thought it was hilarious.

As a rider, and particularly as a team manager, I pushed the rules to the limit and may have stretched them a little beyond that now and again. There's an old saying in racing that you should never fall behind in your cheating, but never get too far ahead, either. The fact is that every team bends the regulations as far as they'll go. If they don't they're handing an advantage to everyone else who does. Apart from running James on a big engine at Donington, I don't believe we ever outright cheated. I just seemed to acquire a reputation for being dodgy.

The job wasn't just about policing the rules. I also had a role in creating a framework of regulations that would be fair, realistic and enforceable. This was the more fascinating part of the work. At the time British and World Supersports regulations were significantly different, so much of my work was aimed at reaching parity through meetings with the FIM. The trackside business of actually trying to catch people out – people who were doing the same job I'd been doing only a couple of years before, with the same hassles and limitations – was something I didn't enjoy so much.

Inevitably, everyone sees the implementation of the rules from their point of view. There would always be complaints that some teams were being picked on, which was totally untrue. If someone was winning regularly, their bike would be checked more than most, although often the team concerned preferred to see this as some sort of vendetta. We'd bend over backwards to be seen to be transparent and even-handed. So before every race I'd say to Barry Hibbert, the chief scrutineer, something like 'right, we'll check the fuel on the guys finishing first, sixth and seventh and the cams on third and fifth' – numbers picked in advance totally at random off the top of my head. What we absolutely didn't do was let paddock gossip or shifty 'words in your ear' dictate which bikes would be singled out.

Not that we didn't hear the whispers. Paddocks are so rife with tittle-tattle we'd have had to be deaf not to. So over the two years I had lots of people whispering in my shell-like about so-and-so up to no good. Sometimes, I'd wander out on to the track and watch the 'culprit' for a couple of laps. As often as not his bike *was* quicker down the straights – but only because he'd come out of the previous corner better and got on the gas before his competitors. So my response would usually be, 'If you think he's cheating, put your money down and make a proper protest.' To me, sneaking around making cheap allegations was as reprehensible as actually cheating.

Perhaps the worst episode involved a bit of both, and probably left the worst taste in my mouth of anything in those two seasons. James Toseland, who's since been world superbike champ, was then a kid riding for Mick Corrigan in the one-make Honda 500 Cup series. Not surprisingly, in view of his subsequent success, he was doing well. I was sure that any edge he had was down to talent.

Unfortunately his bike was illegal, although I'm convinced James knew nothing of this. The Honda's head gasket was the usual laminated arrangement, and some of the layers had been removed, increasing the compression ratio. The advantage would have been too small to measure, but both he and his bike were thrown out of the results.

One of the more obvious innovations I introduced was the use of a rolling road dynamometer at meetings. Using the dyno we could determine within quite small margins what power a particular production-based bike should make, so that if one made significantly more it was likely to be a wrong 'un. As well as being a useful tool for us, it was far simpler and less expensive for the teams than random strip-downs. Usually an engine would be stripped only if the dyno raised questions about it.

Jack Valentine's V&M bikes were usually front runners, so he had more reason than most to think he was being singled out. The irony was that if anyone was steering close to the wind, it was usually Jack. He was canny and didn't miss a trick, which is one reason V&M enjoyed such success. He probably wouldn't thank me for saying so, but he was very much from the same sort of mould as me, if a few rungs further up the ladder.

After one Brands Hatch production race, both of the V&M bikes were revving 300 or 400rpm higher than they should have been and were thrown out of the results. Jack appealed, claiming the original ignition units had packed in on both bikes. Since they'd run out of spares he'd appealed to spectators to lend him ignitions from their road bikes – so how could he reasonably believe they were anything but legit? Since he got his result back on appeal, he was obviously right and I was wrong – and Japanese electronics are clearly random as standard.

There were, though, more ups than downs. I like to think that my input helped to put some sense and fairness into the racing rules. And it felt good to be back amongst all the drama and adrenalin of the track.

Halfway through my second season of gamekeeping, Russell Savory asked me for help. His Supersports CBR600, ridden by Marra Brown, was having some handling problems that neither of them could figure out. In the process of getting it sorted we established a bit of a rapport and he invited me to join his team. Obviously it was unthinkable to do that whilst I was still under contract to the MCRCB, but I committed myself to joining them as team boss the following season – back on the other side of the protest tracks.

To most racers, rules are there to be pushed as far as they can be bent. When I'd run Suzuki's official race team, even though our annual budget would barely buy a fish supper for the entire team, we couldn't really afford to be found cheating because it would have reflected badly on Suzuki. I'm not saying we didn't do marginal things. We did, as did pretty well everyone else, and they always will. But we simply couldn't afford to do anything blatant.

My attitude to protests is that it's always best to put your money where your mouth is and check it out. If you are cheating, then you deserve to be found out. And if you aren't, then it's the greatest compliment in racing that everyone thinks you must have been.

Sometimes it's hard to know whether you're cheating or not. As standard, the GSX-R1100K launched in 1989 was almost lethal. At speed over bumps it was even money whether it stayed on the grey stuff or spat you on to the grass. Our response was to re-shim the compression damping. As far as I was concerned this was totally legal, since no machining was involved, We even gave instructions for the mod so that Suzuki could pass it on to their dealers. Because Reg Marshall would be running a GSX-R1000 at the TT that year, I also made a point of passing the information on to Nigel who would be prepping his bikes.

Reg didn't like production bikes at the best of times, but for whatever reason the mods never made it into his forks. To this day you can watch the result on video. Mez came rocketing down Bray and over Ago's Leap ... whoosh, straight as a die. James ... ditto. Then came Reg, weaving from kerb to kerb at 160mph, more off the bike than on. It was pretty obvious no one had touched his forks. Afterwards he buttonholed me about it but only had himself or his mechanic to blame. James, who's probably no expert on production regulations, still thinks that fork mod was dodgy. I stand by it.

The year before, the issue hadn't been forks, but tyres. The production rules allowed us to run either the 750 or 1,100cc GSX-R, although at most circuits James preferred the 750's nimbleness, even though it was well down on power. At the Carnaby meeting Michelin turned up with a pair of prototype road tyres for us to use (they'd later become the Pilot range). After just a few laps, James came in glowing with praise.

'That front tyre,' he enthused, 'amazing, I can win on that.'

It was one of the scariest things he ever said. True, any team boss is happy when his rider's happy, but at the back of my mind I was already budgeting for the mangled fibreglass.

James, for once, was right. He just cleared off and left all the 1100s in his wake.

Now I'm not actually sure whether the tyres were legal. The rules called for street tyres, which these undoubtedly were, although at the time they weren't exactly available to Joe Public. Michelin wanted us to run 'em, so we did. As far as I was concerned it was up to the officials to decide if they met the rules or not. A couple of riders went in to Peter Hillaby's office to register a protest, emerging a few minutes later with their tails between their legs. Lovely chap that he is, Peter wasn't generally interested in the minutiae of regulations, so long as the gate receipts were good and the fans got a good show.

In 1991, the next stop after running James on the big engine at Donington, was Pembrey for a British championship round – which definitely limited us to 750cc. Our newly rehabilitated rider was quickest in practice on both the 750 and the RGV250. The next morning a deputation consisting of Barry Symmons, Colin Wright and Ray Stringer appeared at our pit. I later learned that someone working at Cosworth had tipped Ray off that we'd bought a set of big pistons. Not unnaturally he'd put two and two together and assumed we were using them in championship events.

'Look,' they said, 'we think you're running a big engine.'

It was hard not to smile. 'Oh you do, do you?' I responded.

'Yes. But we don't want to cause ripples. We'd just like the bike measured after the race.'

There was no threat of a formal protest, which seemed a bit mealy-mouthed. If we weren't cheating, it would all have been hush-hush, with no reflection on them. But if we were, they'd be sure to make a song and dance about it. Not surprisingly, they'd also sent their deputation so soon before the race that if we had been cheating, we'd no time to slot in a 750cc engine. In other words, they were hedging their bets and thought they couldn't lose either way. In reality, of course, since the bike was 100 per cent legal and correct, I was the one in the happy position of not being able to lose. Even so, I'd much rather they'd put their money where their mouth was by lodging a proper protest.

So we raced, and James won. In the meantime I'd put *MCN*'s race reporter, Norrie Whyte, in the picture and invited him along to witness our humiliation at being found out – which never happened, because the engine measured up exactly as it should.

Ironically, later the same season many of us suspected that John Reynolds was running an oversize engine in his Kawasaki. The irony was redoubled by the fact that the team was managed by the same Colin Wright who'd put in the 'unofficial' protest at Pembrey. For meeting after meeting it seemed that Reynolds's bike was visibly quicker than that of his team-mate, Brian Morrison. Eventually, at Cadwell, the rumours looked like coming to a head. On Friday morning Rob McElnea, then still a rider, approached me with the opinion that Reynolds's engine was illegal. I told him I'd been suspecting exactly the same. Unfortunately I had to dash off to South Africa that same afternoon to pursue a sponsorship deal, so whatever we might decide to do about it I couldn't be a part of until my return. Rob decided he'd 'have a chat' with Colin about his suspicions.

'No, don't do that,' I urged, 'wait until next week at Oulton, and we'll put in a joint protest.'

Presumably still thinking he held all the aces, Rob went to see Colin, who's always been one of the shrewdest cookies in the paddock.

'We think you're running a big engine,' he accused, or words to that effect.

Whether Rob was anticipating shame, denials, or bluster, I don't know. But he certainly wasn't expecting what he got.

'Yeah, I am,' retorted Colin, brazen as ever.

Whether this was true or not, we'll never know, but it seems to have knocked Rob on his arse.

When he'd picked himself up, he let the matter lie. The episode wasn't actually fair on Kawasaki, since it gave them no chance to exonerate themselves. But it seemed to me at least, that for the rest of the year Reynolds's bike didn't have its earlier edge.

Rounding off this game of mechanical charades, late in the season Colin protested Rob Mac for running too big an engine at the end-of-season Brands Powerbikes meeting – and won.

Mind you, even Colin didn't always get it right. He wandered up to me at one meeting to tell me he 'had reason to believe' I was cheating by running an illegal ignition box in our RGV250. At the time the ACU had just made unleaded fuel compulsory, so anyone running two-strokes, in particular, was suffering massive detonation problems. Our RGV was nibbling pistons almost faster than we could throw in new ones. Luckily we had plenty in stock, but since a dodgy ignition seemed to be the only way to make the engine deliver any power without self-destructing, Colin was absolutely correct. Our ignition box was bent. Not that this was something I'd admit to.

Colin told me he wouldn't do anything official at this meeting, but if he believed we were running the same kit next time out, he would definitely protest. Since he rarely says something he won't deliver on, I was in no doubt that he would.

Luckily I was well in with Rod Kitchen, who makes Scitsu rev counters and is generally very clued-up on ignition electronics. Rod made up a rig from which we plotted advance curve graphs from both the legal and illegal ignitions. Apart from one tiny blip, both curves were identical in shape, but one began about 13 degrees before the other. So all we had to do was throw away the Woodruff key holding the ignition on to its taper, and re-time the standard ignition timing to mimic the illegal one. Since this involved no dodgy electronics or machining, it was perfectly legal. Better still, probably through lacking the curious blip of the racing ignition, when we tried the re-timed stock ignition on the dyno, it actually gave two more horsepower than the 'trick' ignitions, which cost around £350 a pop.

Now I was happy to admit to Colin that I'd been cheating. 'Thanks, mate,' I told him. 'You've just given us another 2bhp. And saved me money.' I don't think he believed me, but it gave me a warm glow, all the same.

Unless you're a privateer, as a rider your role in protests is totally different. You might see what you suspect is blatant cheating, but it's up to someone else – your team boss – to do something about it. In my last season of race management, we had an issue with the supersports 600s. Marra Brown and Steve Plater, riding our CBR600 Hondas, were neck and neck in the championship with John Crawford's Suzuki. I think the Suzuki was marginally the better bike but our riders had the edge.

After two seasons as MCRCB gamekeeper I had a pretty good idea how the policing ought to work, and that didn't include someone having a quiet word in the chief scrutineer's ear 'ole. My view's always been that if you have a serious suspicion about me, put your money where your mouth is and put in a protest. If you do that, and you're wrong, it's a feather in my cap. If you're right, fair dos – you've caught me red-handed. The truth is that half the paddock are happy to gripe but want someone else to do their protesting for them.

In this case someone from Suzuki had a word with Barry Hibbert. After the race both our bikes were stripped to the last nut and bolt. Nothing was wrong with either, but to me that wasn't the point. To me that was an underhand way of going about it. If Suzuki had stumped up their £300 for an official protest, no problem. But to go about it that way was cheap and two-faced. I was livid, but there was nothing I could do – except store the memory for another day.

Come the final round of the series, Plater and Crawford finished level on points, with the Suzuki rider taking the title through scoring more race wins. This was always likely to happen, so I was prepared. At the end of a race you have precisely 30 minutes to lodge an official protest. In order that Suzuki couldn't respond with a tit-for-tat protest of their own, I hung about outside race office until 29 minutes had elapsed and then slapped down my £300 and a written allegation that the Suzuki's valves were underweight.

Now it might surprise you to learn that I actually had no suspicions that the valves, or anything else about the Suzuki, were the slightest bit dodgy. But I also happened to know that the scrutineers had no immediate access to precision scales. In the 24 hours it took to throw out the protest, no result could be declared and Suzuki's celebrations were put on hold. Call me petty if you want, but that was worth every penny of the protest fee.

My first official protest was against the only bloke in racing who was generally as dodgy as me. At Snetterton for the '85 Superstock series, Steve Parrish seemed to have found an extra bit of speed from his F750 Yamaha and won the race. For some reason my race boss, Rex White, wasn't at the meeting so it fell to me to do something about it. I stumped up the fee and protested. It turned out that a miniscule bump in the choke of Stavros's carbs had been illegally smoothed and he was thrown out of the results. I felt terrible. The mod would have given him no measurable advantage. His bike was quick for the simplest of reasons – he was riding it well. Luckily Stavros was always fairly laid-back and took it in good part.

During my first year with Russell Savory's Sanyo squad, the big production championship boiled down to a battle between David Jeffries on the V&M Yamaha and Glen Richards on our Honda. Word got about that V&M had steepened the head angle on their R1 Yamaha. On the eve of the final round of the series, I was buttonholed by

Roger Harvey, Honda Britain's race coordinator. He'd heard the same rumour about doctored R1 frames.

'What are you going to do about it?' he asked.

'Nothing … until Sunday. If we win the title, there's no point. If they win, we'll protest.'

Paddocks are hard places to keep secrets and I suspect that word got about. I think Roger may even have confronted V&M directly. Whatever they'd had before, by race day, the R1s definitely had the right frames.

Yes, people do go over the line. I did. Others did, and they always will. It's a fact of racing life that the biggest crime isn't doing it. It's being found out.

CHAPTER 21

RACING AGAIN

During 1997, while I was still working for MCRCB, Russell Savory asked for help setting up Paul 'Marra' Brown's supersport Honda. Russell was a good engine man – his engines won the Irish Regal series on maybe five occasions. But he was the first to admit that chassis tuning wasn't his bag. He'd recently changed from running Yamahas, so the Honda was a bit of an unknown quantity. Yet when his crew got the hang of the Honda, Marra made it fly, beating all the importer teams to win the British championship. He was kind enough to say that my input was crucial to the success.

Because of my policing role I couldn't do more than offer a few tips, but Russell and I got on well, and when he asked for help with his TT effort, I jumped at the chance.

At the time I happened to be pressing David Jefferies's case for help from Dave Hancock at Honda. I'd known the lad for years, of course, having raced against Tony, his dad, since around the time DJ was born. As well as having won the British production championship on a Honda, David Jefferies had taken the TT newcomer's award on his Island debut the previous year. Astonishingly in view of that, and what he'd later achieve, he had no rides at all for the 1997 TT. Honda had already exhausted their dealer support budget, but were keen to promote the new VTR1000 road bike. Hancock agreed to let us have one and spares worth £10,000. The obvious guy to run it on the Island was Russell.

Russell was pleased as punch but he didn't have much TT experience so his next question was whether I'd look after the bike's chassis. No problem. Off went our entries, and the 'Jefferies Honda VTR1000' was ready to go – until a week before practice when David broke his collarbone after baling off at Donington. 'That's that, then,' I thought, before learning – not for the last time – that Russell was not a man to be deterred by such trivia: 'No worries,' he said, 'we'll get someone else.'

That 'someone' turned out to be another man who'd make a name for himself over the Mountain, Adrian Archibald. On his Isle of Man debut in the Manx Grand Prix the previous September, he'd been less than seven seconds away from winning the Senior, averaging 115mph.

Due to commitments elsewhere I couldn't get to the Island until the Tuesday of practice week, by which time Russell had rung me with the not very encouraging news that the Honda was handling like a camel. By the time it was in fourth gear, evidently nothing Adrian did could persuade it to go in a straight line. Since it had six gears, this wasn't the best of omens, but I smugly told him I'd be over the following day and was sure we could sort it out.

When I arrived, we took the bike to Jurby airfield and I galloped off on it down the runway. True enough, by the time you reached fourth gear, all you could see above the tachometer was a line of ambulances waiting for business.

We spent all week getting nowhere. Since it was entered in the Formula One race, we had plenty of scope for modifying the bike. Yet everything we tried – even getting the head angle changed at an aeronautical engineers in Onchan – made little or no difference. On road tyres, it wasn't quite so bad; but on slicks it was scary, utterly unrideable. Yet even treads would only last a lap before the bike was weaving from kerb to kerb. All we could do was make the best of a bad situation and find the treaded tyres that were least bad. In fact the only consolation – not that it seemed so at the time, especially to Russell who had to rebuild it – was that the engine kept flying apart. It was a toss-up what would pack in first: the tyres, the motor, or Adrian's shredded nerves. Adrian, bless him, could justifiably have told us to stick the Honda where the sun doesn't shine. He had rides in four other classes, so had enough on his plate.

Worse still, ever since I'd finished with Suzuki I'd always regarded the TT as a bit of a holiday, yet here we were grafting until 2.00am every day on a project that we all knew wasn't going to work. By the end of the week, I was almost on my knees.

On the night before the race – too late to do much about it – we discovered that the bike's wheels were out of line, which seemed strange for a company like Honda. During my time doing development work for Suzuki, I'd got first-hand experience of how bikes end up as they do, and in particular that what the engineers want doesn't always end up on the final product. Costing and marketing considerations often prevail. Honda had mounted the VTR's swing-arm on the back of the engine casings, probably for no better reason than that's how Ducati did it – and Ducati was the bee's knees of the sports V-twin market Honda were trying to break into.

Trouble was, the bearing area was simply too narrow. As Russell was labouring yet again to pull the engine out of the Honda, I noticed a group of wear marks where the swing-arm had been rubbing on the crankcases. The set-up looked altogether like a cost-accountant's afterthought, rather than properly engineered as you'd expect from Honda. Later in the week I spent a day cruising the streets of Douglas, stopping VTRs at random and offering up a straight edge to their wheels. In many cases, their back wheels, too, were 15 to 20mm out of line with the front. On a road bike, it probably wasn't such a serious issue, but with slicks and a bit more power, it was lethal. Under the circumstances Adrian rode brilliantly to bring the bike home in 13th place – over 4mph slower than he managed on his supersport 600.

Once we got back from the Island, a local fabricating shop knocked up a pair of substantial 'ears' which we welded to the engine cases. This not only increased the bearing area but put the wheels back into line and allowed us to run a longer swing-arm. I took the prototype to Bruntingthorpe airfield and ran the Honda as quick as it would go on slicks, without a steering damper. It was rock-steady. Problem fixed.

Honda took a different view: if we hadn't fixed it, it wouldn't have been broken. They didn't seem too happy that we'd highlighted a problem they'd rather not own up to. During practice there had been something else they weren't overjoyed with. Russell had wanted to put air-ducts on the bike to get a bit more power. This was vetoed, at least partly on the grounds that the next year's model would have the very same ducts as standard!

What we did learn at the TT – apart from never letting a marketing man near a race bike – was that as a team Russell and I worked well and I had no hesitation in joining him for 1998. As well as Marra, we had a new rider. At Brands for the final round of the 1997 series, Marra had spat himself off, seemingly throwing away a championship that had been in his grasp. Luckily for him a rookie name Steve Plater nipped past Dave Heal at Clearways, gifting Marra the title. Russell was so impressed he signed him for the following season.

My interest has always been suspension and handling, whereas Russell's passion is for engines. It was a perfect fit. Although Russell usually had a reasonable sponsorship package, we never had sufficient budget to draft in technical specialists – except for the likes of Ohlin's and White Power, whose service was part of the deal. But between us we could cope with most things.

That's not entirely true. Russell's a very persuasive and engaging character. He gets things done. When he's bubbling, it's hard not to be fired by the same enthusiasm. He's also accumulated a lot of contacts in the higher reaches of the engineering business.

One of these was Graham Langham, Ilmor's Formula One valve train boffin, who over the years found himself helping us out with valve springs, cam profiles, air ducts, you name it. The ducting was especially striking. We'd often test the bikes at Bruntingthorpe in Leicestershire. As they howled towards you down the two-mile runway, the noise they pushed ahead of them was totally different from anything else, so efficient was the intake ducting.

Especially with that sort of help, Russell definitely knew his stuff. Glen Richards finished second for us in the 2000 Superstock championship. By 2001, when the bike to have was definitely not a Honda Fireblade, he'd worked magic on ours. By the end of the season Gary Mason had it coming out of corners faster than the supposed top dog, Yamaha's R1.

By that time Russell had the Blade revving to 15,500rpm, maybe 1,500rpm more than anyone else, which is why we had such success. Even at lesser revs, most teams were plagued with snapped con-rods. Russell worked out that the problem wasn't with the rod itself. The bearing would always seize first. So when he built a set of crankcases, he'd torque up the crankshaft bolts, measure each set's out-of-round, then reassemble – this time not to the specified torque but to bring each journal back to round. Only the centre bearings were suspect because when one picked up, the debris would go to centre main. These he gave a greater clearance – 70 microns rather than 35. All the bolts would be marked and dotted so, as long as they went back in the right place, rebuilds were simple. In comparison, my job – a click here, two clicks there – was a doddle.

For the 1998 Production TT we had the services of one 'Mad Dog' Jim Moodie. It couldn't have been more different from our experience with the VTR the following year. Jim had a bit of a reputation – not only as a hard man, but as a rider who liked to do things his own way. A few eyebrows were raised by people who wondered if we could work with him. The truth was that he was the total professional, absolutely brilliant to work with.

Earlier in the year we'd had a meeting with Tadao Baba, the chief engineer on the Fireblade project, spelling out, amongst other things, the fork springs we wanted in Jim's TT bike. Perversely, it arrived with a front end which was totally standard in every way. Before Monday evening practice I adjusted it as best I could, explaining to Jim that the suspension would probably be a good way out. It had standard forks, standard springs, standard air-gaps. We all expected a few fireworks from Jim when he got back.

After two laps, he pitted.

'How's that?' I asked with a tremor in my voice.

'Brilliant. Don't touch it.'

He didn't ride it again all practice week, by the end of which he wasn't even one of the favourites because everyone else had gone quicker, leaving him eighth on the leaderboard. Come the race, he led from start to finish, winning by 30 seconds and annihilating Phil McCallen's lap record to give Honda their 100th TT win at their 50th anniversary party. His fastest lap, 120.7mph, was the first 120-plus lap by any production machine.

The odd thing about that 100th win, the Fireblade's third, was that beyond the odd T-shirt it never seemed to occur to Honda to cash in on it. Russell had other ideas, persuading them that we should build a special edition 'TT100 Evo Fireblade', which we did the following winter. In six weeks Russell took it from clay model to finished bikes. The Evo was full of trick stuff – forks, brakes, carbs, handlebars, rear-sets, you name it – and sold well. Our only regret was that the fastest we ever got it to go was 197mph. Later we did a similar limited edition Joey replica VTR. All 26 – one for each of his TT wins – sold out in a fortnight.

Meanwhile, back on the shorts, Steve Plater more than repaid our faith in him. The half-mad giggling idiot you may have seen on the telly is exactly what you get in the pits. Apart from his embarrassing practical jokes, he's simply a great lad to work with who, much like Whitham, always gives everything on the track. He finished the season as British Superstock champion and second in the Supersport series when Suzuki's John Crawford edged him out of the title on count-back.

So far Russell's squad had effectively been the official Honda entry, but out of the blue Honda themselves set up their Castrol Honda squad for the 1999 season. We had no problem with them paddling their own canoe, except that they gave us so little notice that we had nowhere else to go ourselves. After a couple of seasons of fairly good support, all we had now was a few spares and a couple of cars. Our riders were Plater, again, and Wolsey Coulter. Yet again, Steve placed second to Crawford in the championship, but at least we had the satisfaction of beating the official Honda team.

In 2000 we'd first got backing from Dire Straits's Mark Knopfler, who's mad keen on bikes but under no illusions that he'd ever make a racer himself. He's a lovely bloke who was simply keen to be involved in the sport. At any rate, I can't imagine his involvement ever sold a single Dire Straits CD. He was, though, committed to trying to bring young riders along, so early the following year we put an ad in *Motor Cycle News* inviting would-be Junior Superstock racers to send us their CVs. Something over 100 applications arrived. Some were handwritten and barely legible, others must have been professionally produced for a small fortune – but we were looking for content, not packaging. We whittled these down to a short-list of eight who were invited for 'interview' at Mallory Park.

We had one bike, a CBR600 which was bog-standard, apart from tyres, rear shock and racing handlebars. And eight kids. Of the eight the most awkward and clumsy was Craig Jones, despite having already won a couple of mini-moto titles. He'd fire into Gerrards at a mad rate of knots, not even thinking about blipping the throttle, with the back end flapping all over the shop. His mechanical sympathy was zero, but there was obviously something special about him. If we'd have wanted to win the next year's championship, any one of the others might have been a better bet, but not one of them wanted it as badly as Craig. He was almost in tears at the thought of losing out. To my mind racing is full of talent. What's less common is real hunger. For me, that was the clincher, so we took what Mark said to the letter, and signed him up.

His first season with us began well. Craig finished sixth or better in every race, climbed his first rostrum at Brands, then smashed into a bridge at Oulton Park. He was pretty mangled and missed the rest of the year. The bike was even worse: not a single piece was salvageable, so we threw it in a skip. The next year he dominated the Junior Superstock series, taking the title with six wins and eight lap records. Craig went on to race in world superbikes and world superports, but was killed at Brands in August 2008. A very black day. He was a great kid.

Before Craig we had another youngster who went on to do even greater things. Early in 2000 I was plagued by calls from Barry Sheene about this hot young Australian prospect. 'I've got this lad,' he'd enthuse, 'he's going to be good ...' Eventually we paid the lad's fare to the UK. After picking him and his mum up at the airport, we took them to Calafat, where he rode rings round everyone. Even a German team also testing there were impressed. 'Who is ze kid?' they asked.

The kid was Chris Vermeulen and we signed him at once.

The 2000 TT, in contrast, was one to forget, for the drama dragged all the way to the courtroom. Again, our rider was Jim Moodie, and the bike was another Blade – but this time a Superbike. Supposedly.

As with the Fireblade in 1998, we'd met up near London with Honda Britain and Tadao Baba, the Blade's designer, to sort out the schedule and specification. Baba-san obviously knew his stuff. We enjoyed working with him and by this time had established a good relationship. As the Japanese usually do, he laid out all the discussion points on a blackboard. The engine, we were assured, would produce 170–175bhp and we'd have all the parts we needed by the beginning of May. That was wrong on both counts. Everything was late and we finally took the bike to Cadwell for its first test setting, literally on the way to the TT. The engine had arrived complete from Japan and was supposedly ready to go. As well as Jim, Iain Duffus, who'd also be riding a Blade, was there – plus Joey Dunlop with his Honda SP-1. The Blade was a mess. The carburetion was all to pot, the slipper clutch was slipping the wrong way. Duffus rode it first, and by the time Jim climbed on the clutch was barely working at all. Meanwhile, Joey was lashing round having a great time on the SP-1 with Colin Edwards's world superbike engine, looked after by Aaron Slight's mechanic. We left Cadwell with two very disgruntled Blade riders and Joey grinning from ear to ear.

Our job was just to supply and look after the hardware. Roger Harvey was in overall control of Honda's TT effort. Russell was so backed-up with work he was practically building engines on the boat to the Island. He wasn't best pleased when he got there to be asked to get Jim's engine out, remove the close-ratio gear cluster, slipper clutch, ignition and some special bearings, to pass on to Tony Scott to check why the bike was down on power. We had just one spare close-ratio box and one spare fuel tank, both of which we were also asked to pass on to another team. For reasons we couldn't quite fathom, Jim was to use one of Tony's engines for practice. So, having just got one engine ready to go, we now had three engines lying in bits around the workshop.

It got worse. Russell had built our engine using inside information direct from Baba-san. Evidently the Blade's cranks had to be built in a particular way, or they blew. Unfortunately Tony Scott, who's a brilliant engine man, wasn't privy to this information when he'd put his engines together. Sure enough, half a lap into the first session, Jim's engine blew. It was chaotic, a crazy way to go racing.

Come the opening race, Formula One, Jim rode his nuts off to finish fifth, almost three minutes behind Joey. At the time Jim was the outright lap record holder, so this wasn't exactly a fair reflection of his ability. What it did reflect was that the engine had nothing like the promised power. The dyno gave it 152bhp – around 20 down on what we'd seen on Baba-san's blackboard. My suspicion was that Honda had experienced problems during development, and simply couldn't get the Blade to produce 170-plus horsepower reliably.

On the eve of the Senior race, Russell and I were tucking into our first sit-down meal of the week at the Chinese near the tram terminal when Jim called from his motorhome in the paddock.

'Can you come up here? It's important.'

When we scuttled up to the paddock we learned that he'd decided not to ride the bike. It wasn't competitive, he reckoned. He couldn't win on it, and it'd be dangerous to try. I didn't entirely agree with his logic, but all we could do was respect his position.

It was a bit of a bombshell. What the hell were we going to do? Our contract was to prepare the bikes, so to honour our end of things all we could do was get them scrutineered and have them ready to go in the paddock, so that's what we did.

Jim's arrangement with Honda was that if it rained he wouldn't ride. Inevitably, it rained. Then we heard that Jim had been sacked for declining to ride – which seemed a bit premature considering that if the weather stayed as it was, he'd have good reason not to.

The race was postponed and scheduled for a re-run the following day. We scrutineered the bikes again and warmed them up, even though it seemed futile. As expected, Jim didn't turn up.

Jim's thinking was that far from him betraying Honda, they'd betrayed him by not furnishing a competitive bike – which to my mind they definitely hadn't. I suggested that if he wanted to take it further he should have a word with Simon Taylor, Tom Wheatcroft's legal eagle, who I happened to know quite well. He did, and that's how we ended up in the High Court in London. Russell and I were among the witnesses for Jim.

The two central arguments were about whether the bike was 'fit for purpose'. Jim's case was that Honda had won the Formula One race for the previous umpteen years and he was entitled to expect a competitive bike from them, one that was appropriate for the existing lap record holder. Honda reckoned they'd done precisely that.

When it was my turn in the witness box, Honda's barrister admitted he didn't know much about bike racing, but he knew a bit about Formula One cars. He could probably corner at 5g on his sofa. He invited me to compare Jim's bike with the Minardi which used to trundle around at the back of the Formula One field.

He wanted to know if the Minardi was raceworthy. I agreed that it probably was.

Then surely Jim's Honda was raceworthy, too?

The difference, I suggested, was that Jim was a class rider whereas the Minardi pilots were also-rans incapable of winning in any car. Put Michael Schumacher in the Minardi and he might have a different view about whether it's raceworthy. You could paint it red and smother it in Ferrari stickers, but it would still be a dog.

Honda's second point was that they couldn't have done anything to give Jim a competitive bike, anyway. They had one SP-1, and that was earmarked for Joey to ride, and that was that. For once in my life my memory came to my rescue. Amongst the evidence we'd had to go through were three huge cardboard boxes full of ream upon ream of documents. Somehow I remembered spotting an e-mail from Honda Japan referring to a second factory engine for Joey's bike. Since the bike Joey rode was a bitsa assembled in Britain from factory suspension, factory swinging-arm and a more or less standard frame, there had been nothing to stop Honda assembling a second SP-1 bitsa if they'd had a mind. Jim certainly didn't expect Honda to hand over Joey's bike to him. All he wanted was a competitive machine.

After much lawyerly rifling of papers, the point was made. It was a telling moment but probably wasn't going to win the war. British justice is such that the guy most likely to win is the one with the biggest budget – and that definitely wasn't Jim. The best he could hope for was an out-of-court settlement, which is what he finally got – along with a confidentiality agreement preventing him from telling his side of the tale. Luckily that doesn't stop me having my half-penn'orth.

Jim's wasn't the only controversy surrounding the 2000 TT. In the past I'd often been at cross-purposes with the ACU – not only about start money, but also about their take on TT safety. I'd had words with them before about their policy of allowing nothing but normal road tyres on production bikes, but by 2000 the sheer power of 1000cc sports bikes was making for a very risky situation.

On principle I didn't mind the 'street tyres only' rule in the least, but anyone can see that a modern sports tyre is basically a slick with just enough grooves to make it road legal. The power the big bikes were then producing – already far more than any factory bike I ever raced – would have ripped a well-treaded tyre apart in no time, which wouldn't have been acceptable to a bloke doing 10,000 miles a year on the street. I'd discussed the issue with the major tyre manufacturers, who were in agreement but for obvious reasons couldn't explicitly admit to the limitations of their tyres.

Not just the bikes, but the road surface had changed, too. The old stone-chip covering had a lot more mechanical grip in the wet than the newer hot-rolled tarmac. And ever since the hot summers of the mid-Seventies, in the wet several sections had been polished more like skid-pans than race tracks. In my view street tyres would be plain dangerous if it rained, in which case treaded racing tyres should be allowed.

This was a big enough concern for me to put it in writing – repeatedly. Over the next few months a stream of increasingly angry letters went back and forth between me and the ACU. It got very bitter, but the ACU wouldn't budge. Jim Parker insisted that they were road bikes which should therefore run road tyres, and it was as simple as that. It just wasn't informed or realistic. As so often before, the dear old ACU just didn't get it.

Eventually, presumably having realised that they couldn't shut me up, a special meeting was convened during practice week, where I pleaded that for safety's sake they had to amend their rules. If it rains for the race, I told them, going out on road tyres would be nothing less than suicidal, because they'd just aquaplane everywhere. Maybe racing wets wouldn't last the full three-lap distance, but even if they were completely knackered after 2½ laps, all you'd do is wobble to a standstill. Unlike the thinly-disguised sports slicks riders were required to use, they'd be neither unpredictable nor dangerous.

'Do you mean to say,' I was asked by one crassly complacent tie-and-blazer official, 'that the manufacturers fit tyres that aren't safe?'

'At 170mph in the wet, that's exactly what I am telling you.'

'I find that difficult to believe.'

If he'd ridden a Japanese road bike in the Seventies, when not just the tyres, but the brakes didn't work in the wet, he might have been a bit less trusting.

The street tyres-only rule stood.

Sure enough, the production race went ahead as planned – in pouring rain. David Jeffries won a shortened race on the production Yamaha R1 with a fastest lap of less than 100mph. Wet-weather specialist Michael Rutter, who finished third, admitted to being 'very frightened' by conditions which even a hyper Jefferies called 'bloody awful'. What DJ didn't know as he savoured the win was that way back down the field Les Williams had died after aquaplaning out of control near Ballaugh. Another rider was seriously injured in a similar incident.

DJ unknowingly compounded the ACU's folly in his post-race interview by saying how much he'd enjoyed slithering around the Mountain Course. But this was a top rider, at the peak of his craft. I'd had a similar experience in winning the 1981 Senior on a slick rear and intermediate front. When it rained for the last two laps, the bike was spinning up in top gear – but, like DJ, I was on top of my game and could cope. Fortunately, since the outlawing of wet races – ironically following the safety review after David Jefferies's death in 2003 – it's a situation that can't arise any more. But I'm still convinced that both riders might well have emerged unscathed if they'd had a more appropriate choice of tyres.

A court might have been convinced, too. Simon Taylor, the then chief solicitor for the MCRCB, had helped me draft my letters to the ACU. Naturally, he'd seen all their replies, and said after the race that with the evidence contained in their responses, they may well have had a case to answer for negligence, which could conceivably sink them. For a while I agonised over whether to make the correspondence public. On the one hand, the sport's organisers should be held to account; but, on the other, without them who's going to run our sport? In the end I didn't go public. I still wonder if that was a mistake.

CHAPTER 22

IF HE HAD A BRAIN HE'D BE DANGEROUS

When James Whitham joined us at Suzuki in 1988, he wasn't joining the best-supported squad in the paddock. But he was the sort of rider who was definitely better off in an organised team, even one as skint as ours, than running his own show. The previous year at Carnaby he'd blown up an engine in practice, and for reasons I still can't fathom his spare engine was 40 miles away at home.

'What bloody use is it there?' I demanded. 'Go and get it, you dickhead.'

From then on, I started calling him 'DH'. Before long, Butch did the same. It took James a few weeks to ask what it meant. He probably thought it was something flattering.

'It stands for dickhead, 'cos you're a dickhead, you dickhead,' I told him.

Mez was the opposite – about ten years older, far more experienced and, along with his mechanic, Malcolm, far more able to look after himself. And yet when he first came to us, his results were very ordinary – far less impressive than his performance as a privateer suggested they ought to be. Something was very obviously amiss, but when you tried to get to the bottom of it, his pat response was always 'The bike's all right. It's just me.'

That just didn't wash. Mez was a better rider than that. So I pressed him and pressed him, as gently as I could. 'There has to be something wrong. What is it?'

He was such a lovely lad, but strange-looking. He had a chronic skin condition which meant, amongst other things, that he wore a wig. He was pretty insecure and so didn't want to say anything negative about the bike, the team, about anything. It took an age before I finally dragged it out of him. 'All right' in Mez-speak was actually 'not quite right' at all. At last! Now we could start fixing it.

James was much more direct, but just as self-critical. His standard post-practice comment was 'the bike's fine, it's me that's crap'. In the long run, that wasn't helping him, or the team. But it's the sort of thing you accept in a rookie rider as you nurse him along.

What James had in abundance was commitment. I've always had the notion, with mechanics as well as riders, that the one to go for wasn't necessarily the most talented, but the one who really wanted it. That's precisely why I'd hired Nigel Everett, and that had worked out pretty well. James was keen and eager, desperate to succeed – much like Craig Jones 15 years later. If that eagerness leads to a few get-offs, that's just part of the price. With a young rider, especially, crashing is just part and parcel of the business, something you've got to accept. If nothing else, I knew he had the bottle to pick himself up and get back to it. He'd already shown plenty of that. Not all riders are so robust.

Yet I could never understand how someone so articulate and obviously bright as James could do so many downright stupid things. I guess it was just a gift he had. In the early years in the racing team I'd sit him down and try to talk him through various race issues and strategies … tyres, what his main opponents might do and how he might counter it, and so on. At Mallory when Brian Morrison was going through a spell of winning everything, I told James to just stick on his tail and do what he could with a lap to go. James took me a bit too literally and spent the entire race halfway up the Honda's exhaust. When Brian high-sided at Devil's Elbow, there was nowhere to go except down. Both of them landed in a heap.

'That's the last time I listen to you,' he said when they carted him back to the paddock.

'I said follow him, you pillock. Not ride pillion.'

James's fundamental problem was being the last of the great brakers. I was forever on at him to brake a fraction sooner, arrive at the corner in some sort of control instead of twisting the bike in knots, and get back on the power earlier. For all that it sank in, I may as well have been talking in Urdu. He'd roll his eyes, give me a 'here we go again' expression and do what he always did.

This was still going on in '89. The big tussle that season was between James and Loctite Yamaha's Rob McElnea for the British Superbike title. I knew Rob well from our days as team-mates with Suzuki. He was a mature, canny rider who'd done dozens of grands prix and knew what was what. At Oulton Park, he wandered over for a chat.

'Why don't you tell James,' he suggested, 'that if he didn't use his brakes so hard he'd go a lot quicker?'

'Ferchrissakes,' I spluttered. 'I've told him till I'm blue in the face, but he doesn't listen. Why don't you tell him?'

So I beckoned James over and suggested he have a chat with Rob.

Just as they are now, the Superbike races then were over two separate legs at each meeting. The first race, James won easily. Afterwards, Rob wandered over for another chat.

'Bloody 'ell,' he groaned. 'Me and my big mouth. He did exactly what I told him and I couldn't get near him.'

'Brilliant,' I thought. 'At last he's listened to somebody.'

Come race two, positions were reversed: Rob first and James second. Afterwards – you've guessed it – Rob strolled over, but this time smiling.

'Back to normal!' It sometimes made you want to give up.

Hare-brained braking aside, our set-up worked for us, but I'm not sure James had the confidence to take it on from there. In fact he still seemed to have some of the same mind-set years later when he rode for the Suzuki

World Superbike team. His team-mate, Pete Goddard, who could read the ink off a datalogging sheet, would still be rabbiting to his mechanics three hours after James had finished with his. I suspect James honestly thought himself incapable of giving high-quality feedback. Yet which of them was always quicker? That's the acid test, and James usually passed. Not only that, but he'd go progressively quicker through the qualifying period. That's the only real yardstick that says you're doing the job right.

But for the most part James was a pleasure to work with. He never, ever blamed the bike when he screwed up, and never gave less than everything he had. Since the dawn of motorcycle racing there have been lots of riders who blamed falling off to the bike 'jumping out of gear' which, before the arrival of datalogging, was impossible to disprove. James never once did that. If he said it jumped out of gear, then that's exactly what it did. Neither of us could understand riders who did otherwise, because it was so self-defeating. Every mechanic he ever had would tell you exactly the same thing – just as well when they were working into the small hours putting his broken bikes back together.

The only time I really got angry with him was during pre-season testing at Nogaro in the south of France. I sent him out to do a few laps on the GSX600, with instructions to be very, very careful: it was the only one in Europe and we didn't have so much as a spare brake lever. Two laps later I spotted him larking about on the back wheel, followed by the usual hideous scraping noise as the GSX smashed itself to bits. When he trudged back to the paddock I gave him the biggest bollocking I've ever given anyone.

Years later it was a case of James giving the bollocking to himself. At the 2005 Goodwood Festival, he paraded Bruce Anstey's TT-winning Triumph 600. Being James, he decided the crowd deserved more entertainment than a bunch of fogeys droning up the hill, so did most of it on the back wheel. If it hadn't been for the oil on the track he might have got away with it.

I'd finished my run some minutes earlier and was leaning on a fence chatting to Freddie Spencer when there was the most enormous bang, followed by half of a Triumph cartwheeling into the top paddock. This was followed almost instantaneously by what was left of the other half, followed by James, who landed more or less at our feet. There was claret everywhere, but all he had were a few bumps and a broken nose.

After James scuttled home in embarrassment, I rang him to ask how he was. Still mortified, was the answer.

'Mick,' he said, 'the worst thing about it is that you already knew I was a twat. But all those other guys … Ago, Spencer, Doohan, Schwantz … they didn't.'

I suspect he was wrong. No one leads that sheltered a life.

The honesty that typified James worked both ways. As a manager I always tried to be straight with riders, rather than fib to them in the old Joe Craig mould. That might work now and again, and it might work better for someone more accomplished than me at mind-games. But to my way of thinking it ultimately does more harm than good. Whenever I've set riders on, I've always asked for everyone to hold their hands up to mistakes. The same applies to mechanics. Riders get it wrong and trash machinery, mechanics occasionally drop bollocks which put riders on the deck. As long as it's not a regular thing, you can accept it. But whatever's gone wrong, you're not likely to fix it unless you know what it actually was.

As a former rider I'd learned this the hard way. If you crash and know why, it's a great deal easier to get back on and still ride hard. Crashing for no apparent reason demands a lot more faith.

Once, during practice for the Hutchinson 100 – the 'wrong way' around Brands Hatch – I came out of the hairpin on the back wheel of the Kawasaki 500, just as I had every other lap. But this time something was different. The instant the front wheel landed, it pitched me down the road. It wasn't a big crash, but it unnerved me because there was no logical reason for it: I was doing the same as I'd done every previous lap and had no idea why it suddenly went to pot.

Weeks later, over dinner with Stan Shenton, I just happened to mention that the crash was still nagging at me.

'Oh,' he said, 'we didn't mention it at the time because we didn't want to upset the mechanic. But we were trying some new aluminium front discs. We think they'd been fitted wrong, expanded and jammed in the calipers.'

OK, maybe I would have thrown a tantrum if I'd known at the time. But ten minutes later, everything would have been OK. To me, they'd put short-term harmony ahead of the long-term view.

Arriving at Donington Park for a World Superbike round in 1990, we already knew the bike well enough to know it would have a particular problem. We'd had it before and knew how to fix it, but I didn't want to dial it in unless it actually proved to be an issue. Sure enough, halfway through the first practice session, Roger Burnett came in to the pit complaining of chatter at the front end. Click … click … click and we sent him out again with quicker rebound damping on the forks.

A few laps later he was back.

'Don't know what you've done, but it's brilliant. Can I have some more?'

This sort of thing always gives you a dilemma. If I'd dialled in more of the same – or even just said I had – Roger would probably have gone quicker. But it would have been purely a placebo effect – speed through confidence rather than because the bike was actually working better. Whilst there's nothing wrong with bolstering a rider's self-belief, it's the wrong policy because it's a con. Practice ought to be about making the bike better, not pretending you have. If boosting confidence was all that mattered you may as well abandon practice altogether and put a shrink on the case.

To the best of my memory I've only outright conned riders twice. As far as results went, it worked both times, but the second one I regret even now. The first, of course, was running James with a big engine early in 1991. The second was at Thruxton in 2000, with Chris Vermeulen. By then we'd had our Supersports Hondas for a couple of years, knew what worked and what didn't, knew them inside out.

As I've mentioned, my practice as a manager was never to bullshit riders, never try the psychological game. In the long run, being straight with them always worked out best, and with fewer problems created along the way. But on this occasion I took the soft option and lived to regret it.

After practice Peter Vermeulen, Chris's dad, arrived in the garage complaining that 'we' – meaning Chris – were getting front-end chatter. Now chatter – judder from the front end going into turns – was an endemic problem on supersports bikes. This was because the front suspension is essentially road kit, not sophisticated enough to completely get rid of it. But over time we learned enough to make it go away most of the time. Chris's chatter was showing up on worn tyres, when you most expect it, so I wasn't the least bit surprised.

We knew how to fix this. If the forks chatter going into a corner, as soon as you give the bike any throttle, the chatter disappears – so obviously lifting the front end has a beneficial effect. From both theory and experience we knew that a stiffer spring and reduced rebound damping would largely fix the problem. Peter thought he knew better.

'We want a softer spring in,' he said, 'a 0.85.' His logic was that a softer spring would react better to the bumps. That made sense as far as it went. But it wasn't the bumps that were causing the chatter so much as the tyre and front-end geometry.

'That'll make it worse. It wants a 0.95.'

Even as I was saying it I was thinking that we had the makings of a tricky situation. If I let them get their way, the bike would chatter for the whole race and we wouldn't get a result. If they ran a 0.95kg spring, it would only start to chatter as the front tyre went off in the final few laps. But if I insisted that Chris used that spring, he'd probably ride badly anyway, because his dad will have told him it won't work. So I took the easy way out and told him we'd put 0.85 springs in the forks. He actually stood there and watched as Chris's mechanic, Nathan, put them in. As soon as he'd left the garage, I had Nathan put the 0.95s back in.

Come the race, Chris placed a really good second.

'Any problems?' I asked him after the race.

'Nah. Perfect. Those 0.85 springs were spot-on.'

As team manager I'd got the result and by that yardstick had done the right thing. But as far as I'm aware, to this day Chris still thinks a 0.85 spring is what he ran. And the problem then, of course, was that in his head his dad was right and the team boss was wrong, which is no way to run a race team. Riders need to have faith in their crew.

This had been sharply illustrated a couple of years before. In early season testing in Spain both our riders, 'Marra' Brown and Steve Plater, had been flying. Their bikes had worked perfectly and both had beaten the existing lap record. On the drive home, Marra had been full of it: 'Couldn't be better … perfect … can't wait for the season to begin.'

Reality dawned after the first two meetings, at Brands and Oulton, when neither rider could get any rear-wheel grip. Marra came in from one practice session, stepped off the bike and spoke directly with 'Wellie', his mechanic. That wasn't the way it worked. Normally, he'd speak with me.

Later, I took him aside.

'What's the matter. Have you no confidence in me?'

'Er … yeah. No.'

It was a kick in the guts but you have to face up to it. You're not doing your job right if you can't accept constructive criticism. If a rider comes back and says that the bike is unrideable, then you have to accept it. If you don't, you can't even begin to get it sorted. And the hardest bit in the whole equation is finding out exactly where the problem lies. After that, the solution's easy. It's like taking a bad back to the doctor's: there might be any one of a dozen or more causes, but not until he identifies the right one can he begin to fix it.

So I asked Marra if he preferred to soldier on with just him and Wellie looking after the chassis, rather than debrief through me.

'Yeah.'

Next I took Steve to one side, explained what had happened, asked if he wanted to go the same route. He didn't.

Poor Marra had problems with both ends early that season: with grip at the rear and chatter at the front, even on new tyres. Previously I'd been trying to help Wellie get his head round it, but he didn't have much of a clue about suspension settings. Leaving the set-up to him put me on a hiding to nothing: if Marra did well, it'd be down to Wellie; if he didn't, it'd all be my fault.

I checked what springs they were running. According to Wellie the springs were right – the same 0.95kg jobs Chris Vermuelen wouldn't want a couple of years later – and everything else was just as it should be. Trouble was, I didn't believe him. So I asked Wellie to take the fork legs over to Andy White who did any re-valving we might need. Twenty minutes later I learned from Andy that the springs had been 0.85s all along.

Marra and Wellie carried on with their own thing until the next meeting at Thruxton. Steve won, miles ahead of Marra. From then on it was back to normal.

Effective debriefing is crucial. Some riders you can debrief right off the bike. Others are too hyper. In either case, it's usually no use just asking what the problems are. That's too loose a question. You have to focus in on specifics. As I got to know James's style, after each practice session I'd give him ten minutes to cool down, then get a sheet of paper, and go through everything line by line. Only then did we start to get some real information. James was actually quite good at this. He didn't dress it up in jargon or with his interpretation of why things were happening, but he was sharp and sensitive enough to tell you what the bike was actually doing. From there, it was my job, not the rider's, to come up with a diagnosis and solution.

It's actually worse in my experience to work with a rider who is technically switched on – or, worse still, just thinks he is. Glen Richards, who rode a 600 for us years later, was a case in point. He was a smashing lad and quite smart, quite technical – far better than most riders I've worked with at setting up a bike. But he tended to be looking to the next qualifying session rather than the race, and inclined to give diagnoses rather than symptoms. In other words, by the time we sat down for a debriefing he already had preconceived ideas of what the problems – and thus the solutions – might be. It sometimes felt that I was spending more time arguing about his problems than fixing them. This brings you back to a situation similar to the one with Vermeulen: if his diagnosis is right – and sometimes it was – all well and good. But if it's not, he's likely to have an inbuilt prejudice against any solution I come up with. On the whole it's better that they don't know, or even care, what you've done: their job's simply to report whether it's better or not.

In the Sanyo Honda team we even went so far as to keep our two riders separate after practice sessions so they couldn't contaminate each other's opinions. Russell would do the engine debrief, I'd do the chassis. The two of us were the only ones who knew the settings. All the riders needed to know was whether the bike was the same, better or worse, than the previous session.

338

I'm sure there are others, but the one rider I encountered who could do his own thing and make it work was Jim Moodie, who rode for us at two TTs. Jim was a real thinker, very analytical but always pragmatic. He'd turn up at the pit each day with a list of things he wanted doing. With some riders, this was a recipe for endless debate and lots of wasted time. True, there were times when I had to cajole him a little, but mostly he was spot-on. And if you gave him what he wanted, he'd usually do the job.

Then there's the language thing. You'd think that English-speaking managers and riders wouldn't have much trouble communicating. But there's no dictionary for the type of slang we use to describe what a bike's doing. For ages I wrestled with Chris Vermuelen's complaints about his 600 'not hooking up'. To me this meant that he wasn't getting grip out of turns – which is how American dirt-track racers use the expression. Only after a couple of meetings did it dawn on me that he was actually complaining about the bike running wide through turns. Since you deal with my interpretation by changing the damping and maybe geometry at the rear, yet with his interpretation you might dial in more trail at the front, we spent a frustrating couple of weeks chasing our own tails. Once we began talking the same language, his problem was simple enough to fix, but in the meantime both of us were getting increasingly frustrated – and doubtful of the skills of the other.

Plater-speak was earthier but, once we worked it out, easy enough to interpret. According to Steve there were only two conditions a race bike could possibly be in. It was either a bag of shit, or a pile of shit. A bag, we might just get to work eventually, but a pile was beyond redemption. If we could just get the poo into a bag, we were getting somewhere.

Even if he won, it didn't get much better.

'How was the bike, Steve?'

'Bag of shit. Doesn't grip, doesn't turn. Bag of shit.'

At the end of a particularly good season for Steve I eventually asked Benny, his long-suffering mechanic, what he actually said about the bike.

'Oh,' he replied, 'he always says it's mint to me.'

Once you got the hang of his sense of humour, he was fine. Besides, whatever it is that's in most racer's heads, Steve had something extra. Years later, when he was X-rayed following a road accident, they discovered embedded in him a chunk of metal, presumably from a huge crash he'd had at Stirlings Bend years before. I'm no neurologist, but doubt it helped.

Of course to come up with any sort of solution, you need at least a hint that there's a problem – preferably in good time. At Donington, halfway through a race in which he'd been with the leading bunch, James pulled into the pits for no apparent reason.

'What's up?'

'It's jumping out of gear. Same as last wee ... Oh shit. I didn't I tell you, did I?'

He'd never mentioned a thing the previous week.

As well as 'DH', we used to call James Lead-foot Larry for his gearchanges. We never found an adequate way of describing his brain.

When James did remember, he took responsibility. His other asset was that whatever else he might be he was a realist. All race set-ups are working compromises and rarely can you make a bike perfect. That might be what you're aiming for, but sooner or later towards the end of practice you realise it's never going to be. You have to settle for having done as much as you can. At that point I might say something like 'that's as good as we're going to get it. Now you've just got to ride it as it is.'

James accepted that – probably better than I used to do as a rider. You never got moans or if-onlys. He'd just say 'OK' and you knew he'd go out and make the best of the bike as it was. And I can't remember a single occasion when he gave less than everything he had. Plater was much the same, except that he'd have a gripe about his 'pile of shit' just out of habit before riding it off its wheels. And that, especially compared with many other riders, is just wonderful to work with. In contrast some riders I've worked with have just pulled in halfway through a race on a bike James or Steve would definitely have battled into the points. Inevitably, a couple of those were sacked.

No one ever begrudged going the extra mile for James or Steve, because you knew that however much effort you put into it, they'd put in the same – and more. Nigel, who worked for James in Suzuki's World Superbike team in 1997, says exactly the same. He was the perfect rider to work for – unless he had one of his brainstorms, of course.

A lot of racers – probably most of them – view racing strictly in the here and now. Mention anything to do with the history of racing to them, and their eyes roll up and they practically fall asleep. Rob Mac was like that. To him, Stanley Woods may as well never have existed. Bike racing didn't even start until Freddie came along – Spencer, not Frith – because he could slide the bike at will.

To any rider who does have a historical perspective, this is strange. Stanley was not only a great rider who would be a top dog if he were riding today, but he was also the man who did most to make racing a professional sport. In other words, he was the man who invented the jobs Rob and I were so happy to have.

In 1986 I rode Stanley's factory 500cc Velocette for an Isle of Man parade lap. It had girder forks, primitive swinging-arm rear suspension, next to no grip and even less brakes. Nonetheless I went as quick as I could, and since I'd only quit racing the year before, I was still fairly sharp. The Velo was pretty much flat-out everywhere, and I managed about 90mph.

Stanley, who was a lovely man, was there as a guest of honour and after the lap wandered over to chat.

'That's impressive,' he said. 'You went as fast as I did in 1939.'

No it wasn't. Not at all. Compared to the circuit he rode on nearly 50 years earlier, the 1986 Mountain Circuit was practically a motorway. Far from showing what I could do, what that lap really did was dramatically prove just how hard those guys were riding then.

Yes, sliding's spectacular. But just because it wasn't Stanley's habit doesn't mean he couldn't have done it. If you put Valentino Rossi on a 50 horsepower Manx Norton, he wouldn't be backing it into corners and he wouldn't be sliding it on the way out. He'd just get the most out of the bike, much as they used to. And he'd still be a winner, too.

There are certain riders who can manage on their own, and others who need someone by their side giving them a tap on the shoulder now and again, keeping them pointed in the right direction. If Steve Hislop lacked anything, it was probably that sort of figure. That's certainly how James was in his earlier years. Later Rob McElnea played the same role, and did it well. But when James rode the RC30 for Honda Britain in 1990, he had a miserable year – and, I suspect, less of the sort of guidance he was used to.

James's team-mate that year, Carl Fogarty, whilst not exactly setting the world alight on the Honda, at least acquitted himself much better than James. The difference between the two wasn't so much pure ability. Foggy wasn't technically switched on, but what he seemed instinctively to be able to do was modify his riding style to suit a particular machine. James was more inclined to plug on in the same old way and – that year, at least – have the same old crashes. So whilst Foggy's confidence increased that year, James's disappeared down the toilet. So much so that by season's end, he was close to packing in.

The other bugbear of management is riders' dads. Whenever Barry Sheene and I went back to Scarborough to do vintage parades, it was just like the old days: him carving me up and me returning the favour, but always with lots of mutual respect. The only time I ever had any real bother with him was after Chris Vermeulen joined our Sanyo superports team. At the time Chris was only 16, which caused me to make a fundamental blunder. I told Barry I'd happily give the lad a test ride, but since it was a race team and not a kindergarten we were running, we wanted a parent to accompany him. I should have kept my big mouth shut.

Initially Chris arrived with his mum, who joined him when we tested at Calafat. Later, when he arrived back for the season proper, mum stayed at home and father, Peter, was chaperone. The first meeting, at Brands Hatch, gave a taste of what was to come. I'd be debriefing Chris after practice, and Peter, stood by his side, would answer. Now in the entire history of racing, no one ever made a bike quick by asking the rider's dad how it handled. But, since Peter had announced his intention of returning home after the first meeting, for diplomacy's sake I bit my tongue and put up with it.

Even so, Chris scored something like a fourth and a fifth, a very solid showing at his first British championship meeting. A day or so later I got a call from Barry.

'What the fuck's happening?' he demanded. 'The bike's slow, doesn't handle, doesn't …'

'Barry, old mate,' I cut him off, 'you should know better. This is his first round in the toughest 600 championship anywhere, and he's finished fourth and fifth. The kid's started well and can only get better. So what are you on about?' It turned out that all the negative crap had come from Peter, the ultimate schoolboy dad. He kept saying he was going home after the next meeting, which unfortunately never seemed to come.

By the fourth meeting, he was still there. Eventually I rang Barry, spelled out the problem, and my belief that the responsibility was partly his, since it was he who'd sent the Vermeulens over. He'd certainly have understood the syndrome, having seen it often enough during his career. I believe he had a quiet word with Peter to make clear who was running the team – and who wasn't.

Later in the year Neil Tuxworth wanted Chris to ride for his Castrol Honda squad in a couple of World Supersports rounds. But instead of asking me as team manager he went direct to Chris. Naturally, Chris was delighted. What up-and-coming rider wouldn't be? But our sponsors, who were few enough to begin with, were paying to see our bikes with our riders and livery, not to see their best rider galloping around on someone else's bikes. As a team manager Tuxworth ought to have understood this. It was always my belief that once you sign a contract, for as long as it lasts you concentrate on it and do that job. So I had to tell Chris he couldn't ride, but ultimately, after a bit of arm-twisting – Honda was our machine supplier, after all – we had to let him go. In the long run I'm not sure that could have helped Chris's reputation, either. It's better having 'honours contracts' on your CV than the opposite.

When Chris came back from his one-off rides with Castrol Honda, some of his appetite for domestic racing seemed to have gone. This came to a head at Brands when he pulled out of the 600 race with 'gearbox problems'. On the Superstock Fireblade he pulled in when lying second to Glen Richards, who won on our other bike, complaining of 'no horsepower'. I put both Fireblades on the dyno immediately after, and Chris's bike actually had a couple of horsepower more than Glen's. A day later, I thrashed the 'problem gearbox' 600 up and down the Bruntingthorpe runway for 20 minutes. With or without the clutch, it never missed a gear. Russell and I presented these home truths to him later, after which he was no problem for the rest of the year. But he was just a kid. The following season, when Chris joined Castrol Honda full time, Peter was kept very much in the background. Other than that, Chris himself was no bother at all. On his own he was a delight to work with and an obviously emerging major talent. I still look back on his performances that year with satisfaction.

Schoolboy dads are one of the biggest pains in racing, although if you're watching from the sidelines rather than trying to run a team around them it's probably easier to have sympathy for their concerns. Obviously as a father you're doing the best to bring your lad on, as well as your budget and abilities allow. That's natural enough and there's absolutely nothing wrong with it. But if the lad does begin to make the grade and move on, the paternal ability that really matters is the one that allows them to recognise the time to let go. Otherwise, what's the point of them being in a professional team?

Chris was only a young lad. None of this was his fault. For a while Chris and even his dad stayed with me and Carol. We did our best to make them feel at home. Later, Chris shared an apartment with our other rider, Glen Richards, near Mallory. Glen reckoned that on his own Chris rode fine, but as soon as dad arrived he fell to pieces.

Craig Jones's dad, Steve, was another out of the same mould as Peter Vermeulen – a lovely bloke, but a nightmare in the team pit. I've already described how keen and hungry Craig was. Trouble was, Steve was keen and hungry, too. He wanted an input on everything. After losing my rag and calling him an arsehole a couple of times I gave him a choice – either leave Craig to us because you think we're best at this job, or go back to what you were doing before. There is no middle ground. Eventually we drew him up a set of team rules. He was allowed to walk through the team garage to the pit wall to signal for Craig, for instance – but absolutely not allowed to stop on the way. I don't suppose he liked it, but I think he came to understand. Racing dads have generally put a pile of time and effort into bringing these lads along – and obviously they must have done a fairly good job otherwise they wouldn't have got where they are. If only they knew when to let go.

Of all the riders I've been associated with, Craig and Steve Plater wanted it the most. Neither had the most pure talent, but both were fierce competitors. In contrast Vermeulen didn't have as much hunger as either – he just had talent to burn. The most baffling was Gary Mason, who never seemed to put in the same performance during a race as in superpole. Naturally I asked what was the difference.

'Well,' he said, 'in Superpole I'm shouting at myself for the whole lap.'

I'd happily have kept him in throat lozenges if he'd shouted at himself for 20 laps. He was a nice kid with a real sparkle to him, but I'm not sure he wanted it enough.

On the other hand, my most frustrating season was managing Roger Burnett, who was a smashing guy with immense talent. But by 1990 he'd done what few racers do and worked out that there was some sort of connection between falling off and pain. Some riders can get through an entire career without making the link, but Roger, bless him, was also fairly bright. So he was always on at me for new kit for the bike … like a set of Billet brake calipers which could make him a second a lap quicker. When we busted the budget to buy them, he lapped at exactly the same speed as before – but a second safer. Too smart by half, our Roger.

CHAPTER 23

TRIALS AND
TRIBULATIONS

Despite almost 20 years of road racing, my first love has always been off-road, and especially trials. In fact I only started racing at all because I couldn't afford an off-road bike. Back then, trials and scrambles bikes were pretty specialised, whereas you could convert almost anything into a passable club-level road racer.

It probably wasn't true everywhere but, in Yorkshire, if you were into bikes you couldn't help but be close to trials. The county is almost trials' homeland. Malcolm Rathmell, Martin and Dougie Lampkin are all local men who've won world or European championships.

Back in my days at art college I had two or three outings on an old nail of a Greeves I'd borrowed from a mate. Later, whilst working for Jim Lee, who was making Dalesman frames for Wassell at the time, I managed to pick up a Dalesman cheap. It must have been some sort of development bike, which didn't make it trick – just badly knocked about by anyone who'd ridden it. I managed to fit in the odd trial on the thing, usually with Terry Wright, the Dalesman works rider, who'd regularly drop round to Jim's workshop. He won the Manx Two-Day on one, so it can't have been that bad.

I was keen, but almost completely useless. If those days sliding round a field on Chris Bradley's dad's Triumph Tiger taught me anything, it should have been that I wasn't a natural. Chris had all the talent. I was pure aggression. He'd float up slopes and over obstacles as though born to it; I'd usually end up in a mangled heap in the attempt.

Yet there's something about trials that eggs you on. Skills, or the lack of them, are much more transparent than in road racing. If you have the kind of mentality that wants to have another go after failing miserably, it becomes addictive. It's also true that it usually doesn't hurt quite so much when you fall off.

As I managed to get together a bit of spare cash, I'd usually have a trials bike lying around. Trouble was, I obviously couldn't use it in the summer since practically every weekend was tied up with road racing. So each October I'd jump on a trials bike I hadn't ridden for six months and make a prat of myself in almost every section. It'd take me five months to get the hang of it again, by which time I'd be off to Daytona and barely sit on a trials iron for another six months. So getting any better was a long slow grind.

The two trials I could usually manage mid-season were evening events during TT week and the Manx Two-Day, which was tagged on to the Manx Grand Prix. Over the years Malcolm Rathmell became a good friend, and often we'd do the Manx together – if you could call it 'together'. He'd been European champion a couple of years before and was still a Montesa works rider, so it was all so easy for him. He'd drag me out on the razz in Douglas, get the pair of us shit-faced, and still clean everything the next day. I'd be tumbling around sections like a drunk, getting fives with my face, and cursing the day I ever started trials riding. There are drawbacks in having talented pals.

As I mentioned, it was addictive, but frustrating – yet I couldn't let go. Maybe out of a sense of revenge, when I was team-managing, I'd try to persuade my riders to have a go. If you rode for Rob McElnea, you had to play golf. With me, it was trials. Trouble is, while I'm hopeless at golf, Rob's actually a pretty handy trials rider, too. I've never beaten him. Not once. Mind you, watching

Whitham or Plater trying to kamikaze a section made even me feel good.

Whitham and I once did a trial at Rob Shepherd's farm. At the time I had a Yamaha, he was on a Vesterinen replica, the last of the Bultaco Sherpas. The Bultaco, if not its rider, was capable of anything. Vesty could ride it up a gable end. But not James. He managed to launch it off the side of a big rock, cartwheel off the edge and landed pinned to the ground by his bike. As he lay flat on his back, groaning I leant over and said, 'another discipline mastered, I see'. Call me callous, but that was one of the highlights.

Whitham's revenge came the day he dropped round at Lepton when I just happened to have finished rebuilding my HT-5 Ariel. It was a lovely bit of kit, the culmination of endless hours in the workshop, and I was proud of it. I should have known better but said, 'Here, have a go on this.'

James never needs much encouragement to wreck something, so jumped on the Ariel and razzed up the lane. A couple of wheelies, then back down. Then a stoppy – which went on for ever until he endo'd the bike and slammed it top-first into the tarmac. He claims the brake locked on. It turns out that he was right, but at the time I reckoned all that locked was his brain. At least he had the decency to look embarrassed.

So, usually, the laugh was on me. As well as spending much of the early Seventies battling it out on tarmac, Tony Jefferies and I were also friendly rivals at trials. His father was the great Allan Jefferies, so he – and brother Nick – had trials in their genes. The famous Scott trial was practically family property. Other than the Scottish Six Days, the Scott was the most gruelling meeting in Britain. The pinnacle of many trials riders' careers was winning a 'Scott Spoon', the equivalent of a TT replica. Like everyone else, I coveted one, but never got close. The nearest I came was the year Tony arranged for someone to follow me around with a board offering 'Scott Spoon for Sale'. As I clambered out of each successive section, spitting feathers and dripping mud and the prospect of actually earning one disappeared ever-deeper into the peat bogs, the price went up. That bastard McElnea, needless to say, won a Spoon at the first attempt.

One of the best things about trials in recent years has been the growth of pre-1965 twin-shock events – sort of classic racing, but slower. For a while I rode both modern and twin-shock bikes, but the technique is so different between the two that it's tricky to do justice to either. For the last ten years or so I've confined myself to twin-shock events. The other bonus is that it's so much more rewarding to buy some old nail and turn it into something competitive than it is simply to walk into a shop to buy the latest kit.

The truth is that with a modern bike, there is almost nothing you can do to it that will achieve anything but make it worse. There's none of the satisfaction of buying an old hunk of scrap and turning it into something that actually works – and, riding apart, there's nothing I like more than messing around in the workshop. Eighteen years of this has produced what is unquestionably the finest twin-shocker in existence, anywhere (although I may be biased). My 500cc HT-5 Ariel began life as half a ton of useless scrap. Now it weighs less than your missus and simply floats up sections. Yet it still manages to give me the odd downer. The other week a Lancashire lad called Chris Gascoigne had a ride on it. He normally uses a similar machine, except that his is about three tons heavier, so he was impressive – and impressed. In fact, he must have thought I was a bit of a numpty for not winning on mine every week.

There are high spots. I get the odd class win. But nothing comes close to the time I tackled the first day of the Scottish Six Days Trial in 2000. I was on my usual hiding to nothing riding with Malcolm. He breezed over everything, whilst I panted in his wake. The sections were just too tough for my level of talent.

The Trotter's Burn section must have been particularly difficult, because as Malcolm reached the end of it I heard a huge roar of applause from the gallery. 'Oh, no,' I gulped, waiting for my turn to make a mess of it. 'It'll be "After the Lord Mayor's Show" and I'll end up flat on my face.'

Determined not to make a *complete* dick of myself, I eased out the clutch and chugged into the section. Every eye in Scotland seemed to be on me, including those of Rhoda, Malcolm's wife, stood about ten yards away trying to work out where I'd come unstuck. I'd never once felt this much pressure road-racing, yet somehow I cleaned it. The crowd simply erupted in delight. Later I found out Malcolm had had a dab, which made it even better. That's one of the joys of trials. You can ride like an utter plonker and mess up almost the entire day – as I had. But get just one section right, and it feels like you've conquered the world. And it sure beats sliding down the road on your arse at 120mph.

It may be wishful thinking but I am getting better. I ought to be: the Ariel is that bloody good.

I get more bad results than good ones, but the good 'uns make it all worth while. And trials is a sport where you can keep improving, even at my age. A good friend, Peter Gaunt, is 73. He used to be a professional trials rider, but even at his age he's riding better than he ever has. There's great camaraderie in trials, too. Although it's obviously an individual sport every bit as much as road racing, it's altogether more matey. 'Opponents' routinely help each other to plan their way round sections. Of course they just as routinely take the piss.

Despite everything I've said – and meant – about my ability, inside me there's a guy who still thinks he can be world trials champion, because somewhere out there is the absolutely perfect bike for me. It's total bollocks, of course, but most of us think the same. Well, something has to keep us going when all the evidence is telling us to pack it in.

I was lucky to leave road racing with the most precious thing: my health. Lots of guys I competed against weren't so lucky, so if I'm to dedicate this book to anyone, maybe it should be to them. But for me, and perhaps for them, death was not the thing I feared most. It might sound awful, but when I was racing the prospect that always worried me most was ending up in a wheelchair. I'm not at all academic. I couldn't just spend all day by a computer or reading books, much less watching daytime TV. To pitch up on the Isle of Man and leave in a wooden box was never the game plan, but to anyone even half-realistic it was always a possibility you had to accept. Coming away in a wheelchair I couldn't. Trials, unless something truly freaky happens, just doesn't carry those sort of risks.

Along the way I've been privileged to enjoy the ultimate in racing – success in a good team with good people around you. Team managing comes a poor second to that, partly because – even though you're the boss – you're nothing like as much in control as you were when it was your hand on the twistgrip. Yes, there's lots of fun in it, but compared to racing it's a great deal of responsibility without quite the same buzz. And, because you've been there, done it and said it, you know the bullshit behind the excuses even before your rider has opened his mouth. And a long way back in third place comes selling bikes.

So that's my motorcycling career these days. That, and the odd classic outing and cruising around on my Yamaha FJR1300. The workshop still hums – friends needing the odd bit of welding or machining see to that. Thanks to John Caffrey, the Ariel's just got a new, even lighter frame. For reasons I'm not entirely sure of the restoration of a Greeves RES Silverstone is almost complete. And Carol still puts up with me.

In 1996 at The Haymarket in London, James Whitham was being interviewed after receiving the *MCN* Man of the Year award. 'I'm lucky,' he said, 'to be making a living out of racing bikes. Fact is, I'd do it for nothing.'

I got to my feet and heckled, 'Shut up, you fool.'

He may have let the cat out of the bag. But I'll tell you what: he was dead right.

RESULTS SUMMARY

1965

First competition, Baiting's Dam hill climb, 350cc Velocette.

Some scrambles meetings, 250c Cotton.

First road race meeting late in the season at Croft, also on the 350cc Velocette.

1966-67

Club racing, 500cc Velocette.

1968

Still club racing on the Velo, now gaining regular top three placings.

First Irish road race meeting at Carrowdore.

1969

First win at a Batley Club meeting at Cadwell Park on the 500 Velo.

First Manx Grand Prix, finished the Senior 48th and last, also on the Velo.

1970

Riding for Jim Lee Racing Components with a BSA Gold Star, Norton
  Commando and Yamaha TR2, all with Lee frames.

Regular wins at club level on the TR2.

TT debut: 18th in Junior on the Lee Yamaha, averaging almost 90mph.

1971

Jim Lee Commando and Yamaha TR2.

First National road race win at Cadwell Park on the Commando, ahead of Charlie
Sanby. Regular national rostrums on the TR2, usually chasing Steve Machin.

First International win, at Scarborough, also on the Yamaha.

First TT crash, at Signpost, when I torpedoed Keith Heckles.

1972

Padgett's Yamahas (plus private Yamahas for second half of season); first factory ride on the JPS Norton.

First TT rostrum, 3rd in Junior, same again in Senior, behind Agostini in both.

First dices with Barry Sheene on 250/350 Yamahas.

Gave Norton their first Superbike win at Scarborough in September.

Thruxton 500-miler: 1st with Dave Croxford for Norton.

British 350cc championship: 1st.

British 500cc championship: 2nd.

1973

Privateer Yamahas, sponsored by Brian Davidson.

Some outings on the JPS Norton, including another Superbike win at Scarborough and second place in the Formula 750 TT.

First Continental grands prix at Hockenheim, Monza, Spa, Assen and Anderstorp. Best finishes: 4th on 250 in Holland, 6th on 350 in Sweden.

1974

Privateer, again sponsored by Brian Davidson.

First TT win, on 750c Triumph 'Slippery Sam' in Production race.

Some grands prix. Best finishes: 6th on 250, 5th on 350, both Sweden.

1975

The first of four seasons as a factory Kawasaki rider in domestic and world Formula 750 competition.

North West 200: winner of 500cc and main events.

New TT lap record, 109.82mph, finally breaking Mike Hailwood's mark from 1967.

First Senior TT win (500 Kawasaki).

British Superbike championship: 1st from Barry Ditchburn, Sheene.

1976

Kawasaki in domestic and world Formula 750.

British Superbike championship: 2nd (to Sheene).

1977

Kawasaki in domestic, some grands prix and world Formula 750.

KR750 Kawasaki timed at 191mph at the TT.

250cc grands prix: Holland 1st; Sweden 1st; Finland 2nd.

1978

Kawasaki in domestic and grands prix racing.

Grands Prix results:

Spain: 250 6th.

Holland: 350 7th.

Sweden: 350 9th.

Finland: 250 7th.

GB: 250 4th; 350 3rd.

1979

Honda GB riding Formula One and (Suzuki) RG500; Honda Japan
    developing NR500.

British Formula One championship: 3rd behind Ron Haslam and Graeme Crosby.

1980

Honda GB and Honda Japan again.

Winner, Formula One TT.

World Formula One championship: 2nd.

British Formula One championship: 1st.

1981

Privateer: TZ350 and TZ750 Yamaha, F1 Harris Suzuki, GSX1100 Suzuki in
   Streetbike challenge, plus F1 and RG500 Suzuki at TT, plus occasional
   outings on a 250cc Armstrong.

500cc winner, NW200 and IoM TT.

1982

Suzuki GB

World Formula One championship: 1 Joey Dunlop, 4 Grant.

British Formula One championship: 3rd to team-mate Roger Marshall and
   Wayne Gardner

1983

Suzuki GB

British Formula One championship: 1 Gardner, 2 McElnea, 3 Grant.

World Formula One championship: 1 Dunlop, 4 Grant.

1984

Suzuki GB

British Formula One championship: 1 Gardner, 4 Grant.

World Formula One championship: 1 Dunlop, 5 Grant.

1985

Suzuki GB

Last TT win, 750cc Production, Suzuki GSX-R750.

British Superstock championship: 1 Grant.

British Formula One championship: 1 Marshall, 2 Grant.

World Formula One championship: 1 Dunlop, 2 Grant.

ISLE OF MAN RACE RESULTS

Year/race	Machinery	Posn	Avg speed
Manx Grand Prix			
1969			
Senior	Velocette	48	n/a
TT Races			
1970			
Junior	Lee Yamaha	18	89.17mph
Senior	Velocette	DNF	
1971			
Formula 750	Lee Norton	DNF	
Junior	Yamaha	7	86.5mph
1972			
Senior	Kawasaki	3	97.03mph
Junior	Yamaha	3	97.57mph
Formula 750	Yamaha	DNF	
1973			
Senior	Yamaha	DNF	
Fastest lap	M. Grant	21:40.8	104.41mph
Junior	Yamaha	DNF	
Lightweight 250	Padgett Yam	DNF	
Formula 750	Norton	2	102.56mph
1974			
Senior	Yamaha	DNF	
Junior	Yamaha	2	102.8mph
Formula 750	Kawasaki	17	n/a
Lightweight 250	Fowler Yam	2	93.2mph
Fastest lap	M. Grant	23:08.0	97.85mph
1000 Production	Triumph	1	99.72mph
Fastest lap	M. Grant	22:28.2	100.74mph

1975

Senior	Kawasaki	1	100.27mph
Fastest lap	M. Grant	21:59.6	102.93mph
Classic	Kawasaki	DNF	
Record lap	M. Grant	20:36.8	109.82mph
Lightweight 250	Kawasaki	DNF	

1976

Senior	Kawasaki	DNF	
Classic	Kawasaki	DNF	

1977

Classic	Kawasaki	1	110.76mph
Record lap	M. Grant	20:04.4	112.77mph
Junior 250	Kawasaki	7	96.20mph

1978

Senior	Kawasaki	DNF	
Classic	Kawasaki	1	112.41mph
Record lap	M. Grant	19:48.0	114.33mph
Junior	Kawasaki	DNF	

1979

Senior	Suzuki	DNF	
Classic	Honda	DNF	

1980

Formula One	Honda	1	105.29mph
Classic	Honda	2	112.40mph

1981

Formula One	Suzuki	DNF	
Classic	Suzuki	2	113.11mph
Senior	Suzuki	1	106.14mph
Fastest lap	M. Grant	20:0.4	112.68mph

1982

Formula One	Suzuki	DNF	n/a
Record lap	M. Grant	19:41.8	114.93mph
Classic	Suzuki	DNF	
Senior 500cc	Suzuki	DNF	

1983

Formula One	Suzuki	2	113.20mph
Senior Classic	Suzuki	5	111.76mph

1984

Formula One	Suzuki	DNF	
Classic	Suzuki	3	114.68mph
1500 Production	Suzuki	6	102.87mph
Senior	Suzuki	6	110.80mph

1985

Formula One	Suzuki	DNF	
750 Production	Suzuki	1	104.36mph
Senior	Suzuki	DNF	

INDEX